The Wine of Absurdity

By PAUL WEST

Criticism

Byron and the Spoiler's Art
Byron: Twentieth-Century Views (ed.)
The Growth of the Novel
The Modern Novel
Robert Penn Warren

Poetry

Number Seven: The Fantasy Poets
The Spellbound Horses
The Snow Leopard

Fiction

A Quality of Mercy
Tenement of Clay

Memoir

I, Said the Sparrow

The Wine Of Absurdity

Essays on Literature and Consolation

by PAUL WEST

The Pennsylvania State University Press
University Park and London   1966

The Wine Of Absurdity

Essays on Literature and Consolation

by PAUL WEST

The Pennsylvania State University Press
University Park and London   1966

For Reg and Barbara Foakes

Contents

The body, compassion, the created world, action, human nobility will . . . resume their place in this insane world. Man will find again the wine of absurdity and the bread of indifference which nourish his greatness.

(*Albert Camus*)

Preface

Anyone who engages in the writing of criticism finds himself sooner or later looking into books and authors he had never thought of reading. After going off at tangents he returns to his center, but it is usually a modified one. In this familiar process of self-education he is constantly obliged to articulate for himself the interrelationships of a ramifying, deepening body of reading. Gradually he discovers what he believes in, and from whom, over the years, he has gathered the views, attitudes and criteria he values most.

This collection is the outcome of the process as I have experienced it over the last ten years or so during the composition of essays and review-articles. I have selected related studies and arranged them to illustrate some aspects of twentieth-century literary consolation. The book is meant to be neither a compendium nor exclusively a personal "testament." Some of the pieces are polemical, some are not. In some instances I have written new sections or have considerably revised essays that seemed out of date or weak. The result is, I hope, a substantiated review of writers who have helped me to clarify some things for myself. I resort frequently to contrasts and some of my juxtapositions may strike the reader as wilful or even harsh. All I can say is that I have not consciously distorted the views of any writer I discuss. A personal book will always be to some degree whimsical and the reader will quickly perceive how intense some of my reactions have been. Although I now think more sedately about certain writers, I have left in some of the extremer reactions to show what those writers can do to a young, or fairly young, reader. The main thing, I believe, is to keep the opinionated from becoming bigoted, and this I have tried to do. Of the writers discussed, many have consolidated their positions, recanted or died since I first encountered their works: their careers have assumed patterns one could not always have predicted. In each case I have tried to bring the record up to date and place it, hard as this is, in some sort of perspective. No-one's view is perfect and very few critical views ever get perfected. Especially to the literature of one's own time one's responses are unlikely to be tepid or wholly balanced (see, for example, the writings of such different task-masters as F. R. Leavis, the Chicago Aristotelians and Leslie Fiedler), and I am aware that in some places I am being dog-matic or perhaps trying to "place" an author or a book too soon. What I say here is based on the best honesty and discrimination I can manage at the present time. I trust a consistent point of view emerges. Naturally, I do not regard any of the verdicts as final although I imagine some of them are so idiosyncratic as to have to stay that way.

Idiosyncrasy is something we can always try to control but something we can never wholly beat. If we *could* beat it we would no longer be ourselves. I have always thought that tem-perament is the deciding factor in our responses, no matter how balanced, sane and judicious we aim to be. It is what makes the somewhat clinical business of writing criticism a human activity like cooking, singing or sculpture. Criticism is creative; it is a personal matter, and we should not try to make it too objective or too impersonal. The fine criticism, to take two conspicuous examples, of Northrop Frye and Wayne C. Booth, has excellent virtues: urbanity, thoroughness, a kind of easy magistrality, and wit. In both *The Anatomy of Criticism* and *A Rhetoric of Fiction* we find the unmistakable sound of a sane man speaking deftly. Yet, somehow, both Frye and Booth arrive at an objectiv-ity which is not always good for literature. There is an absence (in these books at any rate) of partiality, an attempt to be all kinds of men, which is no doubt a magnificent feat of self-discipline by two commentators whose love of literature is never in doubt. Some people, somewhere, have to write this kind of en-cyclopedic criticism so that the rest of us can get things straight. But some of us are too egoistic, too "romantic," to achieve it, and we believe that reading books is an activity that calls for opin-ions, liking and disliking; and a criticism that remained coolly impartial, even when dealing with acknowledged masterpieces, would all too soon evoke the computer or the robot. The critic offers, as I with some lack of humility offer here, response as a stimulus or invitation.

Absurdity I take to be life's incomprehensibility, its fusion of meaninglessness and meaning; or, to quote Camus, the "division between the mind that desires and the world that disappoints." Different people respond to the absurd in different ways. Some regard it as a merely temporary condition, a prelude to a heaven where the "division" will not exist; these either persuade themselves or let organized religion tell them. Others, who cannot believe in any reality beyond this world although the origin of life remains inexplicable to them, either despair or try to make life make sense—whether that sense is social, political, ethical, philosophical or aesthetic. I am concerned here with various refusals of the absurd, some heretical and some orthodox, and some of both kinds more successful than others. I have excluded the dramatists of the absurd—Beckett, Ionesco, Genet and others— because they are more or less content to express the feeling of absurdity rather than to propose means of subduing it.

Each of the writers I discuss here devises or accepts something that mitigates the absurdity of being human; and the wine of absurdity is the imaginative effort entailed, as well as the imaginative end product. In some instances the wine blurs (as in the early Camus) ; in others it induces dogmatism (Sartre the politicist) and grandiosity (Malraux the writer on art). But in all instances it is the wine of human imagination which is at work: both the heretics and the converts create the wine and console themselves with it, not always making sense but not always arriving at nonsense. I am using Camus's phrase fairly loosely but always, I hope, in the spirit in which he meant it. Such wine is a means of accommodating ourselves to what seem immutable facts, and in the long run what orthodox religion and heretical literature have in common is imagination.

I am grateful to the following magazines and their respective editors for publishing what I wrote, for sometimes persuading me to write when I had not intended to, for giving me a chance to write on the new books of authors I was already interested in, and for allowing me to reprint the pieces appearing here: *Canadian Forum, The Chicago Review, The Dalhousie Review,*

Essays in Criticism, The Hibbert Journal, The Kenyon Review, The Nation, the *New Statesman, New World Writing, Queen's Quarterly, The Southern Review, The Times Literary Supplement,* and *The Twentieth Century.* I am also grateful, to The Johns Hopkins Press, who commissioned the essay on Yeats, and, for many helpful suggestions and many other kindnesses, to Walter Allen, F. W. Bateson, Kenneth Burke, Arthur Crook, Arabel J. Porter, and John Crowe Ransom. Additional thanks go to those long-suffering persons who, at one time or another, have been generous enough to read and comment on parts of the manuscript, especially W. M. Frohock, Brian John, Cecil Day Lewis, Charles Mann and Philip Young.

May 1965   P.W.

A New Religion

Yeats is full of contradictions—of self-contradicting doctrines—from the beginning of his literary career in the 1890s to his death. He learned much from Pater and, unlike the majority of the Nineties writers, realized exactly what Pater meant by "quickened, multiplied consciousness." Here I consider some of the reasons for Yeats's turning to Pater's doctrine, for his eventually finding it inadequate to his religious needs, and for his final decision to create "a new religion, almost an infallible church, of poetic tradition." Lawrence comes up here as a less exquisite mystic than Yeats, although they are nearer each other than at first seems likely. Yeats is less of an aesthete than is suggested by the kind of company he kept in the Nineties; and Lawrence's rather loosely conceived notion of dynamic prose is closer to art-for-art than his own version of "quickened, multiplied consciousness" has let us see. Both Yeats and Lawrence mythologize whatever is at hand in order to create a private religion which, as they seek to demonstrate in sermons of messianic imprudence, bears also on the lives of all men. They both have considerable, perhaps too much, respect for instinctive forces in man, and they both, despite their frequent lapses into the esoteric, exhibit a lively concern with something "tragic" in human life. This "something" they relate to race memory and race clairvoyance. Such comments as the following exemplify their common bonds: "can we not . . . understand that the unthinkably sensitive substance of the human intelligence could receive the fine waves of vital effluence transmitted across the intervening space . . . ?" It is Lawrence, on "The Spirit of Place," but it could so easily be Yeats, affirming in his own cranky way the mystery of being alive.

W. B. Yeats

In May 1887, when he was almost twenty-two, Yeats went to live in London, feeling there very much the provincial and bumpkin but forcing himself to brave the metropolitan *hauteur,* the condescensions of Oscar Wilde and the age's requirement that anyone pretending to be anyone at all cultivate what James Joyce, growing up in the same years, called "the enigma of a manner." It was a bold venture for the youth from Sligo. He hated London and his bleats against it remind one of the bleats of Dylan Thomas, the youth from Laugharne. Nevertheless, fortified by periodic retreats to Sligo, Yeats survived his initiation and began to get on, fortified in this by what he knew at first hand of simple, peasant life—a far cry from the posing sophistication of the London literary set. It is not too much to say that what at first he thought vocationally profitable—what gave him a kind of pastoral egregiousness—saved him from becoming just another trite, attitudinizing rhymer. Sligo was his amulet, his material and his still center.

The two sides of his personality appear, pointedly contrasted, in his story "John Sherman" in *John Sherman and Dhoya* (1891). Sherman the dreamer whose only ambition is to marry a rich woman finally surrenders his rich fiancée to Howard, the curate who oddly enough is a man about town, and returns to a childhood sweetheart with whom he can farm and dream in the west of Ireland. It is Sligo *versus* London; and Sherman, who obviously has Yeats's sympathies, yields to Sligo, its calm routines and the ritual patterns of its agriculture. But of course Yeats really wanted the best of both worlds, to be William Butler Sherman-Howard Yeats if he could, and in his actual life settled for neither but became a floater, a hoverer, a commuter almost, expressing his self-transpositions, his ambiguous longings, in plays which take on trust, and present without formal or intellectual manipulation, the natural, time-vindicated vision of Irish peasants. Yeats was holding fast to what he knew and not yet troubling

5

about dramaturgical ingenuities. Later, he was to concern himself more with lyrical unity than with actualities.

On 30 January 1889 he was shaken out of this almost voluptuous ambivalence by his first encounter with Maud Gonne, the type of the beautiful, commanding, busy female who always intrigues men more given to brooding than to action. For the first time in his already erratic life he had to formulate severely to himself the split in his personality. Maud Gonne was a public woman and, as Yeats knew, he too would have to become a public figure to win her. In this he had a start because one part of him did covet fame of a literary sort, and he had already, like a sublimely appointed, gifted rustic, made sorties upon the literary capital of England. On the other hand, the ineffectual dreamer in him—the private Yeats who came into being in resistance to the euphoric rationalism of his father and his father's Dublin circle—could not die that easily. And to go the way of Maud Gonne was fundamentally to espouse the views and assumptions of his father: to become practical, down-to-earth and committed. The only scope for his mysticism would be in the revolutionary movement's fervent nationalism.

So Yeats stalled, longing for Innisfree, place of neither sea nor land, and stayed much of the time in bed. Then, to impress Maud Gonne, he forced himself into the role of revolutionary and, to strengthen his resolve, redistributed his characteristics. Now, he thought, the man of action could know through passionate public activity more than Sherman the recluse. And, paradoxically, the recluse was just the man to break out and do things. But he quickly learned that dynamic behavior guarantees no greater degree of self-definition than withdrawal does, and he began to formulate the rationale of his new, more complicated dilemma. He could never, whatever he was doing, suppress his imagined version of its alternative. He even began to anticipate consequences, to pre-empt the failure of plays and political enterprises, and before long he transferred his problem—essentially that of the self-analyst—to the plane of metaphysics. Thwarted love, thwarted revolution, and thwarted desires for peace all seep into his thought in the Nineties and send him, as his interest in drama sent him, from the physical and immediate to the spiritual and transcendent.

In some stories he composed during his thirtieth year he created new personages. Sherman is replaced by Michael Robartes who wants to enlist John Aherne (the new Howard) into the Order of the Alchemical Rose, although Aherne, the Catholic who is intending to become a Dominican monk, always manages to draw back in time. But now, the mystic who formerly was Sherman has become a ritualizing figure of daring initiative (Robartes) and the religious orthodoxy (Howard's High Church), far from animating, merely represses in the same way as the rationalism of Yeats's father. Yeats's sympathies are no longer obvious; he has achieved a wider ratio of involvement and is therefore harder to pin down to any one character.

His work gained in impersonality and his demeanor became more confident. Still the split man—busy Irish nationalist and mystical member of the Order of the Golden Dawn—he needed both a mask and a metaphysical principle. Living in Woburn Buildings, Bloomsbury, he was widening his already extensive set of literary and mystical acquaintances, running *Beltaine* and the Irish Literary Society, and contributing prose and verse to a wide variety of journals. By now he was becoming something of a name and was seeing to it that he kept the name up. On the one hand he busied himself with such ancillary chores as an edition (with Edwin J. Ellis) of Blake's mystical poems and inditing an introduction to W. T. Horton's book of woodcuts, *A Book of Images* (1898). On the other hand, realizing he could not dabble indefinitely, he intensified his efforts to evolve a principle or scheme that would integrate not only his somewhat divided self but would also fuse his personal and public lives in perpetuity. How he did this is a matter of some interest because it shows him in his true originality as well as in the role of a careful reader of other men's works and an ingenious aspirant to greatness.

The eighteen-nineties teach us many things, most of which we have learned well by now, and not least the fact that, of all the self-thwarting forms of human endeavor, aestheticism is the most confused about means and ends. On the one hand it knows what it wants and acknowledges what it cannot have. It has small faith in, or care for, the world at large: it aims at perfection, at a perfected ecstasy, in a limited area; and its conspicuous attitudes—of snobbish pessimism and incautious contempt—are clear. So far so good or, rather, consistent. On the other hand, however, and especially in the Nineties, the aesthete, having decided there is a wilderness and an incorrigible one at that, often elects to be a voice in it, destined to cry in vain but somehow getting an extra thrill from doing so. It is an odd paradox and one that leads us, I think, to the real meaning of the "decadence." The means to an unattainable end became an end in itself and crying for what one cannot have—for what the aesthetes would not have wanted even if by some miracle they had got it—became a pantomime in which they bemoaned their minority and derided the *hoi polloi*. They did not really want art to be popular; they did not really want to convert the masses or even the bulk of the bourgeoisie. They dabbled in obloquy, pique and precious narcissism, and our only sympathy with them is that which we give anyone who, forced into a painful position, compensates by rebuking other people for not being in it themselves.

I make these few abstractions because, if we are to see Yeats clearly, we have to be fairly clear what was going on. Much of what in the Nineties passed for crusading purported to support some abstract principle: reform of public taste, enrichment of human experience, conservation of the unspoiled or the ineffable, and so on. At first glance, Yeats fits in well. He wrote snobbish essays against "popular poetry"; he spoke constantly of passion and intensity; he used colored language to rebel against the drabness of ordinary discourse and, like many of his contemporaries, he flinched away from the externals of industrialism and technology. He even, as the age required, devised spectacular externals of his own: the long black cloak drooping from his shoulders, the soft black sombrero, the voluminous black silk tie, the flapping trousers, all of which made George Moore think of him as "an Irish parody of the poetry that I had seen all my life strutting its rhythmic way in the alleys of the Luxembourg gardens." Such a man could have had little difficulty in being a pain in the neck to almost everyone. All the same, as I hope to show, he was flamboyantly embarking on something serious; something which, at that time, he could best achieve by fellow-travelling (he wasn't very sure of himself anyway), but which was a respectable destination he shared with no-one else.

What we find, if we read carefully his poems, plays and prose of the period, is a triple process. He inherited his share from Rossetti and Pater; he endorsed complaints made by Arthur Symons, Henry Harland and Laurence Binyon—all of them militantly disdainful of the "common man"—and, third, he fought and wangled his own way towards a guiding principle of the kind a man finds it hard to abandon once, and if, he finds it. This is why Yeats achieved a stature that impresses us for reasons neither antiquarian nor chic. He had enough genius in him to go on writing for the rest of his life without, however, disdaining the basis of his apprenticeship. As F. R. Leavis observes, his best work "is full of a bitter sense of thwarting, of sterile, issueless inner tension." Yet that "thwarting" is the result of his trying to maintain contact with life at large on the national and even racial level, whereas the dead-end frustration we find in such as Symons, Wilde, Beardsley and others is really the fruits of narcissism. Yeats is thwarted by life's awkwardness and his mounting interest in "the fascination of what's difficult"; they are thwarted because they attempt only what they find easy. It is only natural if we prefer the embattled Yeats to the cloistered boy poets and the posing rhymers. But it is not clear, I think, how resolute Yeats was unless we stand apart from the fascinating and colorful lives of the time, from the minor pageant of minor particulars that Holbrook Jackson renders so well in his book on the period. If we stay under the spell of the Nineties, bemused by the off-beat dottiness and the tiny bleating, the grandiose scurry of small talents and the social patina, Yeats seems to belong to it more than, intellectually, he did. It is only when we consider ends and means, theirs and his, that he comes away whole and functioning on lines of his own. He was a maladroit young man learning not only how to write but how to become a part of the literary world, and it was predictable that he would use whatever was to hand while getting his literary and social bearings.

Yeats was luckier than he knew. Several of his contemporaries had permitted a fastidious sense of art to involve them in refining delicate ideas to the point of meaninglessness. Too curiously searching for originality, others had merely brought forward the grotesque. They chose catch phrases or seductive aphorisms and worked them to death. They knew what Pater said and they thought they knew what he meant: "While all melts under our feet, we may well catch at any exquisite passion. . . ." The passage is well known. What Arthur Symons made of it, although less known, is exactly what one might expect. "A man," he contends, "who goes through a day without some fine emotion has wasted his day, whatever he gained by it. And it is so easy to go through day after day, busily and agreeably, without ever really living for a single instant." The adverbs make a plaintive point, and we may scoff: burning always with that hard, gemlike flame can amount to a kind of psychological arson, and people get tired.

That is one response to Symons's idea. There is another, however, vulgarly recorded in the commonplace assumption that we all like to feel we are getting the most out of life. Some people try harder to gain this feeling than others do: the relentless capering of F. Scott and Zelda Fitzgerald is an extreme case in point, like Gide's voluptuary treadmill or Aldous Huxley's recourse to mescalin. The heroes of Malraux or Graham Greene want to feel things keenly, not to go to death partly unaware of where they have been and aware only of chances, potentialities, irrevocably wasted. The craving to live intensely—and that need not mean only debauchery and high jinks, or even these things at all—is something we should not underestimate. It gave rise in the Nineties to many a desperate and pathetic *vie de poète* and, in its more up-to-date form as the fear of waste, of wasting this one life, underlies much of the literature of our own time. Yeats was in at the beginning of the cult of intensity and he never relinquished his interest in it or lost what it gave him. What makes him different from his contemporaries is his general human concern, the way he thinks about the intensest emotions of all men of all times. His view includes the sharp cut that personal tragedies make and tragedy's capacity to draw men together. In the Eighties and Nineties, especially in the latter, he was not narrowing himself but broadening. When he rebelled against the prosaic quality of post-Ibsen drama he was rebelling not just because the language wasn't gorgeous but also because language of that kind never has a chance of doing the worthwhile thing that drama can do; and that is, as we learn from *The Tragic Theatre* (1910), "a drowning, a breaking of the dykes that separate man from man." In other words, Yeats's aesthetic remonstrances were functional, going beyond a texture that is thrilling to fondle and to mouth, to an almost social anxiety which links up with his initially unfanciful reporting of Irish peasant life. Pleading for an illustrious vernacular, for a subtle medium, for a full-blooded convention accepted as artificial, he was coasting along with the Wildes and Harlands, but with a sober, reasoned-out purpose in mind.

We have to be clear about the distinction; it takes us further. To accumulate cleverly phrased excesses of response was merely to force the moment—of artistic or other experience—to yield its maximum. Yeats wanted it to yield the maximum for a public purpose that would enrich private life even more.

Again, when the aesthetes, wanting to make the most of every experience, overdid the advertising and encouraged the view that art had to be irresponsible and perhaps immoral, they stopped there, whereas Yeats engaged in publicity for a transcendent purpose which exposes the hectic hedonism of the period for what it was. Not that he went uncontaminated; he did not. But he did, most of the time, know where he was going and why, which in itself is a sort of gift and something extraordinary in a young man who was as tentative, psychologically speaking, as Yeats in the last decade of the century.

The Yeats of the Nineties faced something that Pater and Symons could not. He faced it, one must admit, with many tremblings of the veil, swishings of the cloak and much moist exoticism, but he did accept the probability that an intense experience was as well sought among the trivia of everyday as awaited from the hand of the unpredictable future. To wait for the moment of intensest living, of complete illumination, was perhaps to let intensest living pass one by. John Marcher in Henry James's story *The Beast in the Jungle* (1903) epitomizes the dilemma. Marcher is covinced that there is reserved for him "some rare distinction, some incalculable violence or unprecedented stroke." But at the last he realizes that "all the while he had waited, the wait itself was his portion," and that there is "something he had utterly insanely missed." Small wonder that many of the so-called decadents turned eventually to the Catholic Church's rituals and spiritual security. They had been trying to do the impossible. It went like this: "The crowd never really loves art. But only art raises man above mediocrity, enables him to realize to the full his capacity to feel. So down with the crowd; up with ourselves. We will increase our chances of intense experience by undertaking to live hectic lives." Such was the argument within the *cénacle*. Outside, however, was a whole world of new-literates for whom reading matter was being produced at great speed: amateur pianists, car lovers, salvation army officers, school inspectors, factory workers and thousands of other sorts of people who all, in some way, had a chance to apprehend beauty or intensity without coming anywhere near "strangeness" or what the *Times* called "English rowdyism and French lubricity." *The Yellow Book* itself was far from being through and through decadent, and other journals, such as *The Dome,* set out to be catholic—not just literary or artistic or English, but wide, with symbolist poems by Francis Vielé-Griffin alongside solid articles on Velásquez or Van Dyck, with a reprinted Rossetti story along-side contributions by Roger Fry, Delius, Elgar and Yeats himself.

Yeats, whatever we may conclude about his snobbery, his evasive-seeming images, his incapacity to communicate and his posings, did have a sense of the world's motley. In a sense, for his intentions, he has something in common with Ernest Vizetelly who was imprisoned for translating and publishing Zola, or Hardy whose *Jude the Obscure* was called a shocker. His fey tergiversations and his passion for aristocratic attitudes must not mislead us, as they misled some of his contemporaries, into thinking he was effete. Yeats knew what he was doing; he was neither as vacuously snobbish as his onslaughts on "the popular" suggest nor as unworldly as his most contrived tropes make him sound.

"I am very religious," he wrote in his *Autobiographies* (1926), "and deprived by Huxley and Tyndall, whom I detested, of the simple-minded religion of my childhood, I . . . made a new religion, almost an infalliable church, of poetic tradition." His religion, with which he countered all he "detested," had many mansions and many phases. A list of its origins reads like a recipe for nympholepsy; he drew much from many places: Spenser, Blake, Rossetti, the English romantics, Standish O'Grady's *History of Ireland*, Landor, Ben Jonson, Donne, John Addington Symonds, translations from the Gaelic by F. R. Higgins and Frank O'Connor, Lully, Flamel, Paracelsus, Plato, the *Upanishads*, Shri Purohit Swami, theosophy, the Order of the Golden Dawn, Mrs. Yeats, as well as Maud Gonne, peasants, folklorists, Lady Gregory and her tenants, and Arthur Symons. Walter Pater, too, and perhaps above all. An unkind commentator would almost certainly have been right to say that nothing could come of this farrago but a new simple-mindedness without the innocences of childhood; and Yeats himself, when asked about his occult studies, admitted that his "critical mind . . . mocked, and yet I was delighted." It was as if his intellect, to save itself, turned imaginative and eclectic, exercising what Coleridge called the esemplastic power, the power that unifies. The point is that Yeats, alone of the Nineties poets, had this power; he could and did make the one from the many.

From Pater he appropriated the doctrine of intensity, and this led him to recognize what was heroic and divine in profound feelings. It also supplied him with an aesthetic criterion that ruled out Ibsen and justified his own evocations of Celtic gods. During the Eighties the evanescent and ethereal contemplativeness of pre-Raphaelitism had suited his rather static view of emotion; the vein is lyrical and distilled. But after reading Pater and hearing Arthur Symons on the French symbolists, he committed his pre-Raphaelite manner to exemplifying a doctrine that art was man's noblest achievement, was sufficient unto itself, and was the purest form of emotion. In other words Yeats advanced from intoxication with manner to intellectual acceptance of a dogma, from thin-bodied texture to a full body of thought. He did not delay; he knew how much of his long-standing needs Pater's view could supply. Not that, thenceforth, Yeats desisted entirely from the "verbal decoration" of his first phase; he did not: but even that implemented faintly, as Pater's dogma implemented boldly and bewitchingly, the aesthete's protest against commercialization or vulgarizing of the arts, against what Yeats himself considered the "corruption" of poetry. Back of it all, was the complex view that, although poetry should not be vulgarized, it can do a great deal for and about the world at large. And this implies art's capacity to inform the literati of their bond with all men, of their common membership in the human condition, not to mention the divine. In brief, Pater supplied Yeats with a policy.

But Pater's dictum that "our knowledge is limited to what we feel" had its negative side for Yeats. He responded warmly to Pater's plea for "quickened, multiplied consciousness"—as who would not?—and even went so far as to copy Pater's prose style in "Rosa Alchemica." The copying was, however, more than a pastiche; it was a tribute to the master's doctrine couched in the master's own manner. But Pater stopped short whereas Yeats even in the Nineties and certainly later, in *Per Amica Silentia Lunae* (1918), wanted to go beyond subjective experience, naturalistic knowledge and what Pater regarded as the saving disciplines of taste. What attracted Yeats was "the universal and divine life," the one transcendent unity, "the great ritual" which only tragedy's "little ritual" could reveal. Notice his concern for "unity of lyrical effect" (Pater's phrase), for integration, completeness and no conceptual barriers separating either vision from form or man from man or man from the divine. This is why he goes as far with Pater as he usefully can and then supplements his borrowing from other sources of all kinds.

There is another reason for Yeats's concern with unity. He felt, as I have said, divided himself. The hero of "Rosa Alchemica" has tried all the gods because he believes in none. Something eludes him. All he has is "the bitter dream of a limitless energy I could never know"—an energy central to Michael Robartes and his mystic clique. Finally the hero of the story enters the Catholic Church, a decision that saves him from, or deprives him of, genuinely tragic knowledge. Of course Yeats the recluse is on the side of Robartes and finds the Church just as constricting as naturalism (of which Pater's version, except for its hieratic advocacy of art, differs little from that of Herbert Spencer or G. H. Lewes). Robartes is one of those who, as Yeats remarked of

Shakespeare's Richard II, "find themselves where men ask of them a rough energy and have nothing to give but some contemplative virtue . . ." This dreamy side is what bogs down Cuchulain, the hero of the 1903 version of *On Baile's Strand;* in the 1906 version Cuchulain becomes the complete warrior. By then of course, Yeats himself was committed almost wholly to action too. He had not gone beyond Pater—he never abandoned that early lesson about the intensity of art's liturgical aspect—but he eventually described the doctrine of *Marius the Epicurean* as "a swaying rope in a storm." It was, as he said, a doctrine which had done its share in bringing a good many of his own generation to enact the tragic vision in their own lives, and with distressing results.

Only someone as divided, as naggingly pessimistic and as honest-minded as himself, could go beyond Pater's limits to a richer view of created being. Yeats alone understood Pater's doctrine and, where others notoriously misconstrued it into hedonism, made it his departure-point for a lifelong attempt to apprehend the passional lives of all sorts and conditions of men. His pessimism was as much of naturalism as he needed, and his cosmology, both the early and the late, provided him with a spiritual plane on which the tragic sense, the primacy and mystery of human emotion, and his craving for unity—in other words, his interpretive, religious and psychological interest—could come together in congruity. We may remark, as W. H. Auden did, how little influence the Yeats of *A Vision* (1926) has had on poets and how essentially unaristocratic his occultism seems alongside his ceremonious and rather laborious snobbery. Yet, I feel, without arguing speciously on Yeats's behalf or trying to think for him, we can justify his vagaries and accord them a measure of respect.

Like most of his contemporaries, he was on the defensive in an increasingly scientific, technological age. The evasive historicism of such writers as Carlyle and Burckhardt reveals what was developing. Imagination, subjectivity and individuality had been driven into a position about which harassed, sensitive and sometimes deceitful minds constructed a Chinese Wall of indifference, paranoia, disdain and mumbo-jumbo. It was natural that Yeats should embrace a cosmology intriguing rather than "true" and that James Joyce should set about transforming all of life into words and that G. B. Shaw should perfidiously desert rationalism for Lamarckism. The rebellion was metaphorical: its meaning is in the temper of certain refusals rather than in the eventual resting-places of the rebels. The more harried such men felt, the more they inflated their own values and devalued anything said by outsiders. (In 1939 Joyce, who himself in *Finnegans Wake* had reworked the lore of Ireland into a vision of his own, told Jacques Mercanton, "Let them leave Poland in peace and occupy themselves with *Finnegans Wake,*" knowing full well in his whimsically ironic way that his new book—like so much of Yeats's middle and late works—was a pact with the mystery and daily fertility of life; a pact established at large because for the narrower sanction, that of Christianity, there could be no substitute.)

Auden provides respectable testimony when he reconsiders Yeats's cosmology, for it is Auden, more than any of his literary associates of the Thirties, who has tried to be the poet of civilization, of the city, of modern thinkers and modern politics. Too, he himself travelled a similar path to Yeats's, to a more orthodox religious position, but in a similar mood. He realized, as Yeats did, that religion is a private matter for most intellectuals and cannot be written about without myth—a controlling and subsuming image or pattern—which has especial power over the writer. It is no use starting cold, no matter how convinced you are: if you wish to set things down, you have to find an available common ground, as Yeats did in his Celtic myths, Auden in the imagery of Christianity and Eliot in both Christianity and such modern phenomena as taxis, the London Underground and English villages.

All this means one thing: Yeats was not trifling but trying to put to religious purposes the nonmetaphysical principle of intensity he learned from Pater. As Auden says, when traditions no longer sustain men in such a way that men are unaware of being sustained, men have to construct their own *planches de salut* according to the best lights they have. Otherwise the sense of dislocation and disorientation becomes paralyzing. The state of feeling Yeats referred to as "Timid, entangled, empty and abashed" is tragic enough; man cannot for long walk naked or continually beguile himself with patched-up old mythologies about which he has no *intense* feelings. It is to Yeats's credit that, so early in his career, he was scouting around purposefully in order to extend Pater's vital principle into the religious dimension. In this way he could turn mundane occasions into religious observances without posing.

Usually he is thought of as a chameleon, tinkering about with various bits of doctrines and shuffling several not even successive selves almost as if he had set out to confuse biographers-to-come. No doubt of it, he is confusing, but his purpose comes through. On one wall of his main room in Woburn Building hung Blake's "The Whirlwind of Lovers," an articulate parable of what Yeats called "that tragic ecstasy which is the best that art—perhaps that life—can give" and by which man is "carried beyond time and persons to where passion, living through its thousand purgatorial years, as in the wink of an eye, becomes wisdom." That phrase, "to where," the least noticeable in the whole affirmation, is Yeats's own omega-point on which, almost from the first, his inner eye was fixed. It is the point at which the cheques of the metaphysical traveller are cashed into human relevance and seeming gibberish develops an import plain enough to reach everyone. This is as far as he was able to "come through," both in the sense of surviving and of communicating. He is not everyone's poet; not every reader shares his fascination with what's difficult or cares to read hard into the early, Celtic simplicities, hoping to catch the right nuance. But, quibble as we may about Yeats's groaning, his juvenile cult of action and passion, his fondness for the worst, we have to concede that he chose a principle early and kept applying it until it did indeed enable him to look back to "Ruin, wreck and wrack" with renewed wonder at life's richness.

If we ourselves "summon back" his early poems we find, embedded in the resolute poeticality and the filigree of trance, mature touches which disrupt what Yeats called "the purpose of rhythm" (to prolong "the moment of contemplation") by introducing realism, matter-of-factness and a disenchanted modernity. On the one hand there is an array of souvenirs: white deer, boar without bristles, desolate lake, loosened hair, musical silence, the

Rose (varying degrees of secrecy), black pig, Arcady, faery children, Sligo, Maurya's feet, the bee-loud glade, and so on. On the other hand there are bits that distinguish Yeats from his close contemporaries: "The old cracked tune that Chronos sings," "By the stammering schoolboy said," "cloth That has made fat the murderous moth," and "A sword upon his iron knees." These are no more than touches, it is true, but they make their impact; they are the grit in the elated vision and grit, too, in the sense of courage to face life. Yeats may bewail the lost splendor of Arcady, just as he mourned the loss of ritual from the drama and hymned symbolism as a return to imagination. His lyrics of this period are like echo chambers in which a spiral of sound swells and tightens, expressing little, and making its point through fluent simplicity or pathetic-sounding constrictions. He never lost this knack, never deserted it. And, although his familiar manner—the half-grudging, half-rhapsodical drive at an idea—has not yet emerged, the beginnings are there.

After his drawn battle with the drama, Yeats went beyond the peasant life he knew at first hand and groped for what T. S. Eliot in *After Strange Gods* called "a highly sophisticated lower mythology." He would always, after that groping, be self-conscious, even when he managed to clear his head of things occult. After all, he had also urged the *"passion* for symbol" against the *"interest* in life," a tendentious comparison to say the least. He had dismissed subject in favor of texture and form. So he had much to go through before he could substitute for the "alluring monotony" of rhythm the alluring montony of life itself: the fascination of what's difficult. To the end he perhaps remained too much, as Eliot said, "the weather-worn Triton among the streams"—over-conscious of having come through so much; but, his posing apart, he probably felt a little self-conscious about having found, back in the Nineties, the very equipment—verbal and emotional—which eventually led him out of his esoteric maze to the reportorial austerity that is his alone.

D. H. Lawrence

We are beginning to recognize Lawrence in a full sense that exceeds merely acknowledging "the wild, untutored phoenix" F. R. Leavis adopted and canonized almost thirty years ago. Lawrence, to use his own phrase, keeps on coming through, and more of him in different ways each time. Those who wrote on him in the Fifties aimed primarily at getting his life right, and now it is the turn of interpreters and commentators who, when Lawrence died, were still in diapers. Such homage looks like justice—prose justice, anyway, making this his second decade of thorough recognition after the great swindle in which pseudosophisticated opinion imposed upon him some of the least ingenious misnomers and insults ever devised.

Whatever Lawrence's faults—among them prolixity, vagueness and bad-tempered narcissism—he always deserved better. There was so much that was, and is, so good. And now that we have had the shock of realizing what, both in his life and on paper, he was really about, we may with an even greater sense of shock reread the militant essay of 1937 in which Leavis ironically denounces the pusillanimous who presumed to "place" Lawrence as a provincial, a yob, a bogusly puritanical, blood-spitting, wife-stealing, savage-worshipping, ill-educated, ill-bred, working-class upstart who repeated himself numbly, envied the entrenched, jeered at mental discipline, identified love with rutting, and construed the deferential or tolerant attention of well-mannered listeners as a prelude to discipleship. No doubt of it: he shook them. He also, as Leavis says, made them feel inferior; not only because, for all the iterative meanderings of his prose, he was a better critic than any of them, but also because he had a brilliant, vaulting mind and a daunting fund of knowledge. Long before anyone else in England, he had all the equipment—the predisposition, the antennae, the intuitive flair—to understand and state the driving force in American literature and, wonder of wonders,

19

to transform the earthiness and bread-and-dripping tenacity of the North-East English Midlands into fare for the bourgeoisie.

Unfortunately the bourgeois readers approached Lawrence only on the conceptual and vocabularic levels; they could not feel or vibrate between his lines and words (hence his anger with the Cambridge-Bloomsbury literati). "He was," said David Garnett, "a prophet who hated all those whose creeds protected them from ever becoming his disciples." No: what Lawrence hated was creeds which kept their holders or borrowers from being people. His hatreds were blood-judgments against any denial of life and only incidentally, instrumentally, against class, accent and privilege. About his antagonisms there is something impersonal that appears *ad hominem* but is so only for strategic or tactical reasons. For example, when, in that inspired collection of his criticism called *Phoenix,* he springs the trap on Wyndham Lewis—"the utterly repulsive effect people have on him. . . . They stink! My God, they stink!"—he is functioning as a kind of cosmic bailiff, a *bajulus* or porter, who does what he had to do with any egoistic, brittle, life-denying, sex-disparaging, Hitler-admiring fool. Presumptuous of Lawrence? Only if we cannot share, or admit his right to, his intense response to life's totality. Lawrence the man always did the bidding of Lawrence the seer; the man was the medium, the instrument, the catalyst. And T. S. Eliot himself, whose view of Lawrence was always one of continually modified suspicion (ruffled by the man), managed to see this when observing in *After Strange Gods* (1934) that Lawrence the heretic "lived all his life, I should imagine, on the spiritual level; no man was less a sensualist."

In fact Lawrence worried himself about the sensual lives of other people and not so much about his own. He wanted that part of their lives related to all "the passional secret places of life," but he never ignored the joys, the hazards and the humor of sex's being traditionally (though misleadingly) located in certain "secret"—because covered-up—places of the body. Satyriasis and priapism are no more intended in his message than are the Rabelaisian and the Swiftian views of sex. Concerned always in his tense, prickly way for human dignity, he did not want it to be true (though it was) that for every wild untutored phoenix there were numerous mild, overtutored eunuchs (spiritually speaking, of course), and his homilies inevitably developed an iterative grandiosity. Addressing the many, he tended to lose focus. Man-to-man, he rarely got blurred: he had a remarkable capacity for, as the English working class say, not "sucking up." Whatever the G. E. Moore-dominated Cambridge of 1914 thought about him, and later recorded in memoirs, Lawrence remained unabashed by the dipthongizing twitter of fine minds gambolling. No scintilla stuck to him. He came and saw and heard and retched. What Leavis calls "the incontinently flippant talk and the shiny complacency, snub-proof in its obtuse completeness" scared him not at all, but it did sicken him with its lack of reverence and sharpened his primitivism. Man-to-don, he hated the cynical rationalism which, contrasted with Calvinistic solidarity of the mining counties, seemed sterile and parasitical: no heart, no undissimulated self, no life-love. In Bertrand Russell, who knew nothing of Eastwood and Nottingham, he shrewdly detected "the inexperience of youth"; Russell hadn't lived enough and, as George Santayana observed of him earlier, had been so well educated as to "lose the sense in the logic of the words" and make judgments "always unfair and sometimes mad." One can see that what attracted Lawrence to Russell was the passion of the man's intellect, although it led nowhere, and how Russell, Keynes and "the Club" repelled him: "they talk endlessly, but endlessly—and never, never a good thing said." What was it all about? They didn't say.

But now academe is giving Lawrence his due; or some of it, anyway. What he said about passional, primitive and abounding vitality, as against the metallic coffin of machines and systems, is winning respect. At least it is eliciting many thousands of words, a plethoric homage: I cannot help feeling uneasy about Lawrence's graduation into the heads of young academics who, with ingenious deftness of mind, their vocabularies purged of rancid jargon, and with evident relish, sort out Lawrence's ideas, half-ideas, fake ideas and even his intuitions until, bit by bit, they have tidied him up to receive guests. I feel uneasy because a Lawrence who is organized is not Lawrence; but, having felt uneasy, I feel grateful because the young reader-critics have dared and have, on the whole, triumphed with a magnificent display of honesty.

Just look at the problems. It is only right to study Lawrence's abstract formulations with the same care as we study those of Eliot or Wallace Stevens; but Lawrence's most conspicuous brilliances are not in elenchi or in conclusions carefully worked up to; they are in his mind's unpredictable movements—in the written-down consequences of his miraculous speed of perception and connection (as when he talked). He often skidded and swerved; he back-tracked and created ellipses while he was doing so; he thought far forward and, while doing that, repeated himself like a Shylock. But his repetitions do not remedy his ellipses and sometimes, as when using Thomas Hardy for a springboard into diffuse, repetitious theorizings, he goes beyond mere abstraction into a noetic fog. So I think we have to be careful not to manipulate his utterances into a symmetry or a pattern he himself did not reach. He regarded intelligence as a kinetic onslaught on "the greatest issues." He dealt in incandescence rather than in dialectic, and even when he resorts heavily to what seem standard abstractions, or to standard abstractness, he is not retreating, for clarity's sake, from the world of emotion and sensation, but immersing those abstractions, that abstractness, in a new destructive element (D. H. L. apprehending), which is one of the most Dionysiac uses of literacy yet known. He defies cool summary. And if you can read him coolly, report on him at the same temperature and not get so worked up as to enact his own excitement in your own rhetoric, then you have missed the point.

There is more. Not only must the conventional, dry language of academic discourse partly misrepresent even Lawrence the conceptualizer; it must considerably misrepresent his fiction through analyzing, comparing and tabulating where, in fact, the critic's only way out while remaining in sympathy is some kind of impressionism. This is a repercussion of his way, his message. Part of both was his refusal to verbalize the ineffable accurately and much of his vehement prose makes its impact by nothing so helpful as definition but by a collage of overlapping connotations, hints, entreaties and injunctions which entails each reader's supplying his own version of "the primal impulsive being," "the creative unknown," and "the creative mystery." All dealings with

Lawrence end up in one's own temperament. And Leavis, who more than any of Lawrence's proponents takes interpretation as far as it will go, has wisely limited himself to articulating such intermediary, tricky things as Lawrence's views on marriage, society, family, Freud, Cambridge and humanism. Lawrence's driving force, the nature of his bond with nature, and above all the sequence by which he comes to believe he is indefinably justified—these Leavis leaves unquestioned and imports into his own credo: "vital capacity for experience, a kind of reverent openness before life, and a marked moral intensity." Of the man who said, "without a full and subtle emotional life the mind itself must wither," he quietly observes such things as this (and I summarize) : Lawrence makes us test what he says, not against any body of morals or any formal religion but against our own perceptions and personalities; he is neither a philosopher nor overly interested in moral struggle; he is liable to "primitivistic illusion" and excessive preoccupation with sex; and no-one should "attribute the sum of wisdom, or anything like it, to him." Notice how much his most generous, most penetrating, English interpreter leaves undefined although obviously responded to and accepted *in toto*. Trying to relate the individual vitally to the race and to the very source of being, Lawrence resists exegesis even by the sympathetic, throwing much of the burden, as Yeats does, on the reader's intrinsic self. This is why Lawrence is rightly regarded as a personally absent writer. At the center you find emotions and pulsations which, in order to involve the reader, have to be the reader's own. Lawrence gives the general mood and the reader fills in for himself. The remainder—imagery, plot, character, story, rhythms—is only the church into which each reader (better call him celebrant) brings his own experience, if any, of the life-mystery. Expounding Lawrence's doctrines, then, is tantamount to having to say how all the celebrants feel, for his main theme cannot be engaged at the conceptual, disciplined level. As with Dylan Thomas, the words develop centripetal force, urging the reader back into his intimate self and reminding him that the text is a score he must perform for himself. In other words, Lawrence's emotional core, the core of his cry, is inscrutable. *Finesse,* not *géometrie.*

One further point concerning criticism. Some authors we can be *argued* into appreciating because they operate on the plane of common sense, common knowledge and common experience. Benjamin Franklin, whom Lawrence thought "a wonderful snuff-coloured figure, so admirable, so *clever*, a little pathetic, and, somewhere, ridiculous and destestable," is one: he always "derided the spontaneous, impulsive or extravagant element in man," and someone less apocalyptic and more prosaic than Lawrence could conceivably, on grounds of logic, prudence and discipline, make a case for Franklin, leaving nothing unexplained. Franklin is wholly scrutable. So too is H. G. Wells whom Lawrence in *Phoenix* turns inside out on the occasion of William Clissold—"not one gleam of sympathy with anything in all the book. . . . The emotions are, to him, irritating aberrations." And H. L. Mencken, "the nihilistic, stink-gassing Mr. Mencken," being not esoteric, could be made exegetical sense of too, with no recourse to lyricism, guesswork or groping. Franklin, Wells and Mencken, then, are accessible, as Lawrence is not. Lawrence communicates, if he is going to communicate at all, before (and sometimes in spite of) being understood. And even the most scrupulous, articulate, fresh-blooded young expositor cannot help us much toward the primal mystery Lawrence celebrates. Instead (and even this makes Lawrence clearer than he is) we have to adjust in our own way to the electrical collision between his resolve to join in the freemasonry of mankind and his urge to sacrifice all to the arrogance of having a complete, unique vision. His accounts of his vision are never cogent although, to the right person, they may be vividly suasive.

Say what we will, his readers *will* produce critical treatises on him—for reasons sometimes academic and career-feeding, sometimes egregiously personal and sometimes, perhaps always, because Lawrence voices, authenticates, and provides a fictional framework in which there are blanks for, our own dissatisfaction with the rigid patterns of technological society. We have, as it were, caught up with his version of the future without quite attaining to his reverence for the instinctive life.

After Leavis and a few other Englishmen (Richard Aldington, Stephen Potter and Graham Hough force Lawrence the least) it is North American enthusiasts who are doing the most for him in one of the most intriguing reciprocations the literary world has seen. Lawrence set the ball rolling (in some cases bouncing nastily) by writing between 1917 and 1918 a set of twelve essays he first thought of calling "The Transcendental Element in American Literature" but which eventually, after eight of the twelve had appeared in *The English Review* and after much revision in Sicily (1920) and America (1923), he brought out as *Studies in Classic American Literature* (New York, 1923, London, 1924). Both in the United States and England the book's contumacious absurdities, though intermixed with brilliant *aperçus*, had an unfavorable reception. The style was wearingly hysterical. Conrad Aiken objected to the pastiche of Whitman's barbaric yawp; *The Times Literary Supplement* found genius but also "obstinacy, complacency, and perversity"; Edmund Wilson also pointed to the hysteria and Thornton Wilder found "passages of nonsense." The truth is that Lawrence, living at Lobo Ranch, near Taos, was in a bad way when he did the final revisions. Incensed at Mabel Dodge and her Indian husband, Toni Luhan, he was taking out his nervous frustration on Frieda, his friends, animals, America, and by extension the third draft of this new book. Yet, despite its wildness, Edmund Wilson called it "one of the few first-rate books that have ever been written on the subject. . . . Lawrence has here tried to do," he said, "what it would be difficult for an American to do: read our books for their meaning in the life of the western world as a whole."

This much, and more, has become even clearer through the devoted labors of Mr. Armin Arnold who, under the title *The Symbolic Meaning* (1964), has gathered up the previously uncollected first and second versions of the book and collated them with the third. The contrast is startling. The first two versions are good-tempered, explain at greater length, are less subjective, quote more (and more sustainedly), and, from a hostile England that harassed the Lawrences as possible spies and suppressed *The Rainbow*, see America as a paradise. Between 1916 when he finished *Women in Love* and 1919, when he left England, Lawrence's creative energies went into these essays which, in their original intact form as we now have them, amount to a new, more level-headed version of his best critical performance.

Lawrence shows an uncanny sympathy with the American-ness of American literature and is in tune not only with its "didactic" side but also with what he calls its "symbolic import." What he found in such authors as Melville, Whitman and Cooper was blood-consciousness and reverence for life's mystery, neither of which he found in the writings of his English contemporaries. Odd and heterodox as it may sound, it is the Yeatsian side of Lawrence that is attracted to American literature, to the American experience; for his response, like Yeats's to Irish peasants and Celtic gods, is not just atavistic and primal, not just predisposed to the discovery of national tragedy in an abounding human vitality's being applied increasingly to industrial and techno-logical purposes, but also mystical, atmospheric and almost necro-mantic.

The Symbolic Meaning is one of Lawrence's most engross-ing books. Its minor faults are a gabbling repetitiveness amount-ing to anaphora, a tendency to excite one's mind without enlight-ening it, and a trick of insisting *a priori* even when the essay is arranged *a posteriori*. This last characteristic is inseparable from the main fault, which is Lawrence's habit of fitting American authors into a universally valid understanding he thinks he already has. Not for him the presentation of evidence and then an induction; nothing so mundane. Instead, he proceeds in the authentic way of genius, showing not only how the authors exemplify his theory but also, when he does mention them, using them to extend the theory in hand. What we get is not just the "studies" promised in the title of his original version, but a parabolic, declamatory discourse on civilization, religion and "the creative mystery." So it is wise of Mr. Arnold to supply the new title, preparing us as it does for an approach which finds its summary in one of the two essays on Hawthorne. "One of the outstanding qualities of American literature" is "that the deliber-ate ideas of the man veil, conceal, obscure that which the artist has to reveal." It would be hard to imagine a theme more suited to

Lawrence who himself, as recent studies show, can profitably be explored on the same premise.

As well as being one of the incunabula of Myth Criticism (Richard Chase and Messrs Leslie Fiedler and Philip Young, among others, have paid their separate homages to it) *The Symbolic Meaning* reminds us how much Lawrence had in common with his favorite American authors. The introductory essay, "The Spirit of Place," twice the length of its other version, is a lovely magical thing, meditative and logical where the other was shrill and obtuse. In his anger Lawrence really hacked this one about and it is a revelation to have it restored from *The English Review* of November 1918. The Yeatsian vein begins almost at once. The artist, Lawrence says, is a somnambulist "contravened and contradicted by the wakeful man and moralist." Once, "occultists say," there was a universal mystic language known to the priesthood of the whole world, a language expressed in "symbols or graphs," in "the rosy cross, and the ankh," and it may be possible, he thinks, to evolve a similar thing for our own times—"a universal system of symbology" for use in psychometry and psychoanalysis. He then distinguishes between "authorized symbol" and "art-symbol," the one standing for a thought or idea, the other for "a pure experience, emotional and passional, spiritual and perceptual, all at once." Only the first kind of symbol can be didactic, he says, and then he suddenly launches into a dazzling half-dozen pages that sum up European civilization and the migrations to America. Cortes lands, finding Montezuma the mystic "filled with mystic apprehension" and the Aztecs "subject to the fine vibrations in the ether": he is received as a god. A flurry of emphasis ("It is absolutely necessary to realize once and for all") then prepares us for Lawrence's main point that man, lusting to dominate, cannot dominate the life-mystery which precedes him. The New Englanders, Lawrence says, "struck down the primal impulsive being in every man" and in so doing destroyed "the living bond between men." All that remained was the possibility of achieving a mechanical society not worth living in and certainly not the best "reality" America could achieve. There follows a hymn to the American daimon in which Lawrence predicts the disappearance of "mechanical monstrosity," although on what evidence beyond intuition he does not say. "We wait for the miracle, for the soft new wind." We are still waiting. The reality that Santayana called "bumptious, cordial democracy" (raucously denounced in the third version of this essay) has not heeded or vindicated Lawrence yet, and it turns up again in the essay on Benjamin Franklin, this time provoking Lawrence into an onslaught on the notion of man's perfectibility.

About Franklin, as we might expect, Lawrence was not enthusiastic. In both extant versions [1] of this essay he loses sight of Franklin for several paragraphs at a time. He is more interested in resuming his sermon on the precedence of creative mystery and the sterility of mere will. "The religious truth," he says, "is the same now as it ever has been." What he calls "the Presence" has not changed and it alone ensures "the perfect Now" (a curious refraction of Pater's "mystic Now") to which all men can penetrate if they try. He discerns a lyric unity in creation, "rocking at all times," and involuntarily exposes a problem of his own: "oneness with all" *versus* "independent maturity." Finally he pleads against the existentialist idea of "seizing control of [one's] own life-motion" and, after condemning the "practical unison" of stereotypes, concludes "It only remains for us now, in the purest sense, to choose not-to-choose." The only way out—the way Franklin the leveller derided—is to act according to "the creative mystery which is in us," "each man mystically himself." He ends by backing down a little: until the Franklins have demonstrated the barrenness of will man cannot know how to set about being his *"unique*, self, incommutable." Our wills will be so strong, he decides, that we can eschew willing altogether.

On Crèvecœur he is tentative. Version One says it is easier to turn whites into Indians than *vice versa*, but Version Three says the opposite (Lawrence having seen something by then of Toni Luhan). Where Franklin excels in "spiritual consciousness" Crèvecœur excels in the sensual sort, dictates lyrically to himself

---

[1] The early version is logical and calm whereas Version Three (Version Two if it existed is lost) is all exclamation marks and tantrum, and abounds in irrelevant, subjective touches although it does include Lawrence's own seven-point creed along with his list of thirteen virtues and, astonishingly enough, rates Franklin higher than Version One does.

from the head and totally fails to respond to the "otherness" of nature. Like Sartre in *Being and Nothingness* Lawrence emphasizes the terrors of being *known* (Dmitri Karamazov, he says, dies spiritually from being exposed, from being wholly known) and at the same time introduces his theory of love as "the deep, tender recognition of the life-reality of the *other*." He sums up Crèvecœur as a man who, not liking life as it is and being unable to attain to the passional dark, wills into being a fantasy of his own whereas James Fenimore Cooper, who is the subject of two essays, separates the human as a social unit from the human as a pure sensual being. But we must, Lawrence decides, "admit life in its duality." (Writing to Catherine Carswell he alluded unfavorably to the "journalistic bludgeonings of Turgenev. They are all—Turgenev, Tolstoi, Dostoevsky, Maupassant, Flaubert—so very obvious *and coarse,* beside the lovely, mature and sensitive art of Fennimore [sic] Cooper or Hardy.") And the discussion of Cooper becomes a brilliant feat of hagiographical sympathy (Version Three is more facetious and more critical) . He keeps Cooper in view throughout. Where Crèvecœur imagines himself in a wigwam, Cooper goes further, imaginging a whole lifetime in the backwoods: "living in a Louis Quatorze *hôtel* in Paris, lying looking up at the painted ceiling, dreaming passionately of the naked savages." Cooper holds nothing back; his inner man is not a trifler or a *boulevardier* but the hero variously embodied by Natty Bumppo, Leatherstocking, Pathfinder and Deerslayer who, unlike the typical hero of Thomas Hardy, finds a way through duality, not to death, but to his own "blank reality." As Lawrence points out, Deerslayer chooses singleness rather than the engulfing, dissolving passion of Judith Hutter. He lives for others, remaining true to his own mystery but also deferring to that of the Red Man. To Lawrence such singleness is one of the aspects of the natural aristocracy of the soul which, like Yeats, he opposed to notions of equality or the mutual consumption that love can become.

Poe assists him to pursue the same line of thought, so much so that he unquestioningly identifies Poe with the characters in the tales. Hardly an artist, Poe "is rather a supreme scientist" who demonstrates through lugubrious experiments in prose "a little meretricious" that any attempt to be identified with another person leads not to bliss but to death. Poe's Ligeia dies, "a creature of will and unfinished consciousness" who, like most of Poe's characters, cannot recognize that man's craving to merge with someone, something, is futile. The trouble with man is not, Lawrence says, mother-incest (he mentions Jung), but his disinclination to be alone: to be other than everything, everyone, else. To seek through love an absolute identification with the beloved is both mad and mechanical; the only triumph of love, he goes on, comes about when in communion "each self remains utterly itself." Just as God is a mystery, and not a will, so too the individual human being; "if we conceive of God," Lawrence says, "we must conceive of Him in personal terms"—but without trying to define Him.

This holding back, on both the cosmic and personal planes, is what man finds hard, and when Lawrence turns to Hawthorne in an articulate, insistent pair of essays both of which also become rhapsodical, he sucks *The Scarlet Letter* dry, partly to ballast his own notion of myth, legend and romance as "passionally reasonable," and partly to show how Hawthorne deals not in persons but in archetypes and insignia. What a dense, fervent anthem the first essay is, with its half-occult talk of "the great A, the Alpha of Adam, now the Alpha of America" and its harping on man's being the leader of woman. Hester Prynne seduces Dimmesdale; it is not the other way round, and Hawthorne, "a real seer of darkness," without ever explaining, reveals sensational and ideal consciousness in the act of defying each other and tearing Dimmesdale in half. Then, having extolled this novel as "one of the wonder-books of the world," Lawrence damns the surface piety that masks the "lurid lust in sin" underneath and on the same grounds condemns the Brook Farm experiment—"an attempt to perform by pleasant means what Dimmesdale . . . attempted by unpleasant means." On *The Blithedale Romance* Lawrence is both at his best—lithely analytical and in exact sympathy—and at his worst, so that some of his comments on Priscilla read like a textbook on magnetism refurbished into a new cabbala. The second piece on Hawthorne, printed for the first time in *The Symbolic Meaning*, is one of the few surviving examples of

Version Two (the Sicilian revision) . The droning continues, this time about ancient science, whose habit it was not to "seek" but to "compel the material world to yield up its secret to him." Lawrence goes on to discuss Hawthorne's characters in relation to this distinction (surely contravening his own edict against tying things down too firmly) and gives *The Scarlet Letter* all the superlatives he can muster, reserving his deepest tribute, as in the first essay, for Hawthorne the artist over Hawthorne the moralist.

The next essay, "The Two Principles," originally intended as an introduction to the essays on Dana and Melville, but never before published in book form, treats of chemistry, Genesis, symbols, Biblical events and mystical anatomy, and reminds me of Yeats at his cosmographical darkest. The whole thing reads like a spoof although a fluent, well-rehearsed one. Turn to the next essay, on Dana's *Two Years Before the Mast,* and the contrast is sharp. Versions One and Two have been lost and this is the Lawrence of Version Three. He rambles, dispenses with verbs, becomes colloquial and almost slangy, darts about, gets sarcastic or giddy, talks of himself ("I would rather be flogged than have most people 'like' me") and quotes at great length. The gain is a convulsive zestfulness as if the message is being scattered over his shoulder by someone digging or fishing, and the loss is that of a steady rectilinear advance. Once again Lawrence warns against idealizing anything and argues for unintellectual "knowing." Some of his comments are bold ("Americans have never loved the soil of America as Europeans have loved the soil of Europe") and some, especially those on whipping, are sadistic in a juvenile, scoutmasterish way that cannot be dignified by his allusions to Hardy, Tolstoy, Verga and Millet or made entertaining by his invocation of ganglia, salt and phosphorus. The mood—"Let us smash something. Ourselves included"—is disconcerting and tart, but it does at least keep the reader in sight and, through its hostile importunity, awake. Lawrence, like Dana's sea, seems never still, never quite knowable, never quite to be trusted.

There follow two essays on Melville, neither of them published before and both of them patient in manner (unlike their opposite numbers in Version Three) . In the first, on *Typee* and *Omoo,* Lawrence says Melville does not emotionalize in the manner of Conrad but, a creature of the sea (and therefore unsentimentally attached to it), yearns to return through it to the central mystery of being. But, entranced by his Pacific, Melville could not stay on it any more than he could remain with his Typees. The ocean, "like the Celtic Tir-na-Og," draws Lawrence into all kinds of anthropological and ethnological digressions, especially the sacrament of *"oneing"* as known in Typee and so far from (what Melville really wanted) "life as an *idea*." Lawrence felt strongly, as in the 1923 essay on Crèvecœur, that the white man "must remain true to his own destiny." Knowing the Luhans had taught him that much and he expressed it in the third version of this essay. But, however disappointed he feels about western man's incapacity to return to "soft warm twilight and uncreate mud" (Version Three) he can see Melville plain and in Version Two vividly describe him: "Melville is no amateur at living. He is the perfect epicurean, eating the world like a snipe, dirt and all baked in one *bonne bouche*." Tolstoy he dismisses, in contrast, as "half-educated, ill-bred, clownish." What held Melville back was his nominal Christianity, "intact at the back of his head, in a sort of cupboard" and constantly interrupting his blood-consciousness. In the second Melville essay Lawrence turns to *Moby-Dick*, noting the lurid style deriving from "the violence native to the American Continent," quoting extensively, blaming Melville for the oddly Lawrentian fault of "deliberate symbols and 'deeper meanings,'" spotting as in Dana and Whitman the homosexual element and finally suggesting that Melville didn't always know what his symbols meant and that he often abandoned them for long stretches.

The "tiresomeness" he finds in *Moby-Dick* he finds also in Whitman, about whom in this version he is much less disparaging than in Version Three. Whitman, he says, too often plays at being Whitman, and then we are off into an obscure trip round Whitman's principal ideas in the course of which Lawrence talks of high and low planes (not explicitly defined) and seems to rebuke him for grandiosity, lack of logic (!) and then, tiring of his own and Whitman's opacity, breaks into the everyday language of men: "Even if you reach the state of infinity, you can't sit down there. You just physically can't." Lawrence says Whitman enters

"shakily" upon his "love of comrades" phase and Lawrence just as shakily extolls that phase, a little suspicious that marriage, which he prizes and Whitman does not, will vanish before "love of comrades" comes about—if at all. Lawrence isn't sure. He likes to say Whitmanish things such as "the polarity is between man and man" but, lacking Whitman's twisted view of woman, has to work his mystic side hard to justify their implications. The book's end, with Lawrence laboring to produce an elated paean, rings false, echoing the beginning. That "sad, weird utterance of his classic America," where men develop into machines and ghosts, must surely have seemed, except to the deluded, unconquerable by "the miracle, the new soft, creative wind."

For all the *longueurs* of the early versions, *The Symbolic Meaning* illuminates for us Lawrence the mystic and mystical critic. It also reminds us that, sometimes, the critic who can do most for a book, author or an entire literature is the one who, lacking most of the orthodox critical virtues—patience, scholarship, logical-mindedness, capacity to organize and lack of bias—has only a hunch, a feeling, an intuition, of what is going on. This is Lawrence. It is also, in some degree, Anaïs Nin, whose "unprofessional" study appeared in Paris in 1932 at the time when Lawrence, two years dead, was little known. Usually, if at all, his name was invoked to sustain the tradition of juicy obloquy initiated by the obituaries (Janet Flanner's slanderous *New Yorker* piece was one of the most despicable) and countered only here and there by friends (Richard Aldington, Catherine Carswell, Lady Ottoline Morrell), by E. M. Forster, who knew him slightly, and eventually by a handful of critics. Stephen Potter in 1930 published a pertly thoughtful "First Study"; in 1932 Catherine Carswell brought out an enthusiastic piece of sanity, *The Savage Pilgrimage,* and Horace Gregory set a high standard in discernment with *Pilgrim of the Apacalypse* (1933). Even such friendly testimonies as Mabel Doge Luhan's *Lorenzo in Taos* (1932) and the Hon. Dorothy Brett's *Lawrence and Brett: A Friendship* (1933) did him a degree of harm by treating him on the biographical level the sensation-hunting public preferred. And, of course, the capricious John Middleton Murry's *Son of Woman* (1931) and *Reminiscences* (1933), intended as tributes,

33

only succeeded in denigrating and misleading; Murry was too involved with Lawrence to do him justice while vindicating himself.

So Anaïs Nin's little 1932 study, republished in 1964 with all its old mistakes (she three times tries to mention *Studies in Classic American Literature* and in three different ways garbles the title) is historically interesting for its courage and pertinent now for its intuitive approach. She manages in her off-hand, distracted, way to communicate the feel of Lawrence's language as well as the truth that Lawrence's "abstract thought is always deep reaching: it is really concrete, it passes through the channels of the senses." Lawrence, she asserts (she rarely argues), is an example of female intellect. To read him is to "realize philosophy not merely as an intellectual edifice but as a passionate blood-experience" and to recognize that he writes about vital imperatives apprehended impersonally. A great part of his work, she says, is "interlinear" because of "his constant effort to make conscious and articulate the silent subconscious communications between human beings." Naturally enough this approach tempts her into dark trances all of her own; but who is to say she is further from the heart of Lawrence than his cool-headed expositors or his well-meaning, sometimes misleading, friends? Against the ecstatic and impressionistic side of her study we have to set her judicious remarks on Lawrence's being brought up in a "neutral," undynamic Christianity (such as you still find in the Notts-Derby coalfield), his way of reasoning *a priori* from "trifles," and his habit—really his innovation—of making fiction more intimate by conceiving of his characters as artists, as people who make human relations one of the creative arts. His personages, she rightly observes, as Lawrence himself did of Hawthorne's, are "symbolical."

On a less exalted plane she draws attention to Lawrence's essential Englishness (he hated England in a very English way) and carefully—for her—expounds Lawrence's view of a male comradeship that goes "deeper than property, deeper than fatherhood, deeper than marriage, deeper than love. So deep that it is loveless." In a word, impersonal, but more alive than such other ideals as war and peace. Mellors at the end of *Lady Chatterley's Lover* turns to the building of a world, noting relievedly that the building of cathedrals has nothing to do with coition. She brings out most lucidly the Whitman side in Lawrence, a side which most readers in their diurnal sensibleness and undionysian sensitivity prefer to a religion based on the "sacred handsomeness of the sun." It is Lawrence, more than anyone save perhaps Yeats and Dylan Thomas, who clears the way for modern man to realize in his own way "The God who is *many gods to many men.*"

Clearly Miss Nin should be consulted, and the reader must restrain his impatience when, alongside some just, heartfelt remark, he finds a sample of her unreconstructed silliness. Her comments settle into two categories. In one we have worthwhile observations on Lawrence's "cocksure" and "hensure" women, on love's being relative not absolute, on "the field of contact between two personalities," "that worst of male vices, the vice of abstraction and mechanization," the error of thinking soul-mates or mind-mates will necessarily achieve "blood-polarity," and her accurate description of the style of *Studies in Classic American Literature* as "syncopated, with megaphonic insertions." On Lawrence's attempt to convey in prose "the bulgingness of sculpture" she makes good sense, and no-one who feels with Lawrence can dismiss her emphasis on his deliberate imprecision: "I proceed," he said, in *Fantasia of the Unconscious* (1922), "by intuition." She sees that Somers in *Kangaroo* (1923) approximates Lawrence, "The man himself . . . lost in the bright aura of his rapid consciousness," and reminds us that Lawrence-Somers retains the proletarian habit, unavailable to the bourgeois, of "communication . . . silent and involuntary." Most wisely she adds, "This is the sincerity of the people who have not learned enough language to disguise themselves with."[1] She is right, too, to recall Law-

[1] In the Lawrence country, working-class speakers habitually clinch what they say with "like," thus invoking a community of sentiment. For example, when a miner says " 'E were weshin' t' pit-muck off 'is-sen, like" (He was washing the pit-muck off himself), "like" is a nonce word inviting interlocutors to fill in for themselves from common, intimate experience. I wouldn't call this mystical, but it does exemplify the tradition of nonspecific communication that Lawrence calls "the instinctive knowledge of what his neighbour was wanting and thinking." Where bourgeois "tact," as he calls it, restricts, this working-class "tact" touches (a word Lawrence uses reverentially and intensively) everyone eligible. This is a mode of communication, as he said, not "foiled by speech."

rence's admission in his *Autobiographical Sketch* that "I cannot make the transfer from my own class into the middle class" and to contrast British distrust of the arts with the respect they have in Europe. Lawrence, *déclassé*, and trying to articulate for the bourgeois public what the working class took ineffably for granted, ran headlong not into class prejudice but into an English philistinism that took even less kindly to messianic blood-consciousness than to the arts. She concludes by quoting Novalis's "All absolute sensation is religious" and something she incorrectly calls Pater's "pure white flame," setting Lawrence in an agnostic context that makes him seem less isolated than before without perverting his doxy in the least. I think she overrates *Lady Chatterley's Lover* and is wildly wrong when she says "Lawrence was not interested in the cosmos." The cosmos, after all, is not the abstraction it was in the eighteenth century, say, and Ursula's question in *Women in Love*, "Why drag in the stars?" is easy for Birkin to counter. There is every reason for dragging in the stars. And surely this, whatever she intends, is nonsense: "Biologically it has been observed that a man's emotions are concentrated while women's are spread all over their bodies."

Such an approach should embolden other readers to be just as "unprofessional." Surely no-one can read Anaïs Nin's renewed act of homage without feeling hers is the only way to the core of Lawrence's exhortations as well as the only way of making him fructify in our own daily lives. In comparison, Eugene Goodheart's study, *The Utopian Vision of D. H. Lawrence* (1963), seems almost *too* professional, fashionably panoplied as it is in Blake, Dostoevsky, Nietzsche and Rilke, into whose "tradition" of "tablet-breaking" Mr. Goodheart accommodates Lawrence's own "power-urge," his hostility to Christianity and dynamic egoism. It sounds like fun—a doctrinal *putsch* with a doctorate at the end of it. In fact Mr. Goodheart does necessary things. He reminds us (what we often forget) that "The successful action of art is never direct," takes up what Lawrence says about "art-speech" in *Studies in Classic American Literature,* and compares Lawrence's views on symbolism to those of Yeats. Symbolic art, Yeats said, "entangles, in complex colours and forms, a part of the Divine essence," but Lawrence, generally in agreement with Yeats about the emotional and religious force of symbols, "could never," as Mr. Goodheart says, "have contrived the symbolic apparatus of Yeats's *A Vision* in order to re-create the world to his heart's desire." How close Lawrence came to that, though, can be seen in the alchemical-occult bouts in his essays on Hawthorne and in "The Two Principles." Lawrence said that "You can't give a great symbol a 'meaning' " and yet, in his essay on *Moby-Dick*, he assigns a meaning to the whale. Obviously Lawrence wasn't clear in his own mind about this; and one of the reasons was that he was always torn, as Mr. Goodheart points out, between being clear to others and being himself. The two were incompatible for him.

On the one hand, to communicate he had to dilute and modify; he had to formalize verbally (as Christianity does), thus depriving his message or his experience of its essential mystery and arcane quality. On the other hand, to be entirely himself meant that the prophetic part of him would be thwarted. In other words, he had to choose between private fulfilment and public notice. As Mr. Goodheart sensibly observes, his impulse to *argue* for the vision represents an effort to join, in Malraux's phrase, his "madness to the universe." "We respect the vision, but we cannot embrace it as doctrine." The trouble is that Lawrence, the subversive and enemy, did modify his vision so as to get to other people; and that is why, in appearing to argue, he antagonizes trained minds while repulsing readers who base their response on emotional affinity. Lawrence's utopian vision is unattainable, but his arguments and stratagems deceive us into thinking it is not. In *Phoenix* he says, "If you try to nail anything down, in the novel, either it kills the novel, or the novel gets up and walks away with the nail." That, more or less, is what happens with every attempt to interpret Lawrence. The aspiring critic of Lawrence would do well to remember Aldous Huxley's Mr. Propter who, in *After Many A Summer,* observes that "every direct involvement is *notus calor,* with the connotation of the words left open . . . for each individual to supply." Lawrence always returns us to the passionate Now for which there is no program although he, like Pater and Yeats, labored hard in such works as *Fantasia of the Unconscious,* "The Crown" and *Apocalypse* to provide one. If we can only acknowledge such a fact we shall have come a long way from the punitive sniggers of the Thirties. Lawrence, like Byron's Childe Harold, cultivated his own type of "spoiler's art" in order to acquire a full knowledge of paradoxes he had *not* lived; and if such an "art"—mocking or cancelling an intuition even he could not formulate precisely—seems perverse, then all we can say is that the perversity is a literary device intended to teach Lawrence himself and us about the heterogeneous nature of experience. The device is that of oxymoron amplified into structure in order to state the nature of life.

With the publication of *The Symbolic Meaning* and clear-sighted studies that use Lawrence's methods and discoveries upon himself, we shall be able to advance from asking what doctrine he held to what image of man he presents. Then we shall understand why we cannot understand his euphoric side; for that is the side which we must regard as inscrutable, its principal significance being only within a total picture that includes his nihilism. Soon we shall discover his colossal impersonality beneath his idiosyncratic inflexions of voice. And then we shall realize what is so hard to realize: man's nihilism is just as vague as his faith. In her introduction to the 1957 edition of *Look! We Have Come Through!* Frieda Lawrence recalled how, the night after he died, she sat by his body and sang the songs they had always sung together. It is a touching, eloquent memory, but its full import consists in its being juxtaposed with her assertion that "the incentive for Lawrence's writing was love for his fellowmen. Not a sentimental, squirchy, superficial love, but a dry hard one to make people sit up and tackle their job of living." And that anxiety for man to face life, stemming perhaps from some streak in Lawrence of working-class doggedness, is what his writings express most of all. For he saw life, as he saw himself, in its paradoxical, processional roundness. The more we read him the less he explains and the more, in the old sense of figuring-forth in *mimesis,* he reveals. From him we learn that passion and intellect must be generous with each other while fighting their common war against lack of awareness. For, in the end, the fiercest stupidity a man can commit is indifference, and that is what all of Lawrence is about.

Tragic Hope

*I*T will be convenient to make here some points which bear equally on the work of Albert Camus, Jean-Paul Sartre and André Malraux. Action as the means of self-definition is the keynote of their writing, itself the outcome of an historical situation in which, during the German occupation, Frenchmen had to choose between resistance and collaboration. Not that Camus and Malraux properly belong under the existentialist banner; they do not. But they did settle their respective creeds in the same "existential" circumstances as generated the existentialism special to Sartre, and although they do not use exactly his terminology they do think along some of the same lines.

During the occupation, set schemes of values, whether religious or not, could offer little guidance: the individual had to choose by his own lights what he wanted to be. It was a new context, apt for anarchy like the Renaissance and a logical breeding ground for the extremest form of self-reliance and initiative. For the existentialist, man is what he makes of himself; he makes reality, he does not find it, and he makes it in the presence of the inhuman universe that Santayana felt so keenly. He makes it not in vacuo but en situation, basing his decisions and acts on whatever standards he can evolve from his own spiritual, rational and physical experience. It sounds a strenuous, untidy and almost desperate process, and in the writings of Camus, Sartre and Malraux it is all of that; yet it is something more—something not immediately apparent.

Negatively, existentialism says the world is absurd

or meaningless, and the statement evokes Nietzsche (who spoke of the world's absurdity provoking nausea) and Bergson (who pointed out the resistance of mechanical matter). Positively, there is man's power to shape his life through freely-decided acts. Practically, as everyone knows, there is the fact that no act of self-assertion is simple: the merest act has many ramifications and the conscientious existentialist does his best to realize what they might be. Impractically, there is the fact that sometimes, for all their talk of action, rigor and repercussion, of essence and anguish, existentialists indulge in a kind of metaphysical doodling. It is sometimes hard to tell whether these three writers, for all of whom I feel different kinds of admiration, are just playing with words or are propounding seriously-meant programs. In Camus the temptation to doodle shows most when he talks about suicide in The Myth of Sisyphus *(1943)* ; *in Sartre when he works out his doctrines of "otherness" in* Being and Nothingness *(1943), and in Malraux when he writes his own variety of art-history in* The Voices of Silence *(1951).*

Action eventually leads all three back to some kind of mystique or reasoning-out—back to mystery or a private mental coherence. If it did not—and one cannot be robustly, definitively, in action all the time—it would lead to the mind's being dominated by the idea of the absurd: that the whole world is contrary to reason. Camus reviewed that possibility in Sisyphus; *and Ionesco, Beckett and Adamov have, in their attempt to make a new kind of theatre, pushed it as far as it will go. As Ionesco says in his essay on Kafka: "Absurd is that which is devoid of purpose. . . . Cut off from his religious, metaphysical and transcendental roots, man is lost."*

42

Hence the cruelty and literal meaninglessness of his play The Bald Soprano (*1950*) *and the puppet-nature of the characters. Identity and personality have vanished and so has, in Beckett's* Waiting for Godot (*1952*)*, the purpose in waiting. It is against this knowledge of the senselessness of the human condition that Camus's best work is directed; he fights back, as he does against the philosophy of Heidegger, Kierkegaard and Husserl. He tells us to remain lucid and purposeful in face of this absurdity and not, like the heroes of his plays* Caligula *and* The Misunderstanding—*the one deliberately, the other unknowingly—increase the sum of nonsense.*

Albert Camus

Camus, we might think, was one of the most understood moralists of our time, one of the least willing artists. Whereas Sartre's *Being and Nothingness* is both intricate and obscure, Camus's very paradoxicality is clearly stated. But it is involuntary, not reasoned; and if we sympathize with him it is with the baffled *homme moyen sensuel* caught between physical rapture and cosmic dismay, not with such of his other *personae* as the tortuous dialectician who, having once written a thesis about Plotinus's influence on St. Augustine, still sparred excitedly with the noumenal, and the politicist who was concerned more with predicaments and entities than with individuals. Of Camus's lesser roles—the self-conscious osbcurantist ecstatically and apocalyptically commending the aphorisms of René Char; the pompous Camus, dictatorial, vatic and intransigent, of several essays in *Actualities;* the wry posturer "half-way between poverty and the sun"—we are surely right to take little notice. The Camus we like and understand best (the English-speaking world has interpreted him uncommonly well) is the moderate who in 1939 wrote for the *Alger-Républicain* a series of sensible and constructive articles on the economic plight of the Kabyle tribes south of Algiers, and suggested practical solutions for his native Algeria, in *Combat,* as early as 1945. The same man talked impressively and consistently of *mesure,* gradualness, of delimiting a problem, of being stoical—a strange amalgam of sybarite and preacher, country boy and pontiff, casuist and simplifier. He was constant even in his inconsistencies.

It is important to know of the Camus who was born near Constantine of working-class parents, the father Alsatian, the mother Spanish. He was brought up by his mother, a cleaning-woman, his father having been killed in the 1914–18 war. He came under the guidance of two gifted teachers from whom, as from T. B., poverty, golden days on the beaches, a cheap trip to

45

Italy and the intellectual company he found in Algiers, he learned immensely. He also learned early about suffering and how to write. Rejected for military service he sought other ways of proving himself; and, after the Germans had executed a close friend, decided to join the Resistance—while still something of a stranger to metropolitan France. Editing *Combat,* falling out with the Communist Party and Sartre, he explored himself without becoming self-obsessed. Gradually he came to realize that life would not be worthwhile if we could understand it, if it squared with all our ideals: the irritation in the oyster makes the pearl. And, throughout, he lived his life as seriously and as intensely as he could.

Recent studies of his work have tried, with considerable success, to understand what went on behind that worried, high brow of the publicity photographs. His lyricism, his deficiencies, his integrity and his theory of "revolt" have all been considered and weighed, and perhaps we are now at the stage of surfeit: summaries of his plots and ideas are blunting our appetite for the real thing. But we must also remember that he summarizes rather too easily, that we get more than we should from mere summaries, and that this points to a certain lack of texture in his work.

It is always a tricky problem to decide when a society has become too civilized. For baldly to assess the effete nicety of a phase of the arts against such a concept as murder, as would Camus, is not to settle anything. Most people have a pretty definite opinion of murder. The real problem is to decide how far the refinement of feeling must develop, beyond the rejection of murder, towards maximum sophistication. This is, of course, a problem primarily for the artist and not for the politician; and, for the literary critic, it is likely to emerge in the following terms: How far can novels concerned only with delicate sensibilities of cultivated people be said to commemorate what is worthiest in human beings? How far can the adoption of a narrow ideal of beauty be said to have repudiated, and commendably so, what is unworthy in human ingenuity? How far is an artist of any kind justified in cultivating a snail-horn sensibility? How far must a respect for honesty override a feeling of genuine revulsion? And so on. These are questions of *mesure* which Camus might have been expected to review. For he, like Matthew Arnold, had a passion for trying to get things straight, society included. But Camus relinquished the problems of the artist and the armchair politician. He implicitly rejected not only aestheticism but also the artist whose interests are not primarily those of conscience. He became a pamphleteer, and a good one indeed. In *The Plague* (1947) he demonstrated an eternal riddle; in *The Rebel* (1951) and the three volumes of *Actualities* (1950; 53; 58) he explained what seemed to him to be the *unprecedented* aspects of our situation:

Of course, the twentieth century did not invent hate. But it fosters a special variety called cold hate, which is bound up with mathematics and large numbers. The difference between the Massacre of the Innocents and our rules of reckoning is a difference of scale. Do you know that in twenty-five years, from 1922 to 1947, 70 million Europeans, men, women and children, have been uprooted, deported or killed?

For the courage, sense, balance and unwavering humanity of his views, he won just praise and no small amount of envious abuse. He was right to put the facts before us in this way; and to show the workings of his mind while he strove towards a positive view.

According to Camus, the needed view would respect *mesure* and *justice vivante*. He denounced the lie by which a political bargain with Spain was screened by a maneuver from UNESCO. He repeated Arnold's strictures against the petty bourgeois, but he did not display Arnold's concern for the maintenance of taste. He was not much taken with the Malraux cult of spectacular action: if men are too free, they tend to become libidinous; if they are tied down, their proper experience never begins. He had at heart those often traduced "liberal values," including the rights of displaced persons and races; and the needs of the working class which, he was sure, are not best served, if indeed at all, by communists.

Yet, surveying the immoralism of our time, Camus seemed to let his imagination of the moral alternative lead him to discern

that alternative in the life about him. To his preface in *Actualities II* (1953), he added "various certainties the first of which is
that we are emerging from nihilism." He was appropriately cau-
tious:

I shall certainly be wary of giving any universal value to an experience which is personal; and this book proposes neither a
dogma nor a formal morality. It asserts only, once again, that a
morality is possible, and that it costs a good deal.

Certainly, if nihilism had outworn itself, there was point in
having on hand a ready-made and esteemed morality. That point
needs no laboring. But a morality proceeds from a situation: it is
not superinduced. If the new situation is clear, it will suggest its
own morality. But Camus was not sure whether the situation had
changed or not. Elsewhere in *Actualities II* he admitted: "The
historical experience which was ours is perhaps too strange, too
peculiar, to be generalized about." Does he belong, then, with the
fantastic projectors of Swift's Academy of Lagado? Was he not
toying with a crossword puzzle of the politician *manqué?* To
answer these questions in the affirmative would be to impute to
Camus the very motives he attacked in others. He attacked what is
crack-brained and nit-witted and vicious; in short, what has made
some Jews masochists, intellectuals of the Left apostles of force,
and the land of Europe a slaughterhouse. But he attacks, not to
usher a new high-flown theory, but to remind theoreticians of a
few simple, obvious things. Most adults have a sense of what is
right; and act according to it when they are not duped by an idea
or berserk with the crowd. Such a sense need not be inferred from
history, but merely made articulate from the welter of our
intuitions. And a sense of this kind, mawkish as it may seem, and
vague if compared with the dry rattle of the theologian's or
commissar's maxims, is nevertheless good enough for a start.

Various reviewers, French and English, refused to see any
development between *The Myth of Sisyphus* and *The Rebel:* if
Camus had made anything plain, they said, it was that we should
not hope. Camus did certainly say something like that in the
former book. But he developed: not, it is true, from hopelessness
to its opposite; but from hopelessness to a realization that life is

too mixed and inconsistent an experience to justify an attitude so homogeneous as hopelessness. The myth of Sisyphus who pushed the same stone up the same hill does not apply exactly to life as we know it. Sometimes, if we are Sisyphus, and we stop pushing, the stone does not fall. Perhaps, after all, the demagogue on the other side of the hill has it on a string. Perhaps it is a loadstone and he has a magnet. In *Sisyphus* Camus, yearning for an absolute attitude to life, invented an absolute life. But life, though it may not be better, is different. Only an eclectic of resolute disposition can extract from life the elements of a consistency. And to be honestly eclectic is to give the entire situation at least a single scrutiny.

It is hardly surprising that *The Fall* (1956) proved something of a disappointment. *The Rebel* and *Actualities,* monuments of shrewd but solemn theory, were less vivid than *The Plague* and just as abstract as *Sisyphus.* One had hoped, perhaps, for something of a synthesis, something even better than *The Plague.* Instead, *The Fall* confronts us with a successful Parisian lawyer who has abandoned his practice for the waterfront of Amsterdam. He feels he has failed as a man, having failed to prevent a girl from drowning herself and thus having repudiated his bond with all men. So he leaves his job in an attempt to expiate and requalify for human community by interrogating himself in penitence and obscurity. Camus is notably more interested in the story's philosophical import than in its appeal as narrative. It is perhaps too much of a fable, diagram or allegory, and our response is more to lament the novelist in abeyance than to exclaim with indignant relief, *igne me examinasti!* There is a point at which anguished speculation becomes futile, at which a moving narrative satisfies better than the most exiguous searching of the soul.

Various critics reproved Camus for an obsession with merely transitory themes, and for switching abruptly from them to a too abstract formulation of predicaments. In *The Fall* he fastens on the eternal riddles; but he does not cease to traffic with modern reality. He puts political or environmental man first, and fits Pater's idea of asceticism—"the sacrifice of one part of human nature to another, that it may live in what survives the more

49

completely." His intellect has the ascendancy over the rhapsodic side which tumultuously escaped in *Summer* (1954) in a mystique of the sea. Essentially a North African, Camus almost always maltreated his sensual imagination lest it impair the vocation of seriousness. Out of something perilously near to perversity, he misjudged the part of irony, resorting to it as no mere available attitude but only as a weapon in attack; and what endeared him to the student avant-garde was the unflagging seriousness of his views about the present. His progress consisted of a vacillation between the eternal and the ephemeral, between the abstract and the tangible. His characters (Meursault of *The Stranger;* the doctor in *The Plague;* the barrister in *The Fall*) are men of cardboard adroitly deployed in parables. He never quite integrated his chronic sense of morality with his suppressed lyrical gift. *The Fall,* sensuous only in a strained, lapidary way, does not bring him near enough to the world of individuals fitfully alluded to in *Exile and the Kingdom* (1957) . The danger is that to discuss overmuch, as he always did, the predicament of honest feeling, is often to live at one remove from reality. Utopia, having no location, recommends itself by its quality. But even the quality of an ideal has sometimes to be presented blemished by application and testing, and injured by overmuch talk. For all the sobriety and integrity of his quest, Camus never quite realized how futile prolonged discussion can be, and how little that fact affects an art that is largely one of portraiture.

The man has come to have an almost mythological significance, on account of which some people have praised him for writing things he did not write and others have omitted to notice those parts of his writing that fail to square with Camus idealized. Fortunately, however, Camus made his own distillation from himself, aiming partly to debunk the glorified image of Camus the Just, and partly to set in its proper context the image of Camus the Aesthete. *Resistance, Rebellion and Death* (1961) consists of twenty-three essays which Camus himself chose from his considerable output on social, political and aesthetic matters. From *Actualities* the articles and essays he saw fit to have collected together in English translation are these: the impassioned, stiff-lipped *Letters to a German Friend,* two apocalyptic editorials on the liberation of Paris—both from *Combat;* a moving but unsentimental tribute to René Leynaud, the poet and resistance worker executed by the Germans in June 1944; two indignant sermons on pessimism, courage and intelligence; then parts of an address given before the Dominican monks of Latour-Maubourg in 1948: "If Christianity is pessimistic as to man," Camus said, "it is optimistic as to human destiny. Well, I can say that, pessimistic as to human destiny, I am optimistic as to man." Alongside that typically paradoxical utterance, one is glad to see his withering answer to Gabriel Marcel's defense of Spanish totalitarianism and the "Bread and Freedom" speech given at the St.-Étienne Labor Exchange, May 10, 1953. That speech includes the following summary of Camus's views on something he liked to think of as the duty (as distinct from the predicament) of the intellectual:

Thus, in my opinion [he begins], there are two ways for an intellectual to betray at present, and in both cases he betrays because he accepts a single thing—that separation between labor and culture. The first way is characteristic of bourgeois intellectuals who are willing that their privileges should be paid for by the enslavement of the workers. . . . The second way is characteristic of intellectuals who think they are leftist and who, through distrust of freedom, are willing that culture, and the freedom it presupposes, should be directed, under the vain pretext of serving a future justice.

In the long run, as he points out, an exploiting *élite* produces a totalitarianism of taste; and his argument against those who debase the tastes of an unsuspecting public merely to make profits and to finance their own fastidiousness applies also to social systems run by secret police. Genial vulgarization is just as gross an insult to the possibilities of humanity as torture in an Algerian cellar. Camus never lost sight of the variety comprehended under that respectably bland phrase, "the middle way." So, he points out, one can control without crushing; one can entertain without vulgarizing; one can even discuss workers or prime ministers without necessarily idealizing the one or disparaging the other. All he asks for is the extra effort that takes us from a simpleminded position to one which attends to the individual as an individual. No story is more shattering than that of the French priest who is accompanying a truckload of his countrymen to execution by the Germans. The priest, the only one not going to be shot, tries to comfort the youngest, who is only sixteen. Suddenly, the young boy forces his way between the canvas covering and the truck box and is gone. The priest thinks hard, then gives the alarm. The boy is recaptured and eventually occupies his allotted billet in the lime pit.

Here is Camus's comment on that:

. . . it is important for you to know who told me this story. It was a French priest. He said to me, "I am ashamed for that man, and I am pleased to think that no French priest would have been willing to make his God abet murder." That was true. The chaplain simply felt as you do. It seemed natural to him to make even his faith serve his country.

Thus Camus, to a German friend. In the extremest dilemmas, he says, we must be on the side of life; what we do we must do for the sake of the living. And that is the attitude prominent in the other pieces in Camus's last book: a speech of homage to Eduardo Santos, the exiled President of Colombia, commends "all those men . . . whose sacrifice and example every day help us to live"; and Camus confesses to anger and anguish at "the decrease of liberal energies, the prostituting of words, the slandered victims, the smug justification of oppression, the insane admiration of force." The same stand recurs in the group of articles on Algeria: ". . . if anyone," Camus says, "still thinks heroically that one's brother must die rather than one's principles, I shall go no farther than to admire him from a distance. I am not of his stamp."

All the essays in *Resistance, Rebellion and Death* are mordant. They have also the slightly inflamed rhetorical aura of a Malraux; but Camus's rhetoric amounts to an additional way of proving his sincerity to listener and reader, whereas Malraux's rhetoric is too often self-regarding. Camus is at his most savage in his essay on Hungary and the long piece called "Reflections on the Guillotine." The two pieces come together in such an assertion as this:

. . . there is no possible evolution in a totalitarian society. Terror does not evolve except towards a worse terror, the scaffold does not become any more liberal, the gallows are not tolerant.

And the essay on the guillotine is detailed, brutally vivid, both humane and sickening. "What," he asks, "can we think of those officials who call the guillotine 'the shunting engine,' the condemned man 'the client' or 'the parcel'?" But the lurid circumstances are burned away by the white heat of such argument as this: "Retaliation is related to nature and instinct, not to law. Law, by definition, cannot obey the same rules as nature. If murder is in the nature of man, the law is not intended to imitate or reproduce that nature. It is intended to correct it." And the death penalty, as he shows, is no deterrent. The essay ends with a grandiloquent proclamation: "There will be no lasting peace either in the heart of individuals or in social customs until death is outlawed."

Note the grandiloquence: death, he thinks, *can* be outlawed. But it can't, any more than what appalls Camus in human nature can be eliminated; any more than the man of conscience can do much more than give his life or his opinion or his aid, although he knows that the majority don't really acknowledge the facts of barbarianism until it interferes with their own personal routines. This is not to belittle Camus's anxiety that men should speak out when they can: after all, man's first duty is to maintain the tradition of attempting the impossible. Man has to aim too high in order to hit any target at all; if he aims at what the moderate would like, he gets nowhere. So Camus advises a moderation that proceeds, and seemingly succeeds, through pursuing impracticable extremes. In this sense, he offers a kind of charade: against the horrors of recent history, and against the inescapable facts of the human condition, he protests with impassioned accusations, high-flown slogans, low-flown Christianity, political wiseacreishness and paradoxical stoicism: ". . . I am an artist," says Camus in an interview which he gave to *Demain* in 1957, "because even the work that negates still affirms something and does homage to the wretched and magnificent life that is ours." That sentiment is expanded with gratifying clarity in "Create Dangerously," a lecture he gave at the University of Upsala. The artist's service, he says, is compulsory: he witnesses and, in expressing his own feeling of comparative impotence, makes that impotence a little more useful. And if Camus seems at times too fond of political man, too much of a stylist, too vague about his faith, too self-conscious and sophistical a polemicist, we should remember that verbal attack is a solace as well as a weapon. In Camus the humanist has to serve the humanitarian; but the humanist is in no way inferior. Camus believed in putting first things first—even if to say so meant incurring Sartre's gibe about being a prig with a portable pedestal, as well as the charge that he was not a novelist at all.

The self-righteousness, the mythological nature of his so-called novels and the attention both have won for him amount to his revolt against the absurd human condition. These good things, as he himself would say, he added to the human quantity. Certainly, he oversimplified; his notion of "sunlit thought" seems wishy-washy beside his precise arguments, and it is hard to say where it fits in. But, and we should never allow Camus the Just to blind us to Camus the Artist, this man did deal in parables. He had to. That is why the last complete book he prepared gives us the *data* of his experience after we have had the benefit of his imagination. *Resistance, Rebellion and Death* is as close as Camus got to turning the texture of society into art. He lacked the sense of clutter, and his "novels" are much closer in kind to his *Actualities* than Sartre's own novels are to his philosophical writings. We look to Camus for sermons, not for the fertile human muddle or the subtleties of temperament and of psychology.

His thought was always intricately ambitious but, perhaps because of his lyrical streak and his impatience with extreme attitudes as with all fanaticism, seems less coherent in detail than in outline. His work shows all of Gide's care for the individual without Gide's inability to see further: the clarity of Gide's outlines is that of an unmitigated self-concern; Camus's is that of a man more concerned with the predicament of any individual human rather than with himself in particular. A search for moderation has always characterized Camus's much-publicised "positions." His early essays in *Betwixt and Between* (1937) and *Nuptials* (1938) shuttled between instinctive atheism and physical delight. He learned early that happiness is not easily won by the questing mind: between exultation and despair there is only the realization of the absurd—the lack of correspondence between coherent ideals and incoherent actuality. This disparity, as he pointed out in *The Myth of Sisyphus,* can prompt suicide, physical or mental, neither of which is in accord with his view that "the absurd depends as much on man as on the world for its existence." The fact that we perceive the absurd increases the amount of absurdity. For the absurd is irremediable: to this truth men must stoically attend, all the same. We tread a "vertiginous ridge" between self-destruction and escapism; and, it is true, the act of "keeping faith with the earth" is a sentimental choice. It must not be allowed to deceive us into being adamantly idealistic. But, as Camus explains in his own peculiar choosy and occasionally cloudy way, we can revolt: we can "refuse" the universe.

Man has refused the universe in two principal ways: metaphysically and politically, as Camus points out in *The Rebel.* From such perceptions he extracts a resolute humanism that seeks a way between romantic self-deceit and revolutionary inhumanity. Neither self-deceit nor murder (to which all political rebellion leads) makes life any more meaningful or more tolerable. Within each individual there is something that the absurd affronts; that is sufficient reason to go on living, although Camus infers no divine intention from it. To confront the universe, in whatever way, is an emotional gamble, not a logical step. Confrontation has to be based on some such concept as the "sunlit thought" with which Camus vaguely concludes *The Rebel.* The cultivation of the middle way, *mesure,* entails lowering our sights even at the expense of *mesure* itself. Camus really means we should knuckle down to things and not, like the saint or sinner, expect too much.

When we turn to Camus's fiction we find a mind cerebrally alert, and not quite in command of the world of daily triviality. *The Stranger* demonstrates that there are no explanations of life other than those man creates for himself. Such explanations are a form of self-deceit—what Sartre calls *mauvaise foi;* and Meursault, the unheroic hero, the animated robot who accidentally commits a pointless murder, is punished by society not so much for that act as for refusing to utter things he doesn't believe in.

Meursault refuses to fool himself; he is the archetypally honest man, made what he is by the universe as it is. In fact he is the kind of automaton that a society of different automatons lusts to expunge. In his personal life—in his attitude to his mother's death, to his girl friend and his acquaintances—he neither pretends to feelings he doesn't have nor dissimulates those he cannot help having. Ultimately he realizes that his death sentence binds him to all other men; and that realization is the basis upon which Camus constructs his doctrine of charity and compassion. The individual at once counts and does not: because he is thus merged into the universe's consumption of humans, he has a basis on which to operate as an individual entity. Meursault can therefore reject the priest's belief in divine purpose; in the same way the death of the priest in *The Plague*, the novel-fable Camus worked on during the war, symbolizes the irrelevance of religion when all men have united in a common purpose that reflects their eventual common fate.

In *The Plague* nature is implacable; but several men, whom we are to see in close-up, band together to resist. The priest, Father Paneloux, interprets the plague as retribution for sins, but later comes to think it a God-inflicted test in the true epic style. He dies believing this. But another man, Tarrou, the brawny extrovert, who once witnessed a decapitation, sees the plague as just another manifestation of Nature's destructive urge. He firmly believes that good in this world arrives as the result of exerting our will power. He dies hating Nature's brutish ways, and exalting man's power to change the natural order. The main figure, Dr. Rieux, is a dedicated automaton; at least he is until he sees a small child die, and hears the priest interpret its death as punishment. The doctor cannot see how punishment should be indiscriminate. Why should the child be killed when many of the guilty survive? The only one to survive the plague, he compiles his chronicle of outrage and injustice at the hands of impersonal Nature. His work has to go on protecting man against the blind powers of the cosmos. Only in rebelling against the human condition can man prove, as Camus says, his essential nobility.

After relinquishing all hope of epiphany, Rieux accepts the mystique of brotherhood. He and Tarrou turn one night from the plague to swim in the sea. Thus they renew their capacity for joy as well as their will to fight on others' behalf. But this is no leap of faith: Camus offers, instead, the conviction compactly expressed in *The Myth of Sisyphus* that "tenderness, creativity, action, human nobility will take their place again in this insensate world." This conviction defies all plagues, physical or mental: "the wine of the absurd and the bread of indifference" will nourish man's "greatness"—and not necessarily within a theological framework. According to Camus, "there are only two universes for a human spirit; that of the sacred (or in Christian language, of grace) and that of revolt." Hence the near-liturgy, assembled in *The Rebel,* of revolt, mythological, literary and actual, from Prometheus to Ivan Karamazov and Sade. Camus makes faith a deliberate act, excluding from it such irrational leaps as those of the Christian existentialists. But he commends Buber's doctrine of awareness and distance, as well as defining "the sacred" as "that presence felt in the silence during a moment of genuine awareness." Camus the elated pagan continually disturbed the edifice of rational thought erected by Camus the humanist. Perhaps the doves that, in *The Fall,* spiral in the Dutch sky denote something less matter-of-fact than human solidarity; something to which his death added an ironic new twist.

Always, Camus stressed the privileges and commitments of individual self-awareness. It was this fundamental view of man which continually led him to compose tracts disguised as novels and, in *Exile and the Kingdom,* allegories that shimmer in the guise of technically immaculate short stories. In fact, the further he went, the more he attempted the universal and anagogic rather than the particular. From the beginning he preferred to deal in pregnant generalities, occasionally "filling in" with everyday data when his theme became too abstract (which is just what he does in his published notebooks and journals).

Germaine Brée has described an unpublished novel called *La Vie heureuse*—a kind of Dostoevskian *Summa*—which she considers to be the matrix of all Camus's published writings. The hero, Mersault (foreshadowing Meursault) murders Zagreus, a Dionysus figure, as a protest of "revolt" against death. Mersault, for one moment of time, arrogates to himself death's own power; he is a cosmic trespasser. He then goes off to Prague with money the murder has brought him. But in a Prague street he finds a body, returns to Algiers and rethinks his whole position. He falls ill, but welcomes his decay and imminent death as the cosmos's supreme compliments. We are not very far from the English Romantics' talk of being made "one with Nature." The novel is a variation on the theme of the pilgrim's progress; it exemplifies Plotinus's view that all beings have fallen from a state of participation in the source of being and are constantly attempting, through various stages, to return. Mersault's stages are physical, intellectual and spiritual—a common enough triad. He lives out in his own career the three main points in Camus's analysis of the human situation: the universe is "absurd" and provokes "revolt" either nihilistic (anarchy) or ideological (prophetism and revolution), neither of which compares favourably with a hopeful moderateness based on sunlit thought. Camus, in fact, was a true stoic; and the theme of his writings is almost Christian: in tribulation, in this "century of fear," we should seek neither solitude nor utter solidarity; we should be neither maenads nor ascetics, neither men of stone nor mock-gods, but simply "present" to one another and responsible for ourselves.

This positive side of Camus is impressive and heartening. But, from *Betwixt and Between* to *Exile and the Kingdom,* he maintained certain negative habits of mind which have been little noted and little discussed. The key to this unsatisfactoriness can be found in Sartre's rebuke to the effect that Camus loved humanity but mistrusted individuals. He had a feeble sense of social texture, of the stuff that makes Balzacian novels; of love between individuals in all their eccentricity and groping; of the fact that we fear not death, but the possibilities beyond it: rapture without hope, like heroic hedonism, is not enough. We must love life, he says; in his discussions of art, however, we find much talk of fraternity but little delight in man himself. He once gave his "ten favorite words" to a magazine: "world," "suffering," "earth," "mother," "men," "desert," "honor," "misery," "summer" and "sea." This list—taken together with his mythology of exile and fall, victim and executioner (into which groups he thought the whole world divisible), revolt and plague, Sisyphean and Promethean endurance, unresponsiveness and "invincible summer"—suggests a simplified and impoverished view of human nature. The truth is that his mythology and Nemesis, his goddess of *mesure,* depend upon an exigent eclecticism which might have included only Berenson on art, Plotinus, and "the sunlight on the olive-trees." As it is, he ranged widely although retaining little. His concern was to explain how we can, within limits, provide a just framework for our private lives. His plays (still too little known), his cautionary tales and his essays offer foundations, not superstructures. They offer a doxology of noble civics rather than what Lionel Trilling calls a culture's "buzz and hum of implication." In 1952 Sartre apostrophized him in glowing terms: "You were a real person, the most complex and the richest, the last and the most gifted of the heirs of Chateaubriand and the most scrupulous defender of a social cause." But that was the Camus of 1945, the author of *The Stranger* newly revealed as the editor of *Combat.* Sartre, after an unsuccessful attempt to create a noncommunist Left (the *Rassemblement Démocratique Révolutionnaire*), knuckled down to the Marxist march of history. Camus held aloof from both Sartre's project and the French communists. Sartre called him a "reactionary bourgeois" (standard odium unworthy of Sartre's intelligence); but then, Sartre was committed to dogmatic totalitarianism, and Camus firmly opposed all systems and determinisms. *The Plague* and *The Rebel* do seem like postscripts to Chateaubriand's *The Martyrs,* and certainly Chateaubriand's ghost drifts through Camus's intensely colored evocations of Mediterranean pastoral as well as such *romans personnels* as *Nuptials* and *Summer.* Indeed, his emphasis on personal responsibility is a kind of half-way Christianity oddly at variance with his announced hedonism and paganism. There were similar contradictions in Chateaubriand, and one can see what Sartre meant and what, beneath the surface, perhaps antagonized him without his knowing it.

Camus's last book, announced as *Le Premier homme,* might demonstrate whether or not he was incapable of the novel of manners. Moderation's nympholept, he often found his middle way conducting him into an ordinariness his imagination spurned. He always seemed rather unheedful of life's mixtures.

He put freedom of the body before the quality of the spirit, and once quoted Dostoevsky's remark that "One must love life before loving its meaning . . . yes and when the love of life disappears, no meaning can console us." Camus's love of life was selective; he preferred its primitive forms, pastorals and archetypes. When Rieux and Tarrou go off to swim in the sea, they briefly reunite themselves with the beneficent side of Nature; they challenge the horror, complete the picture, refuse an absolute vision. So too Camus, stealing off from the "century of fear" to lavish rhapsodies and abstract ideas. Swimming brought him "the turbulent possession of the sea by my legs"; theorizing often brought him a similarly illusory hold over the world. His synoptic view—of the eternal and contemporary extremes: death, the pathos of aging, summer's invincible recurrence, oppression, cold war and French troops lording it in his native Algeria—has variety but not quite enough for some people. One wonders whether his philosophy was communicable in terms of so much that is muddled and intricate and not momentous, out of which our daily lives are made. *Le Premier homme* sounds as allegorical as ever. Chateaubriand's last and most gifted heir would not, I think, have become a Balzac or a Stendhal without making deep inroads on his previous habits. In *The Gates of Horn* (1963), "a study of five French realists," Harry Levin argues that storytelling fluctuates between two poles: immersion in myth and "a sharp confrontation with actuality." Stendhal, Balzac, Flaubert, Zola and Proust obviously, he says, go for the second type of narrative. And, I would add, Camus went for the first, perhaps because he did not wish to become a bourgeois novelist retailing wads of information for a public that cares less about philosophical statement than about the familiar, or familiar-seeming, minutiae of daily life.

Camus never forgot the working class he came from. Like Lawrence, he felt his childhood and young manhood had created the matrix from which his art came: poverty, roaches and the deafness of his mother provided him with an early vision of a brutal and paradoxical world, a world whose essentials he learned about early and which dominated his response to worlds he encountered later. He always cut through to fundamentals and found them familiar; he had known about them from the beginning, and he never had time to work away from them to what, in some novelists, is a delectable sifting of social particulars, trimmings, mores, manners and topicalities. In addition he always felt, much as Lawrence did, that the writer's task was to speak on behalf of the inarticulate and the silent who confront the stoniness of the world without fuss. Not long before his death Camus declared that he would have achieved nothing until he had managed to place at the center of his writings "the admirable silence of a mother and the effort of a man to find some form of justice or love which could counterbalance this silence." Lawrence eventually got over his feelings about his mother, Oedipal and otherwise; Camus never did, but extended them into a stark apprehension of the human state all classes have in common. The young Caligula says, "Men die and they are not happy." For Camus there is man in his irreducible quintessence and the mystery, the glory, of the cosmos in which he is placed. Everything else is either destructive of man or mere social padding; what is destructive he fights and what is padding he leaves to others to display.

We have to remember that after a childhood and youth which taught him much that was basic about man's nature and place, Camus became immersed in war, which was like learning severe lessons all over again—this time not in the sunlit limbo of Algeria but in France where everything was crumbling and nihilism rampant. A born victim, man victimized himself, losing sight of spiritual ideals and consoling himself only with sensual pleasure. And Camus, who had learned nihilism from Malraux and Dostoevsky while still in Algeria, found himself torn between a voluptuous savoring of the North African litoral and a horror of death. It is no wonder that he developed into a kind of X-ray writer, forever penetrating the appearances and the camouflage of amenities that society invents. There was a streak in him of dogged unimaginativeness; he refused to be taken in, he refused to sing along, and he continually referred everything to what, in the strictest sense, we might call his utopia: a placeless condition in which all men are subject to the same forces and which is therefore the condition of ultimate solidarity. Between 1939 and 1944 he countered his own sense of despair at the French collapse, and the humiliations of being occupied, with an almost desperate commitment to the Resistance. He fought despair—the despair so meticulously expounded in *Sisyphus*—with revolt and militant stoicism. Sisyphus shows the way out, laboring without end but not giving up. And Meursault in *The Stranger* is caught up in a similarly unrewarding, meaningless world in which no-one's account of an event resembles the account of anyone else; he just pushes forward according to his own standards, expecting no logic, no sequence of cause and effect and certainly no understanding. Here once again we have the theme of communication, deafness and isolation; even the syntax of his French, as Sartre pointed out, serves to isolate from one another things that we might expect to see connected. Yet it is—to use a word I introduced earlier—a diagrammatic novel, not a sketch of society.

The Misunderstanding (1944) too is a parable rather than a slice of life; it operates upon us in much the same way as Robert Penn Warren's "The Ballad of Billie Potts," which has the same plot of the prodigal son's returning unknown only to be murdered by his own kin. It is a kind of puppet play, approaching caricature and cartoon; yet the moral—the negated chance of trust and solidarity on a level above the familial—comes through with none of the frivolity that sometimes attends hyperbole. The son, counting innocently on an absence of ill-will to someone unknown, moves into a crazy situation in which people do not murder their sons except under the delusion that the sons are someone else's. It is, to say the least, an horrendous ethic. Where there is no charity there cannot be a sane love, and the son loses more as a stranger than he could gain as a blood-relative. A dead son cannot fight back, of course, but the bereaved emperor Caligula can, and in the play of that name he tries fanatically to surpass the absurd world in absurdity. But, of course, only man can lose by seeking to make a bad into a worse; for the universe does not respond, cannot be hurt.

From this homiletic and allegorical phase Camus advances to one in which his philosophical assumptions and his fictional illustrations do not interpenetrate as neatly. Between, say, 1945 and 1951 (the year in which *The Rebel* appeared and Camus quarrelled with Sartre) he worked his way from the idea of grim, total revolt to an insistence on *mesure*. Sisyphus, Meursault and

Caligula have no middle way, and Camus illustrates this relent-lessly. But the heroes of *The Plague, State of Siege* (1948) and *The Just Assassins* (1949) rebel not against the destined but against accident, seeking to affirm something to go on living by. This is the imaginative version of the theories and sermons contained in Camus's journalism of this period in *Combat* and other papers, of the "Letters to a German Friend" and *The Rebel*. What one misses in these works of fiction is circumstantial detail: the comforting clutter of pastimes, hobbies, little enterprises and minor purchases that people preoccupy themselves with and, metaphysically speaking, set between themselves and what they do not understand. Forces—plague, sea, mortality—overshadow the characters as *people* in a way that we do not find in, say, *Dr. Zhivago, Bleak House* or Malraux's *Man's Fate*. The only charac-ters that seem to have a life of their own and not just for the purposes of this demonstration are such comic-grotesques as the man who spits on cats. I think this is a flaw. Camus is trying to express the arbitrary, rather than the absolute, nature of absurd-ity, and he manages to do this successfully with such concepts as the plague and the siege; but he neglects to show us something we know very well, and that is the inexplicable efflorescence of personality at all times, during hardship no less than during misery.

I am suggesting that his view of the accidental and arbitrary is incomplete. I am not asking for the kind of overspilling eccentricity we find in Dickens or Dostoevsky, but for some acknowledgment of the full spate of human variety and complex-ity. Diego and Victoria in *State of Siege* have no personality with which to counter the pressures upon them. And to this extent I think Camus falsifies: it is not so much the pressures of time, world and mortality that dominate them as Camus's own doc-trinal emphasis. There is a gap here between the facts as we know them and Camus's demonstration. He creates a situation and characters which fit his special talents, and that is right and proper; it does not, however, exempt this play from the criticism that it fails to select a representative pair of people who, as well as making the main point, would also remind us that our world is too complex to be exhausted by one label, one characteristic.

What I miss is density of irrelevance, by which the playwright reassures us he is selecting from a life we all know is more untidy and less predictable than any play can spell out. It is as if Camus is drawing not from life but from the argument within himself, so much so that he fails even to convey the accidental, heterogeneous confusion that forms part of his thesis. The same is true of *The Just Assassins,* a dialectical play which seems amputated from life as we know it. It is not that Camus shirks the big questions; on the contrary, no writer of our time has so purposefully, so relentlessly fastened on to the issues of life and death, conscience and callousness, pain and joy. I complain because he fastens onto nothing else—the ephemera, the trivia, the miscellaneous idiosyncrasy. He fails to give the idea of life's developing, as we know it does, without being planned, and cannot therefore communicate to us the sense of life's contradictoriness which Lawrence does.

In a writer without a sense of humor this would be excusable because he would obviously not be able to render the absurdity of the thousands of juxtapositions that a single day will yield. But Camus did have a sense of humor and of the ridiculous; asked if he thought any part of his work had been persistently ignored, he answered that his humor had. It is there, in some measure, in *Caligula* and *The Fall* and mordantly so in his essays. The answer, I suggest, is that he was writing within a French tradition that includes Racine and Corneille and Voltaire, a tradition that dislikes mixed emotions and disdains Shakespeare as a botcher. So he was obliged to eschew contrast, discordance and medley. Above all he must not mix comedy and tragedy, and he must aim at an Aristotelian purity of exposition: no muddle, no untidiness, no splashes, no loose ends. It is a pity, but I think the circumstances of his early life compelled him to resort to that tradition. The tragic sense came to him early, and war and recurring tuberculosis intensified it. He was, formally at any rate, *anima naturaliter classica,* and spiritually (these are the words that come to mind) intent, serious, earnest, single-minded, objective, deliberate, lucid and spare. There is nothing of Rousseau here. Instead, everything is discernibly organized toward the presentation of highest common human factors until there emerges an image of man, a bare image that carries none of the oddities of nation, society, class or indeed of personal temperament. Such an image travels easily, especially to America where the dominant literary habit is to see man alone and naked against the universe (as in *The Old Man and the Sea* or *Moby-Dick*) ; Camus, like Hemingway and Melville, celebrates man's power to endure what appear the inexorable ways of an inscrutable, impersonal nature. Americans, especially those of the Myth persuasion, prefer fables, and this may explain the success of Camus's stoicism in a country trapped between the ascetic-puritan and the materialistic.

It is fair to say, then, that Camus's writings have a primarily philosophical appeal: they come to us on the level of fable and myth. His life too, from some angles, seems an exemplary fable, especially to those who witnessed the eloquence and intensity of his conviction, the way in which he said what he said as if perpetually conscious of the fact (noted by both Camus and Malraux) that death makes everything definitive and incorrigible. The dominant fact about him is the co-ordination of all his effort: not a word wasted, not a page; and I think it is right to see him as a man with a mission, insisting and never meandering. This is the source of all the non-Communist complaints, mainly from the English, against him. Obsessed with negation, with forces that annul man and stunt him, Camus tended to neglect whatever man finds to fulfill and rejoice him. The obsession with things negative produced in Camus some equally negative oversights, and tempted him into too much thought of death, too much identification of joy with sensual rapture and too much distilling of human nature into abstraction. It is the psychology of the prisoner who cannot shed habits he acquired in captivity. Camus was always a prisoner of what he learned in his formative years, always managing to fit new experiences into the old pattern. Like a doctor (remember Rieux), Camus developed special attitudes to keep himself balanced while dealing daily with life and death; and these attitudes—call them safety measures—took him away from particularity and individuality toward a vastness in which his own pain seemed less his own.

If we compare him with Brecht, which is reasonable, we find that Brecht cultivates exactly what Camus avoids: the mixture of realism and myth, the rational with the irrational; the depiction of life's incongruity not only doctrinally but through characters such as Mother Courage who are highly complex and sometimes betray the very dogma they are supposed to enact; freedom of the actor from his part—so much so that Charles Laughton could be entirely himself while 'performing' the main character in *Galileo*. In his way just as determined to make his point as Camus, Brecht continually found his plays taking on (both as he wrote and as they were performed) a life of their own that played havoc with his theories, his ideology and his conceptual discipline. And when Brecht divides his characters to demonstrate the thesis that it is impossible to be virtuous in this life, he still cannot control the comic inventiveness and the Shakespearean gusto which, in *Herr Puntila and His Man Matti* (1940), draw attention from the ideological duty-character, Matti the Communist, to the ludicrous, egregious capitalist himself. We laugh because he is a funny personage, not a funny capitalist. Compared with such stuff as this, Camus's plays (at least) seem somehow unsophisticated or priggish or simplistic, on the side of ideas rather than of life. And when, in *The Caucasian Chalk Circle* (1944–45) Brecht confronts us with such an "approved" theme as a dispute between two collective farms, he also allows the warm hearted Grusha and the lascivious Azdak to overpower that theme with an abounding vitality I find only rarely in Camus, and mainly in his early works. Camus felt he could not imperil his seriousness and his message with anything that was not functional; he wrote, so to speak, with his muscles and mind tight and thereby, as I see it, deprived his work of the additional convincingness that comes about when the writer's thesis emerges from what looks like a random assembly of items. The casualness of this, the deliberate show of not having picked the best evidence, is something Camus could not manage; and that is why in reading him, and even in agreeing with him, we may feel he tries a little too hard, giving us a truth we assent to intellectually but which we would have liked to infer for ourselves from his facsimile of the world's enduring mass of particularities. The fish he catches is the one he has already placed in the barrel and not one that he takes, pot-luck, from the sea.

Having said these things, some of them harsh, I confess that I do so uneasily. We are always harsh on those writers who give us most and I feel I may have been straining, here and there, to curb an emotional response to Camus's *thought*. It is hard to be cool about this man who addressed himself to the young as neither Sartre nor Malraux has, who worked his way from squalor and through the dark mills of the Resistance up to the Nobel Prize at forty-four, who seemed always an unposing and humble celebrant of good will and who met a cruelly ironic death not long after his major work had begun. I would find it easy to overpraise Camus for his achievements of conscience, for the honesty and gravity of his human concern, for his courage in both war and peace, for his refusal to budge on certain issues, for remaining himself. If any writer can teach those who have to live without God how to do it, Camus can: his devotion is to the best in man and to the best action man can take. He is the least obscurantist of the humanists and (a rather special point) he never lost the feeling of what it was like to be young and joyful. I just feel he had not fully orchestrated his theme; only the philosopher and the fabulist got substantial parts before he was cut down by the car smash. All the makings are there, but we have to take them as we find them, mostly in argumentative form and not deployed in imaginative works of comprehensive, detailed power.

Only in *Exile and the Kingdom* do we find the stubborn hold on detail, texture and the swarming particulars of daily life; he seems caught up, for once, in the actual fabric of things and the quirks, the behavioral spectrum of people accidentally hit upon. The tone is discordant and the method erratic. The places are not places of the mind but sites realized in close-ups that evoke a whole climate. Here are eddies, fluctuations, distractions, objects of impertinent interest, words spoken that do not always attend a visible thesis. Jonas, the workers on strike, and Janine the wife in "The Adulterous Woman," throb with life and complexly so. This book appeared in 1957. By the 4th of January 1960 Camus was dead. So there was no time. In the meantime (as we see it now), he adapted Dostoevsky's *The Possessed* for the stage and chose the texts for inclusion in *Resistance, Rebellion and Death*. One can see the preparations for something new: *reculer pour mieux sauter*. Camus had always given his mystical side a hard time after his early writing days. What I have called "mystique" is there; in *Nuptials* he speaks of "gods that speak in the sun." But pressure of circumstance led him away from such private ecstasies to a reasoned interpretation of what men were doing between 1939 and 1945 (as earlier in Algeria and later in Hungary) and from that to a strictly formulated mode of behavior, "a tragic hope," a stoical resolve to "serve suffering and beauty" simultaneously and to think clearly on such lines as these (from his address at Columbia University in 1946) : "Whoever today speaks of human existence in terms of power, efficiency, and 'historical tasks' . . . is an actual or potential assassin." And: ". . . if we believe that optimism is silly, we also know that pessimism about the action of man among his fellows is cowardly." This leads directly into his dispute with Sartre and his refusal of any ideology (such as Sartre's professed one) that "claims control over all of human life." The writer's task was to face absurdity, reveal it to others and then try to show them how to contend with it on human premises. This amounts to facing death without the solace of the supernatural ("Man is that force which always ends by holding off gods and tyrants") and without Christianity (which Camus found a doctrine based on injustice and brutality).

Camus's attitude to Christianity has much in common with his attitude to Marxism. As Christian commentators have pointed out—some of them rudely, some of them humbly, and some of them redundantly presuming to clarify in their own jargon what is clear in Camus's prose—Camus did a good deal of thinking about the Christian faith. He set down his conclusions in some of the essays in *Actualities* and in *The Rebel*. Christians have not, on the whole, welcomed Camus's scrutiny of what they stand for, but they have applauded his onslaught on Marxism. Unfortunately for them, Camus damns both for the same reasons.

He starts with evil and death, abiding items in man's condition, and concentrates on Christianity's performance as an ethic rather than as an account of divinity. If, he says, there is a God who controls this world, then God is responsible for evil; God is unjust inasmuch as the innocent (such as the dying child in *The Plague*) are made to suffer. He sees Christ as an intercessor, a New Testament effort to mollify the image of God; Christ is God become man and therefore represents God's ostensibly relinquishing His traditional privileges in order to suffer and die as a man. Thus Christianity combined the idea of mediation with that of history and, according to Camus, was at its best while the Hellenic idea of mediation prevailed over the Judaic idea of history. The first Christians impatiently awaited the world's end and then, tired of waiting, set about improving the world *within* history. In the Albigenses and St. Francis, Camus finds no resignation but a "tragic hope." All the same, whether or not God assumes the role of man, if there is unjust suffering in this world, then either God is culpable and men are innocent, or God is innocent and men are guilty. The Christian has to assume the latter and, convinced of this, tries to make the best of the world he lives in.

But, says Camus, in the Middle Ages historical-mindedness took over again and created an opening that Marxism would eventually use. Echoing Matthew Arnold he deplores the ascendancy of Judaic elements over Hellenic. The equilibrium between humanity and nature began to disappear, he says, with the Inquisition and the elimination of the Cathari heresy. As soon as the divinity of Christ was denied—when Christ became a man-God rather than a God-man—a condition had begun to develop in which eventually Karl Marx could become "the Jeremiah of the historical God and the St. Augustine of the revolution." Instead of God we get the Future (from Marxism) which, unlike the Kingdom of Heaven, stands at the end of a history which has no starting point (the Christian Creation). So whereas Christianity is entitled to an end in view, Marxism is a state of eternal becoming. It is here that Camus appeals for values within history and not above or beyond it. Against what he calls the "German ideology" that aspires to an absolute, he argues for a history in which men can be acknowledged as having limits, knowledge its ignorant aspects and values their uncertainty. We must not ask too much of men, he contends; beyond certain limits they revolt and thereby define for all time the human potential. Where historicity says the end justifies the means, Camus says the means justifies the end. He is preoccupied with the here and now, which is the only thing we know. He is pessimistic about destiny but optimistic about man. There is, after all, nothing else to be pragmatically optimistic about. Once men turn their whole attention to the here and now, to history, then abiding values will emerge—abiding, that is, in this life. It is no use judging man (as Meursault is judged) by absolute standards; man himself is not absolute. Small wonder that Camus, desperately arguing for a human standard, should exclude everything that seems not essentially, not universally human, and that, in the concentration of his argument, he should appear to be making an absolute case for relative man. For, as I have said, he pares things down so much, ignoring the inessential. I have to believe that such a paring down is the prelude to a *constatation* after which (as in *Exile and the Kingdom*) the peculiarities of individuals can be reintroduced. It has to be, for if we are aiming at basics such as death and pain, is it not true that there is no man who dies, or suffers, who has not some individual peculiarities? Men do not die as if they were chemical formulae, as if they were all H_2O. In the long run it is not a standard human nature that suffers or dies, but, each time, a unique human being whose children are his alone and whose fingerprints have no double.

Sartre spotted this habit in Camus and attacked him for simplifying the human facts, for removing wealth from the rich and poverty from the poor in order to establish man against heaven. But, as Sartre for all his intelligence failed to realize, Camus habitually dealt in allegories and his allegories amount to a preliminary clearing of the ground. Where Camus fixed on the present he did so because he believed that talk of a future state of secular happiness would only legitimize murder on a large scale. Sartre, who as an existentialist believes in the future only, dismisses the present because "man is always in a state of formation."

It is difficult to define Camus's ethics. In some ways it advances the notion of a vital Now; in others it recalls Comte's positivism and the Mosaic decalogue. Certainly it is not existentialist although its terms of reference are existential, and it is not Marxist. My own feeling is that Camus did not see it as part of his responsibility to provide rules for living but rather to emphasize a predicament in which either enlightened self-interest or self-denial for the sake of others will serve to keep man on the right track—and that is the track of doing things in the present, not of talking airily about the future. At times he talks as if he were proposing a code for the individual but his habitual terminology refers more to a code for the state: he is against historicism, pogrom, mass murder, poverty, totalitarianism, military adventurism, hypocritical alliances and pussyfooting by what he calls the social church. It sounds sensible enough. And what he is for—happiness, justice, moderation, sunlit thought (which amounts to an intellectual reverence for life's fertility) —sounds, as several commentators have said, banal. There is a reason for this: just as he pares things down as far as he can, ignoring the superstructure of life, he chooses not to fill in the details of his ethical outline. It is the habit of the philanthropist; his concerns are too large to permit him to examine, or to recommend, details of behavior. So it is no surprise that he has been attacked for grandiosity, for a smug and ineffectual righteousness whereas Sartre has taken the trouble to relate his ontology to such concepts as shame, fear and anguish. All we know is that Camus advocated revolt and that revolt takes us at once to the question of values. About this question Camus affected the same kind of coy, dissimulating amateurism that Eliot learned from F. H. Bradley. "I am not a philosopher," he tells us. He need not have bothered. He gives us intense moral emphasis without supplying any kind of doctrine; and this emphasis derives, I believe, from his experience of and addiction to the state Gilbert Murray calls *euetheia,* which is primitive innocence and what Serge Doubrovsky in an essay in *Preuves* (October 1960) calls "the *precultural* springs of existence." Camus always felt he was part of nature, whereas Sartre feels nature is alien; Camus rhapsodizes about the sun and the sea and the sand, the mystique of swimming, whereas Sartre pays his homage to manufactured objects. Indeed, sometimes Camus recommends concentration on the body as the site of an earth-ecstasy that relates man to the sources of being. In this he is close to Lawrence, not least because they both formulate rites of passage (Camus being fond of pairs who go swimming together).

But, awed as one may feel by the immensity and fecundity of the universe we inhabit, we find it hard to derive an ethic from the sun, whether under the auspices of Camus or those of Lawrence. And it would be wrong to derive anything in the nature of hedonism: "Self-enjoyment is impossible," Camus says in *Betwixt and Between* because to apprehend our bodies properly is to fuse them with the world about us. We cannot hold our bodies back to enjoy them *per se,* for this would be like trying to get the maximum from a telephone without dialing anyone. It looks as if Camus, for all his litany of moral and civic terms, really belongs with the writers of "mystique." But not quite. He points out that man is the only creature "that refuses to be what he is." Man is always trying to do something beyond himself and being returned to his limits: the return is revolt. "I revolt," says Camus, "therefore we are." In other words, all men know the aspiration (the yes) and its check, whether deliberate or inevitable, (the no). He argues for imperfection as distinct from a perfection that is to come. Whatever we do we must not reject the present or spoil it or waste it. This fairly simple idea comes to us wrapped in ingenious and hyperfine casuistries of the kind the French revel in. It is, I dare say, the view of life which the average ploughman or milkman adopts without knowing it: this furrow, these horses; this milk, these bottles. When commentators say that Camus creates an ethic of "being" as against one of "action," they mean he settles, as John Wain would say, for living in the present. My own mother, a musician with no taste for philosophy at all, has been talking Camus all her life without knowing it: her youngest brother died at twenty-three, and she cites his case because he was a "planner" who always said what he was *going* to do. In her view, you deal with today and wait until tomorrow to plan ahead. It may be banal to mention this, but it isn't any more banal than what Camus says in fancier language. "What we need," he says, "is to define a modest policy, a policy just as free from any trace of Messianism as from the nostalgia of a Garden of Eden." And he defines it as "honesty without illusion, a wise loyalty," which sounds good, but not the sort of thing to run up on posters—*except,* and this is the point, at times of mob agitation, when a banner will transcend the order of banality. Camus will have none of the march of history, but if he has to write on banners—speaking out on Algeria and Hungary—then this is his motto.

Camus's ethics is really a mood. He wants man to be happy:

in tune with nature (a heresy to the existentialist) and with his fellows in what Malraux has called "virile fraternity." All he asks is that happiness should not be a self-regarding, uncommunicating state; such happiness is really self-abuse. And we can see him moving toward a view that occurs in Whitman and Lawrence when they set the self on its journey to the brotherhood of men. What sets Camus apart is his hostility to egoistic heroism and sainthood, to Gidean hedonism and existentialist absolutes. He was unfair, I think, to Malraux, for the heroism in *Man's Fate* is of a quiet kind that chimes in nicely with Camus's desire for moderation. But, by and large, Camus measured his contemporaries correctly and although his own ethics (really a prelude to an ethics) is an intuitive way of asking men to be intuitive (*intueri:* look at, consider) and comes at us discontinuously, we can see what he means by obeying his first plea; and that is to accept that members of any community stand ontologically alone. No man can stand *in loco dei* to his fellows, and no knowable God stands in supervision over the universe. These are our facts, our situations, our *"actuelles,"* which we have to love, or at least learn to defend, in defiance of submen, supermen and those who take such a long view that communication between present man and his future goal breaks down altogether.

I have already suggested some of the grounds of dispute between Camus and Sartre; and before going on to discuss Sartre it will be helpful to recall the debate of 1952 in which Camus had the best of it and certainly the last word. *The Rebel,* Camus said, was meant as "a study of the *ideological* aspect of revolution" in which he explained why he had taken a hostile attitude to Communism. Sartre, it might be added, never did explain his own attitude, whether we call it allegiance, commitment or, more properly, flirtation. *The Rebel* was in the nature of a confession-cum-study, and not, as its attackers in *Les Temps Modernes* for August of that year assumed, a rallying-call on a political plane. Rather, the book was a piece of metapolitics. It charged modern Communism with nihilism of a kind that derived from Jacobinism and sanctioned violence in the name of "historical tasks." Further, it claimed that the cult of liberty had led to oppression in the name of a mythical apocalypse and that it degraded the present and presence of man. Therefore, Camus said, it was time to denounce Communism's invitation to puppetry and murder and to set up anew an old standard by which men made up their own minds in their own time empirically rather than according to ideological abstractions and speculative formulae. We should remember too the pertinence of this argument to the France of that post-Liberation period when Frenchmen, disillusioned with the old political creeds and all they had brought with them, thought of themselves as *disponible* (unattached) and open to suggestion. Camus was admitting certain facts about modern society; he felt they should be recognized even if they could not be abolished. Among these facts was the principle of violence as practiced by both the so-called free societies and the Communist ones. *The Rebel,* then, was a *caveat* against letting human life become even more meaningless than it already was, and Camus, by no means an optimist, argued eloquently against the beguiling historicity held out by Sartre: if men had made a mess, then, Sartre held, why not put the whole business in the hands of the representatives of history? It was an odd notion to come from a man who believed that human consciousness is in gear with no process whatever. Sartre would have been on better ground if he had stressed the assault on nature rather than a salvationary process which more or less took care of itself. Existentialism has always said that human consciousness is independent of history, and yet here was Sartre setting the two in alliance.

This made him easy meat for Camus. The clash began with the June issue of *Les Temps Modernes* in which Francis Jeanson accused Camus of "anti-historicism"; Camus, he claimed, was dabbling with beautiful, ineffectual ideas whereas he should have been supporting the Communist Party's interest in the masses of Indo-China and Tunisia! Camus replied, denouncing "prophetic Marxism" and asking "If there is no human end that can be made into a norm of value, how can history have a definable meaning?" Existentialism could not have both freedom and history; if history was the right standard, then why was history such a mess? And how could apostles of freedom sell out to destiny? It was then easy to point out that the existentialist, denying any such thing as human nature, could not base revolt upon it and so had to go through the same proposals with history, a mere abstraction. Even more trenchantly, Camus went on to mock history seen as a sort of God, complete with priests and Church. Sartre answered in conundrums about freedom's being "nothing but the free choice to struggle in order to become free" and about accepting many things in order to change a few. Obviously he felt uncomfortable since one of the many things was a Communism which eliminated from the outset not only the remainder of the many but also the few. And Camus had detected this monolithic evasion.

Sartre and his group play with Communism in much the same way as Pater played with Christianity: they want to savor the tenets and rituals without buying in, and they steady themselves by fondling their ambiguity. This proves (to them) they are dealing with tough, complex actuality, and so we find them going through Party motions. Sartre and Maurice Merleau-Ponty, for example, refused to sign an appeal for the investigation of the Soviet forced-labor camps circulated by David Rousset, author of *L'Univers concentrationnaire* (1947), on the grounds (stated in *Les Temps Modernes*) that "no matter what the nature of present Soviet society, the Soviet Union is . . . situated, in the balance of forces, on the side of those who fight against all forms of exploitation." We think, rightly, that such explanation is no more than catechistic clap-trap of the exact kind that Camus finds inhuman and nihilistic. It affronts the minds of those to whom it is offered and degrades those who offer it. As Camus saw, you cannot pay lip service without implying inward assent, and this means too that those who are not against Communism are for it.

The quarrel hung fire and Sartre did not answer. In his "Tribute" to Camus in February 1960 he took care to praise Camus in vague terms that verged on the fulsome. Calling him the Descartes of the Absurd, Sartre also accused him of refusing to quit the "safe ground of morality" for the paths of practicality, but then commended his humanism's "human" attitude to death inasmuch as its quest for happiness "implied and called for the *inhuman* necessity of dying." The adjustment in that humanism seems indeed very practical and goes to prove that "practicality" is not confined to the dogma of Communism and might even be discerned in the refusal of many Frenchmen to vote at all. Sartre himself said these men formed the largest political party in France and he proposed the formation of a new Left in order to reach them. Surely here Sartre came full circle, proposing just the sort of thing which, provided it was not a covert stratagem for Marxism-Leninism-Stalinism, "the most gifted of the heirs of Chateaubriand" would have expected from "the scrupulous defender of a social cause." The last few words are Sartre's own description, in 1952, of Camus himself.

Sartre and Others

As we have seen, Sartre rebuked Camus almost to the end for not being practical enough, for being silent and reticent. It is true that Camus is not always too specific as to what should be done on the level of detail and that he did, before writing *The Rebel,* withdraw from public life in order to clarify certain ideas to himself. But it would be wrong, I think, to apply the word "impractical" to Camus any more than to Sartre, for each in his own way felt and responded pragmatically to the existential emergency that France underwent during and after the Occupation. We have to stand at a considerable distance from them—viewing them from some such standpoint as that of English or American empiricism—and see them as men of their time, shaped by an anguish that is essentially European.

Three things then become clear, if we can for a moment set aside the matter of atheistic existentialism in its French, as distant from its German, form. First, both Camus and Sartre readily exposed themselves when the need arose: during the war and after. Naturally their respective emphases differed, but on the question of Algeria (which occupied Camus all his life) they were not very far apart. They were willing not only to "stand up and be counted"; they were willing to count and to exhort others to stand up as well. Second, both offer a philosophy that seeks to redefine the idea of man and to establish a better way of going on. And, third, both lapse at times, in all varieties of their writings, into a form of impracticality that reads like an elegiac sophistry or metaphysical litany of concepts. But this is only to say that, as Frenchmen, they went through the fire (the totalitarian plague) not as philosophers or writers only, but as sensitive men. And their existential pleas can sometimes be read as nothing more, or less, than articulate notes on pain, the pain of being French, human and hopeful. He would be a crass reader indeed who did not respond acutely with both mind and heart to such a reading.

In such writers as these we find something more basic and more serious than the hyperbolical, self-conscious frivolity which characterizes, say, the English novel during the same period. It was like this, they say, and you must never forget.

On the other hand, when we narrow down the existential (which is what everyone has to deal with if he is honest) into existentialism, and find Camus and Sartre at loggerheads, we cannot respond quite as acutely or as fully. It is the conceptualizing that deters us, even though much of it is set down in incantatory prose that evokes Gertrude Stein or even the poems of such writers as Michaux and René Char. And we cannot be blamed for feeling a little impatient with the convoluted ingenuities of *Being and Nothingness* or the Siberian inspissation of such a tract as *Critique of Dialectical Reason* (1960). If we want the *philosophy* of French existentialism at all, as much as we want the humane common sense of Camus, then we shall do better to turn from Sartre to Maurice Merleau-Ponty and Simone de Beauvoir, who both avoid the conceptual stratosphere more than Sartre does and write in a more commonplace manner about more comprehensible matters. Where Sartre idiosyncratically and emotionally subdivides perception too private to be got wholly into the light, they show a greater degree of empiricism and seem just as anxious to communicate to others as to straighten things out for themselves.

Merleau-Ponty, for example, resorts more to history and modern psychology (although he seems ignorant of modern physics) and, where Sartre takes his start from Hegel and Heidegger, takes his from Aristotle and Russell. For this relief alone, some thanks are due. Even more thanks go to Simone de Beauvoir because she has seen how the existentialist obsession with the future can lead to obscurantism; in *The Ethics of Ambiguity* (1947) she says that "The end justifies the means only if it remains present to us, if it is completely revealed during the enterprise itself." She has gone further, moving in fact into line with Camus. In many ways at one with Sartre and Merleau-Ponty, she has argued for "joy" against "nausea" and contends that "If we do not love life in our own selves and through our fellow man, it is useless to try to justify life." She is the only existentialist who has proposed a defined ethics, and she shares with Merleau-Ponty a willingness to think within a framework that can be either destiny or ignorance. Again, this is the sort of thing that Camus thinks about, and it is only fair, in discussing Sartre, to test him from time to time against these two members of his own faith. It is unfortunate that he has overshadowed them because they are, although less gifted in the creative sense (Merleau-Ponty is strictly a philosopher), more accessible than the master. I shall refer to them as occasion prompts.

Existentialism is based on subjectivity, so it is not suprising that it proved a sitting duck for such destructive examiners as A. J. Ayer and Jean Wahl. You have only to take a page of *Being and Nothingness* to see that often Sartre is thinking emotionally when he writes coolly and writing emotionally when he thinks coolly. Always he has to get off his chest something that contorts or drives too far into casuistry his main point. Generally speaking we can assume that he believes throughout that the self confronts a nonhuman world, is ineluctably involved in society, and cannot be classified under any such chimera as "human nature" (there is no such thing, says Sartre) although it can be related to a constant human situation. Understandably both Sartre and Merleau-Ponty originally called themselves "phenomenologists"—the subtitle to *Being and Nothingness* is "Essay in Phenomenological Ontology" and one of Merleau-Ponty's books has the title, *The Phenomenology of Perception* (1945)—thus acknowledging their debt to Husserl, although Sartre seems to have reached him only via Heidegger. Sooner or later, of course, all theory of existence has to return to empirically self-imposing phenomena. The verbs *surgir* (surge up) and *jaillir* (spurt out) recur in the writings of the existentialists, and they admit that there is no way in which man can separate himself entirely from life in order to report on it. The existentialist spectator is always to some degree a participant and therefore all he says is bound to be tinged with the confusions, the shadows and ambiguities of discovering himself while he is on the move, involved or partly imperceptive. The existentialists have the same occupational shortcomings as we find in such early philosophers as Parmenides and Zeno; and existentialism is a primitive philosophy, intended to fructify in *action* and

79

never, therefore, immaculately noumenal. The creative mystery that made us what we are, that placed us where we are, preceded us, as Lawrence said. What existentialism at its most theoretical would like to do is to go back and classify things from the beginning. It is little use trying, as Husserl does (except on the same kind of mystical basis as Gilbert Murray and Lawrence), to reach the preconscious world; the truth is what we live now, and what we see is determined by how we see it while living. Sartre himself, in *Nausea* (1938), expresses this as a kind of mystical disclosure—not a pleasant one, but essential and the only one we can start from. The indecision of the main character is the prelude to the arrested hopelessness or secular *accidie* of the characters in *The Wall* (1939). Therefore, as Merleau-Ponty says, it is appropriate to comment on the world not only in treatises of philosophy but in imaginative works too. Sartre's novels and plays, then, are not only fictions that parallel his philosophical inquiries; we cannot even say they are more colored, more dramatic versions of what he has decided on the plane of the abstract. No: they are independent and equally valid instruments for exploring the world.

So much for what Sartre calls "being-in-itself," which is a meaningless condition until man imposes meaning upon it. As Sartre sees it, the physical world amounts to sense-data and the results of human classifying; he takes no heed of the procedures of the physical sciences. Merleau-Ponty has a wider view. In his basic text of 1943, *The Structure of Behavior* (the word he uses in his title, *comportement*, is obsolete in modern French), he expounds a Croce-like "field theory" in which three autonomous fields—physical, physiological and mental—compose existence without, however, interacting. In its way this is as naive and homespun as Sartre's less elaborate view. It is rather vain nowadays, when we have just begun to learn that particles are by no means as predictable as we thought, to say that quantity characterizes the physical, order the physiological and meaning or value the mental. For the existentialists nature is a constant, inactive backdrop against which consciousness persistently "negates" itself by repeated changes. Sartre cautiously, and not without an echo of Gertrude Stein, explains that "Consciousness is a being for which

80

there is in its being a question of its being insofar as its being implies a being other than itself." This statement, with its euphuistic niceties, is about as far as we can go with Sartre in this subject before becoming bogged down in niceties that do no more than categorize the unknowable.

The human body, for Sartre, is as private as subjectivity. We know our bodies mainly through apprehending their function in the world. I know my body as no-one else can; so the body has two aspects, the public and the private, and I can sometimes distinguish the body from what it is doing—the dancer from the dance. For the most part the body runs its own life, subject to chemical and physical laws, but occasionally, as Sartre says, it "incarnates" us. In sexual activity, we exist individually either using the other body to "exist" ourselves (which Sartre, using the verb transitively, calls "masochism") or to "incarnate" the other person (which he calls, again rather unusually, "sadism"). Sartre is with Lawrence in this; they both assert the autonomy of the self and the impossibility of merging. So we have here, if not an ethics, at least a *praxis* of sex. The body also, for reasons I confess I cannot understand, provokes in Sartre a feeling of "nausea"—"an insipid taste . . . which is *my* taste." Perhaps it is the inertia of the body that worries him because, with Merleau-Ponty, he has a passion for being active and prefers the body when it is engaged in the act of perception. Yet it is hard to see how perception does not include those bodily functions which Sartre finds depressing, such as sex and pain; for both sex and pain are modes of perception. Perhaps he means that the man suffering from agonizing cancer or experiencing sexual desire is man "nauseatingly" dominated by the physical universe, whereas perception entails an active intellectual contribution to the physical act. There is no being sure; Sartre, as I said, is nothing if not personal and emotional, even private, in his severe conceptual formulations.

Of the two forms of existence, then, *être-pour-soi* can change and cancel itself whereas *être-en-soi* cannot because it is nonconscious. The physical world does not, except through the behavior of a few maverick particles, negate itself. The conscious self creates its freedom through action; or so it would seem. Sartre, however, says that freedom precedes action and that what we call motives are really explanations of a decision already taken. The driving force is the *mobile,* the explanation is the *motif*—the subject or theme for development. It is, really, a sensible bit of human observation: we rarely understand our "motives" and one of the useful roles of psychoanalysis is to elucidate them to us. Sartre rightly observes that human judgment is faulty—we cannot be sure of our ability to choose the right course—and therefore we are *"condemned* to be free": obliged to seek our individuality through procedures we do not entirely understand or master. Chance plays a part and so, therefore, must *Angst.* We do not know (1) why we act, (2) if what we advertise as, or tell ourselves is, our "motive" is not just an excuse or an illusion, (3) all the consequences and repercussions of our act, and (4) that outside, unpredicted forces will not modify what we do. This seems a realistic critique of behavior and it bears equally, and heavily, on all codes of conduct. Not that Sartre is arguing for "immobility" (in the general sense of the word, not his) ; he is not. He is pointing out the pain of having to assert ourselves so tentatively and the wisdom of seeking as much control as we can attain of what we do. The principal fear, he points out, is that of acting and, in the process, becoming—or getting the reputation of being—someone we did not intend to become. You set out to attack the enemy but, through some uncomprehended and unpredicted mechanical redisposition of forces, you appear to be deserting. Or, again, you elect to desert but run right into the enemy lines, perhaps winning a medal. Such are the hazards. The worst anguish of all is to realize that none of us is consistent, is stable; always, because our only response to initial freedom is to change, we are becoming different people through adding to the sum of our life's actions. Man, in fact, is indefinitely malleable at his own disposal, whereas the material world is not—at its own disposal or at man's.

At this juncture in his philosophy Sartre makes one of his most useful contributions. He defines *mauvaise foi* (bad faith) as the refusal of one's freedom (trying to evade one's life sentence) , as the attempt to become an unchanging *thing* (a man cannot be a thing) , as allowing others to tell one what to do (say, the social church or a political party) .¹ And in fact it is impossible to evade freedom, the obligation to choose. For even to elect to become a vegetable is to choose, and the inaugurating choice has continually to be backed up. Man is so far from being a vegetable that the effort of becoming and staying one ensures his remaining human. In contrast, Merleau-Ponty proposes what he calls a "semideterminism": man is part of a context against which he defines himself, altering his relation to it although in some ways retaining the same life style, "under the surface," as was imposed upon him from the start by family, class, education, and so on. This is really a bolder version of Sartre's *être-pour-autrui* (being-for-others) inasmuch as Sartre says I start by using the other person as an instrument by which to realize myself but discover, before very long, that other's freedom too. This is the semideterminism of being involved in mankind. From it develops, first, the *nous-objet* (each man being done to) and then, after the group has realized its slavery and has a concerted plan of action, the *nous-sujet* (what Camus calls revolt in common with Sartre, thus establishing a concurrence uncommon in their history). Obviously the Occupation created the *object* situation and the Resistance, to some extent, the *sujet* response, and Sartre seems to think that only emergencies can produce this sense of oneness. The rule is that selves enact their own freedom anarchically although Sartre seems to have forgotten this after the war, insisting upon the old unanimity for political purposes when, in fact, it had disintegrated. But he, like Merleau-Ponty who said his own existentialism was the best kind of Marxism, soon found that the Russians did not envision as much freedom as existentialism did. This is why the two of them retreated forward into a neutral position, neither genuinely communist nor genuinely anticommunist, but favoring the U.S.S.R. over the U.S.A., of which country Merleau-Ponty declared in *Humanism and Terror*

---

¹ Here, as Camus fully realized, is where Sartre falls down: he cannot preach obligation to choose and then espouse Communism without committing "bad faith." He is caught between his passion for action and the rigidity of Communism. The contradiction has annoyed some, but others have welcomed it as a sign of Sartre's being human, "like everyone else."

(1947) that "the principles are humane" whereas "ruse and violence are found in practice." In Russia, he said, it was the other way round. A realist like Camus, with no amateur communism to befog him, found that in both countries principle and practice were part humane and part corrupt. To enter further into such Gallic aphorisms would not be rewarding; once again we are reminded of the *literary* nature of existentialism.

The version of Marxism proposed by Merleau-Ponty sees man as an "historical idea and not a natural species," which would seem to chime very nicely with the Marxist march and the Hegelian predetermination of Absolute Reason. But Sartre and Merleau-Ponty do not quite settle for either. For them, in the last analysis, and as is obvious to every farmer and newsboy, the future is unknown, politics the art or science of the opportunist, and violence the usual outcome of ideologies. Such, in gist, is the tragic view of Camus, largely because he thought things through while retaining *some* faith in man. Sartre and Merleau-Ponty, however, have more use for heroism than Camus had, and their writings reveal an occasional passion for bold, theatrical attitudes that conflict oddly with their advocacy of the universal class. It is like finding a bit of Carlyle in the middle of a Party manifesto. We have to note again that the existentialist emphasis on action has never been fully articulated with the invitations to Party-mindedness, or the existentialist sense of adventure with the recourse to the Kremlin cramp. The odd thing is that Sartre's version, especially, seems the perfect rationale for the carpet-bagger whereas Camus's opinions might fit congruously into the plan of British socialism.

Inevitably, with time and a series of disillusions, both Sartre and Merleau-Ponty assumed more circumspect positions. In a lecture, "The Responsibility of the Writer," delivered at the Sorbonne in November 1946, Sartre complained that too many Frenchmen were silent. He also distinguished between the Russian's deportation of people ("it is a means of arriving at an end. I don't say that excuses it, but it must be considered from this angle") and the lynching of a Negro, which he found an inexcusable act of violence. One can detect here the philosopher's fondness for considering all situations equally on their theoretical

84

merits; whereas, of course, there is no merit, theoretical or otherwise, to deportation or to any other kind of totalitarian conversion of individuals into things. If anything should have struck Sartre, it was that deportation is the worst, most massive form of "bad faith" we know short of genocide. Yet in the same lecture he went on to insist that the writer, who tells other people what to think, should "refuse . . . in the name of freedom—which will not, of course, prevent anything—to sanction any means of violence to establish or sustain an order." How odd that he should not only contradict himself but also lapse into the faintheartedness of, on the one hand, saying "considering" does not "excuse" and, on the other, saying that refusal to sanction is impotent. Surely he might have worked out the relationship, if any, between his inviting an attention that does not necessarily assent and inviting a declaration that is powerless. It is surely "bad faith" to dangle, from a communist position, the conscience and the handicap of liberal humanism by the same string. One can see why Camus revolted and was revolted and why Simone de Beauvoir said "If the satisfaction of an old man drinking a glass of wine has no value, then production, wealth, are only empty myths." And, I would add, that old man has a right to drink his wine, even if it is only the wine of absurdity, in the country in which it pleases him to live and to which he belongs. But she too is confused; compare with this: "Men of today," she says, "will be sacrificed to those of tomorrow. . . ." This is the reformism of the abattoir and the freedom of the castrated.

At this point, however, let us widen our view of Sartre by considering what he has written in his novels and plays to further the idea of being responsible not only for ourselves but also for our fellows. We find his main idea is to restore us to the sense of individual responsibility:

> . . . the first effect of existentialism [he says in *Existentialism and Humanism*, 1946] is that it puts every man in possession of himself as he is, and places the entire responsibility for his existence squarely upon his own shoulders. And, when we say that man is responsible for himself, we do not mean that he is responsible only for his own individuality, but that he is responsible for all men.

He goes on to speak of the "anguish of decision":

All leaders know that anguish. It does not prevent their acting; on the contrary it is the very condition of their action, for the action presupposes that there is *a plurality of possibilities,* and in choosing one of these, they realise that it has value only because it is chosen. (my italics)

Sartre's atheism is beside the point here; his main emphasis is upon action and responsibility, upon conduct and choice. He develops his ethics between twin extremes: awareness of too many responsibilities and action without motive; in other words, between paralysis and nihilism. Such ethics may help us in our own dilemmas but may also introduce us to one of the subtlest modes of evading our responsibilities.

Sartre doesn't distinguish as carefully as he should between choice and responsibility: we are not always responsible for what we accept, or get into, while making the major decisions of our lives. But he is entitled to skate quickly over this point; in theory he is consistent, concentrating as he does on the major decisions. His main difficulty is with what we acquire from the impressionable years of childhood. We do not always choose for ourselves in those years, although they may shape us irrevocably. Of course the emphasis on choice is, in one sense, pointless: anyone can choose; the great thing is to choose well. And about choosing well Sartre, even in his studies of rootless or committed or hovering men in his novels, is rather vague. His main concern is that we should not become something by default. He recommends initiative, coupled with the realization that between the creed (or the impulse) and the act, there is no help. In deciding and in acting we are always alone with our own peculiar way of seeing things: our environment acts upon us, as adults, only in so far as we acknowledge and understand it. Our response to it is purely personal. And, whatever our dilemma, in the last analysis there is no objective account of the situation. At the last moment we are islands, and the last *analysis* we have to perform for ourselves. So he stresses the outline of our condition rather than its quality; the obligation to act, to act in any way, lest we become something accidentally.

In his novel-cycle, *The Ways of Liberty* (1945–50), he

constructs a social panorama, applying to it the extra dimension of philosophy in much the same way as Proust applies time and memory and Tolstoy history. But Sartre's panorama is more limited than that of Proust: not because it reviews a narrower range of society (it does not) but because Sartre fails to make virtue out of his philosophical necessity whereas Proust's theories are made to give all their strength to the narrative. Proust integrates theory with behavior; the two interact and produce bewitching syntheses. Sartre, caught between rather crass demonstration and the need to keep things moving forward, becomes woolly and tentative.

In *Nausea*, Sartre set out to show a character in a state of hopeless indecision. There were few philosophical trappings to this persuasive short work. The same is true of the stories in *The Wall:* the brutal, matter-of-fact close-ups lock home the trapped people; hemmed in by their own circumstances, then by Sartre's relentless concentration on nouns and constant recourse to verbs denoting ineffectual responses, these people have a meaning beyond the immediate. Prisoners all, they are the antithesis to the hero of *Nausea* whose existence nothing justifies, who is at once free and paralyzed. These early fictions are among Sartre's best, and deserve attention. His longer efforts, however, suffer from too much ambition and too little pruning. Perhaps early doses of Dos Passos and Faulkner (about whom Sartre wrote critical essays in the *Nouvelle Revue française*) repeated on him when he began to emulate. In 1943 he published the 700-page philosophical tract *Being and Nothingness* which, towards the end, develops into a rather sketchy theory of psychoanalysis. So, aiming at density and continuum, as well as being philosophically preoccupied, Sartre offered his fictional version of existentialism. Like Proust he held that reality is mental and that love, as a union of two humans, is an impossible and misleading ideal. But because reality cannot demonstrably exist for anything but minds does not mean that it exists only in minds. On the contrary, human reality is there all the time. What people try to do is to give themselves the same definiteness as a thing without losing the human faculty of self-awareness. Those who overdefine themselves (or others) lose humanity; those who indulge in excessive self-awareness lack clear edges. The trouble always begins when we try to define ourselves in relation to what we think the fixed identities of other people; for as soon as we "fix" a person, we have created an inhuman person. Hence the constant blur in which most people live; hence the frustration and nausea of life. It is the old opposition between flux and fixity.

We shall always be incomplete and undefined because man at his most human is tempted to annul his very humanity. The only way out, although Sartre has not suggested it, is to try to cultivate a respect for *things*, so that we respect whatever we have to make of ourselves or of others. It would not then be depreciatory to speak of other people as "the Other." Sartre's main problem is that he cannot forget the difference between what he knows of human consciousness and what he knows of things. Other views, such as those of Lawrence or Santayana, recommend an all-embracing attentiveness in which people and things are not identified but given equal, *thoughtful* respect. After all, as Sartre has pointed out, although we can keep on choosing, our identities will not be completely defined until we have died. From such an agonizing view, ethics must grow although it will be tentative ethics at best; for there is always an unknown element depending on how a multitude of individual consciousnesses will respond to the doubleness of humanity. Ethics does not refer to things; but not all people are more human than they are things. There is no slick answer to all this. Man has to keep on examining his predicament until he has over it the kind of power that only understanding can confer.

So to the triptych of *The Ways of Liberty: The Age of Reason* (1945), *The Reprieve* (1945) and *Troubled Sleep* (1949). A tribute to "the grandeur of humanity," it sounds well and sets us combining social complexity with metaphysical ideas. Unfortunately, for the most part, we come away from Sartre's panorama with social ideas and metaphysical complexity. Historical events whirl the people forward while they are trying to define themselves. Nations at war, nations averting their political eyes while neighbours are invaded, nations wondering what to do and being overrun while they wonder—this is bad enough to provoke an enduring disgust. But the cosmos, with its unheeding renewal

of sap, works on the characters too. So the nausea is both social
and cosmic; the portrait is of disintegration and distraction. This
is the account of life that the Catholic rejects as irrelevant to the
Beatific Vision and that the Marxist explains as merely incompe-
tent arrangement of society. Sartre writes in a transitional period
between a settled and a revolutionary view of man: for various
reasons, and under various labels, rugged individualism opposes
the collectivity; and Sartre is showing how unsatisfactory the
result will have to be. Only this could explain his fellow-travelling
period and the varying degrees of intensity evident in his life-long
attachment to Marxist doctrine. This century has seen the individual beguiled into accepting creeds of world domination,
driven into fierce nationalism against those creeds, fashionably
paying the psychotherapist to adjust him to society, confusedly
turning to the safe, sometimes hermetic world of art and toying
virtuously with noble but apparently impotent ideas. Sartre
himself has exaggerated, at one point claiming T. E. Lawrence for
existentialism, at another laughing at systems from the security of
his very German, very Italian system. (He has German blood
himself, and it is worth noting that some of his personages bear
German names: Hoederer, Goetz, and more recently Franz von
Gerlach in *The Condemned of Altona* [1956]. Perhaps this is a
means of exorcising the bogeyman of your philosophical system.)
In the long run, and this makes any philosopher bad-tempered,
reason outstrips our abilities to put things right. Therefore a
great deal of reasoning is merely intellectual exercise; good for the
muscles but ineffectual.

Not surprisingly the hero of *The Age of Reason* is a young
philosophy teacher, Mathieu Delarue, *"l'homme,"* as his circle of
Bohemian intellectuals call him, *"qui veut être libre."* Exhaustively analyzing himself, Mathieu tries to take full control of, and
full responsibility for, himself. He is not trying to rationalize the
Gidean *acte gratuit,* having indulged in such acts in his youth to
no enduring advantage. He is trying to give a rational account of
all his actions. Unfortunately, however, Marcelle, his mistress,
becomes pregnant and all his good reasoning cannot alter the fact.
After some squalid efforts to muster an abortionist's fee, he begins
to consider marrying Marcelle. He recoils from the idea of

destroying a human embryo; and if he married Marcelle he could tell himself his self-assertion was not ended: after all, he does not have to marry her. Mathieu's brother, a sensible *bourgeois* solicitor, advises marriage; and that is enough to make Mathieu prefer the opposite. He is now infatuated with a young student, Ivich, not least because she is unconnected with his main dilemma. (He fails to realize that, in distracting him from one problem, she is confronting him with another.) Suddenly, however, Daniel, a young homosexual, suggests to Mathieu that he himself is responsible for Marcelle's condition. At once Mathieu welcomes the news; he resents it too: his rights have been infringed. His self-esteem continually battles with his instinct for self-preservation. He wants to get out of complications until he can deliberately bring on himself complications of his own choosing. The unheroic hero, indeed, he exemplifies the futility of theorizing while you are leading any kind of life. A thoroughgoing theorist would have had no Marcelle in the first place; but he might have caught a cold, been mutilated in a traffic accident or become a prey to melancholia. Sartre makes these points almost garishly in sinuous but sometimes deliberately stumbling prose. Finally he makes Mathieu, now bogged down in self-despising indecision, steal the money for an abortion. Too late; Marcelle inveigles him into saying he no longer loves her and then decides to marry Daniel. The cosmic joke is now played in full: a practical, fertile joke, at that. Mathieu has asked too much, trying to cut his physical cloak out of metaphysical cloth.

Characteristically Sartre chooses his examples from an unstable, groping set. Most people could get into the same scrape, but would not approach it or get out of it with such a wealth of theorizing. Sartre is making a special point pertinent to himself and to all theoreticians. Another point, which does not seem to occur to him, is that most people remedy problems with principles or a spin of a coin. His disgust is with formularized living, the *bourgeois* way that a C. P. Snow finds imperative if we are not to have chaos. In *The Reprieve* Sartre turns from his bohemian rebels to the atmosphere before Munich. He exchanges the test-tube method for that of the cinema; rather than tabulating and listing the main events of the period, he jerks us away to the atmosphere of Marseilles, Munich, Biarritz and Paris. The stench of appeasement wafts away from the Daladiers and the Chamberlains to yield creatures of its own making: Gros-Louis the illiterate mental pigmy in the vast physical frame; Phillipe the pacificist, and Pierre who dotes on all his sensations, pleasant or otherwise. Personal tension gives way to national. By now in the background, Daniel has adjusted to marriage; Mathieu has regained the confidence to muddle onwards with Ivich. When mobilization hits, there are disintegrations of a nobler kind than the merely sexual: Daniel, for example, becomes a Roman Catholic. But, they find, war is not coming, after all. Reintegrations do not follow; in fact, this phase of the novel is handled in a deft, Tolstoyan way. The intersection of the international with the personal has rarely been more movingly, more discerningly portrayed. The rebels have been rebelled upon; and their own personal acts of defiance have been engulfed by a crisis which affects a whole nation, both ennobling and destroying. Suddenly, it appears that not only cannot the Mathieus make sense of their own lives; they cannot even in the vaguest way anticipate the collective fate. Hence all the guilt in Sartre's writings: man can conceive of the deliberately lived life but he cannot, individually or collectively, bring it into being. Sartre ties the two themes together in another paradox: "definitions are never settled; one cannot define a man before he has died, or humanity before it has vanished." That is a religious point—the compassionate but brutal answer to all egocentric neurotics who want to postpone their lives until they can be in full control. Neither microcosm nor macrocosm will be entirely sensible until we stop them both and put them right: that is why the universe is absurd. Freedom, as Mathieu comes to realize, is sheer terror—whether on the personal plane or on the national, as when in *Troubled Sleep* the national disintegrates because the known does not indicate in any way the nature of the unknown.

Sartre's vision must ultimately be interpreted as one of the compensatory games we play with ourselves once we have admitted our ineffectuality. His dithering adolescents personify the mind-game. Theorizing is an effective way of cheering ourselves up, but not of constructing principles. Not afraid to get his hands dirty or to present his own type unflatteringly, Sartre has created a contrapuntal type of literature in which the evasions and vain ambitions of a whole era add up to rhetoric while a culture burns. Where do we come out? In narcissism or political action? Sartre implies that the choice is false.

In his plays, as in those of Camus, character is subordinated to dialectic. *The Flies* (1943) retells the legend of Orestes the matricide through whom, in defiance of the Nazi censorship, Sartre managed to issue a powerful exhortation to freedom. In *No Exit* (1944), with its three modern characters locked up together in a tawdry hotel room ("Hell is other people"), Sartre achieved something of the claustrophobic tension of Racine without, however, seeming to get anywhere. Something more than chance has brought them together, as one of the characters says, and it is probably Sartre's own version of the same illustrative relentlessness as we find in Camus. Altogether more horrible in a more obvious way is *Death without Burial* (1946) which is about the torture of Resistance fighters and perhaps, now uncomfortably, reminds Sartre of what happened in Hungary as "a means for arriving at an end." *The Respectful Prostitute* (1946) has a crude vigor in its anti-Americanism and its portrayal of people consciously playing roles; but this is a minor piece compared with *Dirty Hands* (1948) in which Sartre really gets to grips with the Party problem. The hero interrogates himself concerning his murder of a Party boss; he will not disclaim his responsibility and, in so deciding, affronts the solidarity of a Party that sometimes elects to change its mind. Whatever the Party decides, the murder is his and his alone; it is the act by which he has defined and authenticated himself, and he therefore elects—another choice—to die for it. His "motive," which of course is private to him, has become clear with the completion of the event, so he can talk freely of "motive" rather than attribute his act to a "mobile." The play spells out Sartre's theory of intention. But it is only with *The Devil and the Good God* (1951) that Sartre gathers up all his gifts into one creation. This comprehensive play is set in the Germany of Luther, with unrest (which Sartre excels at depicting) and war flickering back and forth throughout stringent, muscular debates about good and evil, human responsibility and the problem of God's existence. Here we have (although with some of the arguments already heavily loaded) a Socratic fresco which seems a prelude for the new humanism Sartre had announced earlier as "without illusions (that is to say, divorced from religious experience), but full of confidence in the grandeur of humanity; hard, but without useless violence; passionate yet restrained; striving to paint the metaphysical condition of man while fully participating in the movements of society." But that humanism has never arrived.

It certainly did not appear in the surrealistic morbidity of *The Condemned of Altona* in which Franz von Gerlach, self-incarcerated in a bedroom in the family mansion, abandons time and spends his life addressing speeches to the crabs who invaded and occupied the earth in the year 3000. "Listen to the plea of mankind," he instructs them. "We were betrayed by our deeds. By our words, by our lousy lives." Incestuously involved with his sister, Franz refuses to see his father who is dying of cancer of the throat. He is a haunted, lost man; he tortured prisoners at Smolensk and thus broke his pact with humanity. The father eventually drives both himself and Franz off to suicide. The play ends with a recording in which Franz attributes the ills of the century to "that hairless, evil, flesh-eating beast" who has sworn to destroy man. The beast, of course, is man himself. About this play there is something destructive and panic-stricken that is hardly surprising. Sartre's pessimism has widened to include a view of man as a creature destined from the outset to assume that consciousness, rather than will to good, made him human. The Sartre who cares deeply about the role of conscience and the nature of responsibility is only one aspect, as is the one who flirts with Communism. There is another, who seems merely morbid, inert and grubbing. And this Sartre, who dramatizes himself or other writers (*Baudelaire,* 1947; *Saint Genet,* 1952), brings me to my next point.

On Baudelaire, except on the malign impact of his childhood, Sartre is reticent; he does not elucidate the "project" of Baudelaire's life but meanders interestingly along as if he is learning how to swim in a new element. On Genet, however, he is more deliberate and more explicit. He reviews the circumstances, the nature of the "project" and then Genet's actual behavior and elected role ("clown and martyr"). Rather than permit the bad faith of accepting a role society imposed upon him (Sartre cares more about *status* than about economic capacity), Genet turned round and chose that role. Caught stealing when very young, he chose to be the thief people thought him. Sartre's analysis of his subsequent development is both voluminous and ingenious, and it is most persuasive on the prerational element in Genet's choice. This type of existentialist psychoanalysis is one of the most fascinating parts of Sartre's achievement, and one which surely should be applied to himself. But, it should be added, in this instance Genet converted censure into a life project only by, in fact, playing into the hands of the conventionally minded upon whom, although Sartre does not always admit it, the existentialist depends for his bearings. When he does admit it he talks like this (*Being and Nothingness*): ". . . the responsibility of the for-itself extends to the entire world as a peopled-world." The word that counts is "responsibility," for it means both answerable for something and capable of judgment. It does not, I think, follow that all those who are answerable for something are capable of judgment; here we have to reckon with what Sartre discerns of the prerational in all choice—as in Genet's.

We may in fact abandon any idea of acting well; and one cannot help suspecting that Sartre sometimes misses his own point. If we are unlikely to act well, since almost always we are impeded, while always obliged to act, then we might well develop a fondness for mere self-study—watching ourselves while something emerges from, or is done to, ourselves the watchers. This amounts to a kind of ethical bird-watching. Sartre, in fact, toys with the intoxication of choice. When he says in *Being and Nothingness* that "everything that happens to us can be considered as a *chance*, i.e., can appear to us only as a way of realizing this being which is in question in our being," it seems that he is more concerned to savor the chance, the moment, the process, than to evaluate morality. Such an aestheticism of ethics is attractive to the fatalist, and will breed fatalists. Something has to turn up; a choice will always seem to be made; so we can regard ourselves as guinea pigs and live, increasingly fascinated but also

94

increasingly muddled, "for the moment." "Look," whispers the self-regarding existentialist, "although I am abdicating from choice, I am having the delicious experience of watching the life-process force out of me something which looks like a change in me, a thing done in my name."

Such is one of the subtlest forms of self-abuse. It is no use arguing that so to regard one's processes is a choice; for choice entails an attempt to take control. All the same, whenever we have had a chance to take control, and have refused it, we remain responsible. We are not responsible only when whatever we do has no consequences; but we are incapable of proving that such a possibility can arise. Even so, if we are careful to separate the existentialist gimmicks from their serious implications for morality (for morality is acts), we gain in constructive self-awareness. For this philosophy makes clear the confusion and "viscosity" of the world in which we are condemned to choose. It also specifies the nature of human self-deception and, although seeming to suggest new ways of deceiving ourselves, at once makes us responsible for falling into those ways. After all, to tell ourselves that we are trying to take control of our lives when, in fact, we are merely watching our own mental drift—this is self-deception: what Sartre calls "bad faith." It is as well to know of such a possibility and to guard against it.

When we shirk we become objects; when we are afraid we try to turn other people into consistent, reliable objects too. Similarly we try to make our codes and systems responsible for us. So there is good sense in existentialism's effort to teach us the difference, often obscured, between the underground man and the outgoing man. The latter is clear about man's place in the world and about man's duty to exert his will according to some standard of benevolence. Dostoevsky's mouse-man in *Notes from Underground* scurries into his tiny room and there beats his head against the wall. He is not a complete failure: this much, this retreat and this self-punishment, is within his power. In *Crime and Punishment* the mouse-man emerges to try his luck in a larger sphere—and finds salvation. Alexey in *The Brothers Karamazov* represents a more dignified version of the mouse-man's capacity for turning the other cheek; but Alexey goes further: he tries to fathom the other person's reasons. And people esteem him for his outgoing interest in them, his sensitivity towards them and not towards himself. If Raskolnikov in *Crime and Punishment* exemplifies how selfishness and solipsism can be overcome, then Alexey exemplifies how the overcoming can be given a positive direction. From self-correction to self-projection, as Dostoevsky shows, is a development necessarily entailing charity.

To Dostoevsky the most important thing was to be outgoing. Father Zossima makes the point clearly:

There is only one means of salvation . . . take yourself and make yourself responsible for all men's sins; that is the truth, you know, friends, for as soon as you sincerely make yourself responsible for everything and for all men, you will see at once that it is really so, and that you are to blame for every one and for all things. But throwing your own indolence and impotence on others you will end by sharing the pride of Satan and murmuring against God.

Compare this with Sartre's bolder assertions in *Existentialism and Humanism:*

I am thus responsible for myself and for all men, and I am creating a certain image of man as I would have him to be. In fashioning myself I fashion man.

A man "in choosing for himself . . . chooses for all men." If there is any philosophy valid for daily living, surely this is it. Overstated by both Dostoevsky and Sartre, it nevertheless calls for the kind of imaginative wisdom, the kind of effort, we would like made towards ourselves. The echoes of "even as ye have done it unto the least of these, my brethren, ye have done it unto me," are obvious: this is not a marginal idea; it is already firm in our moral tradition, not as self-effacement, but as prudent charity. It is an idea that remains valid even when, like Dostoevsky's Grand Inquisitor, we have found Christian standards too high. And it is an idea on which the writer, the humanist, the enhancer of existence, ought to take his stand.

By this standard the so-called objective religion of such a writer as T. E. Hulme stands reproved. If Sartre has too cloying a sense of the many courses of action open to us and tends to savor them in their own right as objects of nearly aesthetic delight, then Hulme, following both Bergson and St. Thomas Aquinas, is too ready to eliminate choice altogether. All very well for him to announce that we cannot define "values" and in "Humanism and the Religious Attitude," an essay in *Speculations* (1924), to condemn modern relativism and extol the absolute values of the Middle Ages. Hulme would de-nature man. He would make him into a perfectly functioning toy. This is to press the doctrine of original sin too far. To Hulme anything subjective is wrong; yet, if we throw overboard our own power to choose, all we have left is codes and systems that once began in subjective, reflective minds. In the long run, in fact, we have to reconcile ourselves to the human quality of systems and the overtheoretical nature of the mind: such reconciliation being impossible for him, Hulme dived back into the irrational. He spoke up for an external authority based on reason rather than on feeling. But if reason aims at certitudes, it also provokes doubt; and we do not always respond rationally to doubt. That is why, in anticipation of our own unruly responses, we may try to train ourselves into automatic charity and constant humility. No system we evolve is capable of coping with our full nature; and a "perfect" system envisions us only partially. The idea, therefore, of a perfect system is self-deception. We always have to return to the agony, the anguish, of choice.

Hulme, preaching order and constraint, omits charity as well as humility. Values, he claimed, could be expressed only in terms of imperatives: any attempt to define would only bring about "amplifications of man's appetites." He wanted order based on absolute values, but couldn't face the spadework of explanation. He was too much aware of the gap between human and divine, and never tried to make a virtue of it. All he could offer as a spiritual source was "dynamic classicism": a military discipline applied to tin soldiers. After all, no humanism is as crassly idealistic as Hulme supposed; no person is as capable of sustained reasoning. The best humanism is the dupe of no black-or-white outlook; the best persons are never homogeneous in the way he prescribed. Where Sartre tempts us to think too much, Hulme would have us think only what we are told. Sartre proposes a surfeit; Hulme, famine. Sartre opens too many doors of possibility, bewildering a man out of his definite identity; Hulme wants to type people, relieve them of responsibility. Sartre opens us up; Hulme seals us tight.

It is not surprising that Heidegger, the most unreadable of the existentialists, has stressed that we live in tension. We may believe in perfectibility, but we may also wish to state perfectible" for what. Hulme, a perfectionist, needed absolutes to discard in favor of absolutes of his own. As Herbert Read says in his essay on Hulme in *A Coat of Many Colours*, "Between the feebleness of mankind and the perfection of the divine Hulme saw nothing but a tragic discord. . . ." But the perfection of the divine is as much a presumption by the mind as the utter feebleness of mankind. We have no decisive evidence for an absolute either way. Hulme tended to forget that the classical attitude—that of Aristotle, Euripides and Menander—was one of compromise; it was no extreme, and the Renaissance had the sense to see it as such. Only our modern irrationalists have offered classicism as an absolute, all at one end of the spectrum.

Yet, if one can see the dangers of taking Sartre too literally, and Dostoevsky too much as the discoverer of a perfect way, one must be charitable to Hulme, the "philosophic amateur" with the "Tory philosophy." Like all stern idealists he felt bound to reject haphazard and unsystematic charity—partly because charity, like mellowness, is irrational, partly because it is so hard to tie down. No doubt he thought he understood the concept of original sin; but, in fact, it was merely a convenient hand grenade to throw at overhopeful, smug humanists. Hulme also thought original sin held the clue to possible means of reform, whereas it is only a device to account for, and describe, man's unsatisfactory nature. In fact Hulme, more than any of the liberal humanists he castigated, believed in the possibility of improvement on the grand scale. "It is only by tradition and organization that anything decent can be got out of him [man]": this is the view of most humanists who want anything worthwhile. The truth of the matter is that Hulme, like the T. S. Eliot who praises him in *Selected Essays*, oversimplifies whatever he attacks. Humanism is vague; it has to be so until it is made to do duty for religion.

Humanism is not a program or a scheme, but a way of living life deliberately. And if, to some humanists, charity seems inseparable from living life well, then charity remains quite unorganized, quite separate from any idea of perfectible man. Perfect things may indeed teach hope; to the sane and the humane they have nothing to do with setting up a regime of reform. Humanism as I am interpreting it here has nothing in common with such wild hyper-Sartrism as Robert Jungk's *Tomorrow is Already Here:* "The stake is the throne of God. To occupy God's place, to repeat His deeds, to re-create and organize a man-made cosmos according to man-made laws or reason, foresight, and efficiency." This vacuous formula is Hulme's view reduced to absurdity; and it does not reduce Hulme very far. Humanism, in contrast, concerns itself with being grateful for what good there is, morally and aesthetically, and with not exaggerating or elevating into an absolute the facts of human corruptness.

A thorough humanism finds itself between Sartre's realistic but bewitching imagination of possibility and Hulme's passion for authority and elimination. Dostoevsky illustrates one way of emerging from self-scrutiny into harmful involvement with one's fellows; it is for men neither daunted by possibility nor demoralized by the presence of the facts of evil or of irrationality. No doubt, in order to acquire a full sense of all we are capable of, we must risk being sidetracked into a voluptuous fondling of alternatives. No doubt, if we are to achieve anything in the world of action, we have to consider in theory such an authoritarian code as Hulme proposes. But between being dazed by the arbitrary and revolted by wickedness, we have a fairly large area in which something generous can be attained.

I now offer a juxtaposition. "Thou shalt have power to degenerate into the lower forms of life, which are brutish. Thou shalt have the power, out of thy soul's judgment, to be reborn into the higher forms, which are divine": thus Pico della Mirandola's God to Man. We must not expect either degenerateness or judgment to be all-powerful. Being what we are, we must not plan too grandly, nor too small. Able to judge, we must remember that action always eliminates alternatives: they no longer exist although memory recalls them and perhaps desiderates them.

"An optimistic vision of man is no necessary feature of Humanism": thus a Dutch humanist, J. P. van Praag, in an essay in *The Plain View*. This is the region of prudence and moderation, where intellectual pleasure meets moral hopefulness, where mania meets degeneracy. Much maligned, this middling humanism is only as absurd as the universe that forces it into being. Neither humanism nor humanitarianism is enough; and humanism plus humanitarianism is not enough either. Not that many men do not have to make do with one or with both. There is, perhaps, something else: some intuition of oneness with nature, some illumination, some kind of vision. This we may call mystical experience; it is not a matter of leaving an open door for it; it would penetrate anyway. The thing is to remain perpetually aware of the incompleteness and unsatisfactoriness of our systems and eclecticisms: to be neither cocky nor despairing. The unappeased spiritual appetite is bound to trouble men who seek spiritual exaltation outside organized faiths; and it is bound to prompt them to create private mysteries—some wild and fantastic, others dry and prosaic. Ironically, the more we develop the ability to tame nature, the less easily do we come to terms with such inescapable items as pain and death. Members of primitive communities and, presumably, animals do not share these civilized difficulties. Perhaps the most satisfying way of meeting spiritual needs that are ineffable is to remind ourselves always of the mind's own inexplicability; but without, of course, priding ourselves too much on the instrument we did not create, although it in its turn enables us to create so much else. The Sartres entail the Hulmes; multiplicity of possibilities brings forward the eliminator. Sooner or later we have to exclude something, unless we are to languish in a perpetual night of indecision. But humanism is the habit of refusing to identify selection with blindness. A Sartre accustoms us to the idea of self-review; a Hulme would deprive us of that idea. Only a constant alertness will save us from floundering or from wishing not to think for ourselves. Charity begins at home; and only a rigorous attempt to establish and maintain what we hold "dear" will enable us to be charitable to others. To respect the "presence" of others, and to be "present" to it, we must first know what it is we respect in ourselves. And what that is we can learn only through consultation with others; the consultation that Sartre's inwardness postpones and Hulme's prescriptions render unnecessary.

Sartre's predicament has become extreme: it is a Sartre *in extremis* who introduces Henri Alleg's horrifying account in *The Question* (1958) of torture and sadism practiced by French paratroops in Algeria. Sartre is horrified; a Frenchman, he says, has only two roles open to him—tortured or torturer, rebellion or complicity. For this is a dichotomy world: if a man does not oppose, then he supports. Not to act is to condone. "I have," Sartre goes on to say in his preface, entitled "A Victory," "always detested those books that involve us in a cause mercilessly, and yet offer no hope or solution." Such a dilemma debunks all sublime talk of "action" and "commitment," and Sartre is driven, in fact, into a strangely Christian position that would have suited someone like Psichari or Péguy. This is a new Sartre, preaching not action but the obligation to suffer. When people are being mutilated, the old gimmicks look pale; and a religious rather than a political or philosophical absolute has to be found. Here it is:

Alleg has saved us from despair and shame because he has conquered torture . . . it is in our name that he was victimized, and because of him we regain a little pride: we are proud that he is French. The reader [of *The Question*] identifies himself with him passionately, he accompanies him to the extremity of his suffering; with him, alone and naked, he does not give way. Could the reader, could we, *if it happened to us,* do the same?

Sartre has had to formulate his agony of choice in terms of capitulation or pain. It is quite simple. And it is astonishing to see the apostle of the active and positive compelled to seek religious allegory in torture, and dignity in the remnant. He is left with an increased respect for man's courage and an intensified sense of evil. But, even so, he is not entirely persuaded that life in this world is wretchedly flawed, that morally we have not improved very much since the Middle Ages and that a thousand years of recurring oppression of all kinds indicates something irremediable in human nature. Instead, he concludes:

Torture is imposed by the circumstances and required by racial hatred; in some ways, it is the essence of the conflict and expresses its deepest truth.

If we want to put an end to the atrocious and bleak cruelty, and save France from this disgrace . . . there has always been and still is only one way: to open negotiations and to make peace.

He is back where he began: after a searing journey through the actual world created by negotiation and peace, he resumes his conceptualizing, hopeful and astute to the last, and invincibly Pelagian in a world in which negotiation has always failed, still fails, but might not always fail in the future.

The longer society lasts the more difficult its habits are to break. This is not to proclaim the decline of the West but to worry about our decreasing inclination to rethink certain policies. Nor is it to assert that we should cloister and give up. It is to abandon such notions as our complete malleability; we cannot shape ourselves according to the noblest ideal in our minds. People might attempt that only at the millenium, under the spell of a perfect being. We must not expect too much, nor yet too little. Tradition dictates much of our selves, but not all of them. An intelligent stoicism, coupled with the assumption that one's fellows and one's politicians have not thrown in the moral sponge, can surely work some local good. But on the international level things are less clear. After an empirical scrutiny, like that undertaken by Machiavelli, we note the evidence of greed in high places. Perhaps the sheer complexity of the modern economic world explains not only Bertrand Russell's statement that "the world has become more like that of Machiavelli than it was" but also Ignazio Silone's chastening indictment of collectivity:

Frankly, I cannot think of a single collective organization today which could be said to be untainted by the leprosy of nihilism. Group living, it would almost seem, creates the most favourable temperature for the incubation of its germs. Human stupidity is so monotonous. The deathly mechanism is always the same: every group or institution arises in defence of an ideal, with which it rapidly comes to identify itself and for which it finally substitutes itself altogether, proclaiming its own interests as the supreme value.

Many indeed are the "gods" that have failed. What remains? Certainly charity in our everyday behavior, for we are not in power either to put things right or make them worse or simply to perpetuate them as they are. Then there is pity, another cherished concept of Silone, who says that "even the revolt born of pity alone can restore meaning to life." There is faith, hope and self-sacrifice. And there is also art; the intellectual, Camus said shortly after the Hungarian uprising, should not spend all his time talking:

In the first place, it will wear him out—and especially it will prevent him from thinking. He should create, if he can, and that first of all, especially if what he creates does not recoil before the problems of his own times.

In this way he can, as Silone says, place "before the minds of men the problems which elude them" and so present them with an honest picture of themselves—even by delineating the fact of despair itself. Thus we find a good deal of literature which records man's heroic ability to die uselessly. This is to find a straw, but a supreme one, in the nihilistic position. Sartre comes near it but is duty-bound to talk of negotiation and Communism as panaceas. His ideal world is one in which nothing may be attempted save the sacrifice of the present to "the future." In the real world, sane arrangements are the merest item and are usually made after bloodshed has begun. We have indeed come to an extreme situation if, in order to justify ourselves at all, we have to compile a literature of hopeless heroism. The real, less spectacular bravery is in learning to cut our cloaks according to the human cloth—according to that cloth's history-long quality. Life must be made humane, must be enhanced; but we cannot expect to do these things without exerting ourselves enormously and taking full account of the fragility of our virtuous instincts.

The final verdict on existentialism is something we can only guess at. It has been a fashionable philosophy for a long time already, and to a certain extent it can never lose its appeal, building as it does its realism on the borders of the incomprehensible and treating of mundane matters that affect everyone daily. Despite its cloudinesses and its habit of presenting the agony of thought rather than its outcome, it occupies a substantial position between the great systems of philosophy and the current concern of philosophers with semantic minutiae. There is about it something vigorous and *ad hoc;* its metaphysics is far from lucid and its ethics is nebulous. But it does, so to speak, register the pressure of the times and elaborate themes which, as Emmanuel Mounier showed in his *Introduction aux existentialismes* (1947), all modern writers of any awareness and seriousness have found preoccupying them. On the one hand, Sartre, Merleau-Ponty, Simone de Beauvoir and Francis Jeanson have kept fairly close together in formulating a system (although they have disagreed among themselves, Merleau-Ponty calling Sartre "an ultra-Bolshevik" and Beauvoir implicitly rebuking Sartre by supplying the ethics he promised but never delivered). On the other hand there are writers such as Camus, Malraux, Bernanos, Mauriac, Graham Greene and Anouilh who all deal with the problems of being alive in the present time; and it is only right to call their concerns existential. Again, it is truer to say that Sartre had begun to form his philosophy before the war began than that the impact of war forced it from him. Rather, the war was the sustained emergency which winnowed his doctrines and sharpened his demands. The time has gone by in which existentialism can be presented as a marginal, *avant-garde, café* movement akin to such later manifestations as hipsterism. The glossy, hungry journals no longer find excitement in this philosophy (although, after the war, both *Life* and, in Britain, *Picture Post* did their share of publicizing the "new" view). Over the last twenty years or so the movement has made its appeals and its conquests outside France, mostly among the British and the Americans. After all, it is both empirical and pragmatic in its emphases and, in some aspects, has affinities with the woolly modernism of John Dewey, with Santayana's "This world is contingency and absurdity incarnate," as well as with Bertrand Russell's outspoken rejection of Christianity and A. J. Ayer's logical positivism.

But neither American pragmatism and naturalism nor British hard-headedness has the theatrical, urgent quality of Sartre's doctrines. Existentialism comes out of Idealism and, when confronted with the unknowable or the incalculable, lapses into a kind of metaphysical melodrama in which it has exaggerated the inexplicability of the world as well as its "facticity." It may be satisfying to fix, as Sartre does, on manufactured articles because they embody a man-made indifference more comfortable than the indifference of the stars or the soil. But surely this is a quibble on his part, just as his disregard of modern physics (which has shown that not only do positive and negative attract each other but also that two positives can be made to join and can be separated only by colossal forces) is an oversight. The physical universe is by no means as fixed as Sartre seems to think; there are still particles that go their own way. He just *assumes* that mind evolved genetically and genesis began from inert matter but, like Merleau-Ponty, makes no attempt to relate the one to the other in any scientific way. Instead he asserts apocalyptically, and this is the key to his thought. His doctrine is psychological, saying how it feels to be alive and basing itself on intuitions rather than upon scientific fact. Existentialism is a philosophy of human assumptions rather than a description of the universe or of the material world. We are returned to subjectivism as seen in the older Gestalt psychology; and Sartre's own doctrine that choice can be conscious yet not deliberate (based on the views of Wilhelm Steckel, a pupil of Freud who broke with Freud) can be turned against him in that his own construction of the world, *being-in-itself,* is prerationally motivated: a hunch only. It is this recourse (if that is not too deliberate a word) to imposed meaning that deters his readers. He presents his hunches as if they were axioms and so creates a determinism of the mind, a psychological metaphor that is the natural outcome of Idealism mixed with phenomenology. Sartre's truth, underived and *a priori,* is set to work to propagate itself unassailably.

What is stimulating in existentialism, as distinct from what is baffling and merely speculative, is its emphasis on initiative and responsibility, and especially its conception of each human life as an undertaking of a high creative order. This is the dramatics of identity and a fruitful basis for the composition of novels and plays. What is daunting and unilluminating is its disregard of the stability all humans glean from their closeness to nature and society. Sartre dismisses too much of the sustaining texture we call *mores* and physical needs, as well as the steadying power of a reputation, a role or a burden. In fact, many people become themselves largely through the slow accretion of these inherited and imposed factors, and not through any agile pursuit of a freedom so tenuous as to seem no more than an atmospheric phantom. Instead of heady disponibility and the grandiose noumenon called "historic mission," most people prefer to stay at ground level with the image most other people have of them. If "negation" is vigor, they will settle for the torpor of routine. We have only to look at such a work as F. H. Bradley's *Ethical Studies* to see how far in the air Sartre flies without coming down. Bradley deals in minute, vivid detail with all kinds of ends and means; he is extremely concerned with behavior, pleasure, pain, self-denial, selfishness, and so on; and Simone de Beauvoir is the only existentialist who has even remotely approached Bradley's care for day-to-day particulars of conduct. When Sartre in *Being and Nothingness* or in his study of Genet permits himself an autobiographical item he quickly transcends it and resumes theorizing.

Simone de Beauvoir, on the other hand, ballasts her theoretical discussions in *The Ethics of Ambiguity* with all the data of a well-read, active and practically-disposed woman who sounds as if she might enjoy cooking. Her analyses of human dilemmas are observant, imaginative and subtle. She writes well against "that flight from freedom that is found in heedlessness, caprice, mania, and passion" and carefully explains that "any dictatorship [on her part] is a fault for which I have to get myself pardoned." Here is a mind that cannot remain for too long on the level of the abstract; she considers, for example, someone approached by an addict friend for money to buy drugs or drink with, and reviews all the gradations between dangerous refusal and helpful capitulation. On the Resistance she is discriminating and humbling: she explains that its guerilla actions were not intended to weaken German material power but to create a climate of violence in which excessive reprisals (a village burned for the murder of three German officers) "created an abyss between the occupiers and the occupied." In other words, as in Paris and Lyons at the beginning of the nineteenth century, or during the revolts in

India, it was the idea of resistance that was kept alive. It is an undeluded, frank woman who recalls reading Hegel in the Bibliothèque Nationale in August 1940 and experiencing "a great feeling of calm." But out in the street again, she says, "the system was no longer of any use to me." We may not quite agree when she says existentialism offers none of the consolations "of an abstract evasion"; some parts at least of *Being and Nothingness* are in the manner of a voluptuary tone poem in which urgency is lost in casuistry. But there is nothing evasive about her own writings (she attributes parts of Sartre's view of sex to the underprivileged status of women), and she emerges concerned essentially with dilemmas and principles.

I cannot help feeling that it is in such disabused practicality that the existentialist passion for self-definition and for responsibility assumes its most available and most impressive form. Her novels, *All Men are Mortal* (1946), *The Blood of Others* (1946), *The Mandarins* (1955), her diaries of travel in the United States and in China, and her other books, including the brilliant study of Sade and her militant essay on women, *The Second Sex* (1949–50), provide a most readable enactment of her theories. She shows how much we are capable of if we are deliberate enough. In *Being and Nothingness* Sartre said he did not exclude the possibility of "an ethic of deliverance and salvation" founded on a "radical conversion"—whatever he meant by that. Beauvoir, less cryptically, makes what is I think the same point: it has something to do with the concept of *communication* as expounded by the Christian existentialists, Marcel and Jaspers. "If," she argues, ". . . each man did what he must, existence would be saved in each one without there being any need of dreaming of a paradise where all would be reconciled in death." The deliverance, then, is not from the snares of this world or from its evil (as the Christians say) but from speculation about death. In this she and Camus are close together. As they both point out, it is mankind that establishes the criteria of true and false, and usually on grounds imperfectly empirical or wholly intuitive. In these circumstances, then, men have only to "glorify" the earth for that glorification to be instantly true. Sartre, on the other hand, stresses "the abortive aspect of the human adventure," as she tells us, and therefore, as far as ethics is concerned, has not delivered the goods.

It is appropriate to conclude this review of Sartre and his disciples with some allusion to *Les Mots* (1964),[1] the first volume of his autobiography, and to *La Force des Choses* (1964), the third volume of Beauvoir's.[2] The story Sartre tells is that of a lonely, protected childhood which, like that of Camus, decided his habitual attitudes and obsessions. But whereas Camus acquired something positive, Sartre tells us that his own boyhood led him to develop an hermetic attitude to literature from which he took thirty years to recover. He dismisses *Nausea* and *Being and Nothingness* as based on invalid concepts, especially that by which the writer aristocratically asserts the meaning of his own life by underlining the pointlessness and absurdity of the lives of others. Here is Sartre satirizing his early period as posited on a neo-Romantic fallacy he inherited from a *bourgeois* upbringing in which the writer was regarded as a medieval clerk. The infant Sartre, "Poulou," had no other children to play with and therefore developed the habit of justifying his existence in isolation; in other words, like Genet and Baudelaire, he accepted the role thrust upon him and did his best to live it. One gathers that the one thing which most "authenticated" him was having his Paris apartment bombed by French patriots because he had spoken out against the French army's use of torture in Algeria.

Another thing that helped him was the opportunity to revile the bourgeoisie year after year (an activity in which Beauvoir herself remains energetic although she reserves some of her vilification, oddly enough, for Camus on Algeria). The C. P. is still there for both of them, tempting, beguiling, rebuffing and just. For Sartre it is literature that is suspect now and, for her, almost anything to do with America. They are both somewhat pessimistic, Sartre the less so, perhaps because he still flourishes on the level of theory and the tide of events has not battered through his defenses as, apparently, it has through hers. Their political hopes are now old-fashioned; the French Left failed to translate

---

[1] First published in *Les Temps Modernes* (October, November, 1963).

[2] The preceding volumes were *Memoirs of a Dutiful Daughter* (1958) and *The Prime of Life* (1959).

the Resistance's spirit of triumphant fraternity into any form of political usefulness (Beauvoir blames America for this, it seems) and it was de Gaulle, the aging praetor, who came along and put their best ideas into action in Algeria. On another level, we find the Beauvoir who now, like some Camus character, awaits death without making recourse to the supernatural and also without pretending she feels fulfilled and gratified by her life. There is no fuss from either of them, but a great deal of honesty and, in Sartre's case, much revision of his attitude. He seems to have spotted at long last the mind-game aspect of his writings up to about 1953; and this piece of revelation, to him and to us, consorts oddly and rather sadly with the pessimism and depression that flow through the end of his lifelong friend's autobiography. In each case the key is to be found in an incapacity to get into action: Sartre was laboring under the influence of his upbringing (he was less than one year old when his father died), and Beauvoir (along with Sartre) has been unable to force the historical moment to do her bidding.

Such are the torments of self-liberation. It is good that these theorists are now revealing what their doctrines have meant in their own lives. One has a feeling of relief that, after so many books and so many thousands of absolute assertions, one can begin to compare—as one must in the case of existentialism—the formula with the life. The pendulum is swinging slowly back. We are already learning how disappointing it is not to have been able to act as you wished, and not to have been as lucid as you thought you were. Tyche, the unpredictable goddess of Fortune, has been at work in these two careers, and it is only now that we can rigorously appraise existentialism as a code to live by. We may discover something new or we may be led to remark, with Malraux, that the age of the fundamental is beginning again. "Life in itself," Montaigne says (it is the epigraph to *The Ethics of Ambiguity*), "is neither good nor evil, it is the place of good and evil, according to what you make of it." Perhaps, in spite of what Malraux hopes for, we shall discover man does not change except for, from time to time, developing a new idea of what man can be, but never is.

André Malraux

I wonder how many of the people who still interest themselves in André Malraux have begun to grow sceptical. His lifelong "search for man" has come to rest in "the imaginary museum," and the lively characters—the "adventurers" of his novels—are beginning to look obsolete. Heroes are more diffident nowadays. Somehow, it seems, Malraux arrived at a failure of hope which is also the apotheosis of theory. It would be neat, but too easy, to explain his coming-to-rest in aesthetics as one consequence of disillusion: of too much de Gaulle and too many civic involvements. It is more likely that this finale has been predictable all along and that his career must be seen as a self-conscious game with masks, roles and aesthetic treasures. I try here to see him plain as a man whose career has been the cancellation of successive good ideas.

Malraux is not given to frequent public statements of his position: he makes few formal announcements of what he thinks about Hungary, Algeria or Vietnam. Instead, he goes about his job in practical politics and leaves the trained inferrers to their game. And the game, as it must, palls into the idle speculations and fictions of the boulevard. But there is another speculation, a more respectable one, that can be conveniently undertaken without detailed knowledge of any of his so-called positions; and this speculation is very much in line with his own habit of affiliating the similar. I do not think he has advanced anything precise enough or integrated enough to be called a system. But he does, I think, suggest a theory of humanism, a theory relevant to other lives and addressed, perhaps, to people more capable of applying it than Malraux. After all, it is common enough for a man to embody his own frustration in hortatory books; and, in so transcending it, to preclude their comparison with his own way of living. At first sight, preaching seems to require the sanction of practice. But we do wrong, I believe, to regard the literature of commentary and self-solace as prescriptive only. Therapy is more to the point. He offers advice; he reminds us of Arnold's dictum: "The greatness of a poet lies in his powerful and beautiful application of ideas to life." Not, as T. S. Eliot remarked in *The Use of Poetry and the Use of Criticism,* a happy way of putting it, but at least an acknowledgement of poetry's ineffectuality: it makes nothing happen, except privately. Arnold went on to say that "morals are often treated in a narrow and false fashion" and, of Wordsworth, that "The Wordsworthians are apt to praise him for the wrong things, and to lay far too much stress upon what they call his philosophy. His poetry is the reality, his philosophy—so far, at least, as it may put on the form and habit of a 'scientific system of thought,' and, the more that it puts them on, is illusion." Eliot called this "a striking, dangerous and subversive assertion." But Arnold was not proposing a slack self-indulgence or the abandonment of systematic thought. He was recognizing the elation that ineffectual knowledge can give. He was directing attention from the powerless idea to the possibility of joy.

So with Malraux: much of his writing is lyrical and exultant; yet many of his perceptions about the history of art, like his earlier ideas about engagement, are not meant to bear the test of action. His is the literature of consolation; the contentment is the reality; the apparent ethics are the illusion. To have acted in vain, as his experiences in China and Spain told him, is only another version of the passive insight recorded in *The Voices of Silence* (1951) with such intensity and poetic fervor. The test of a humanism is its power to console; it has to be privately pragmatic even if it seems publicly effete. So it is that Malraux, writing on art, invites us to share his elation; we may be able to do so; but the theory which prompts the elation is unlikely to affect our own way of life. And, equally, Malraux's return to politics neither contravenes nor quite fulfills his humanistic view. A divided man he may be; but some attitudes of mind need not be reconciled; and Malraux's humanism is an inward seed. It is placeless and timeless. But it is likely to be subjected to irrelevant criticism because it has a philosophical aspect and begs an ethical question.

His novels are of course autobiographical, cannot be separated from his own lively career, and record the worldly sanity of a man who has put himself at mankind's disposal. Unfortunately mankind did not match his expectations, socially and morally at any rate, and he relinquished the novel in favor of art criticism, a move that some have deplored and some have welcomed. But Malraux has been through enough to let this move remain his own business: that is, not to need glossing in interviews or extenuation in self-conscious articles in the newspapers. The fact speaks for itself and, to anyone who has read most of his works, makes a reasonable kind of sense. We may wish Malraux had done otherwise, but we cannot fail to realize what his motives are.

For his novels he is one of the outstanding writers of this century; he shows versatility, depth, passion, and faith in mankind as well as in his own idiosyncrasy. He speaks as an individual: where Camus's rhetoric is politically oriented, Malraux's is private: aimed at the aesthetic sense. His first three novels, *The Conquerors* (1928), *The Royal Way* (1930) and the ample, compassionate *Man's Fate* (1933), all deal with China and constantly suggest allegories of "the human condition." *Time of Scorn* (1935) presents with harrowing conciseness the fate of a Czech communist in Nazi Germany; *Man's Hope* (1937), Malraux's most Hemingway-like novel, is about the Spanish Civil War, abounds in scenes of deeply moving irony and signalizes his despair about man's ability to cooperate reliably, consistently, with his fellows. *The Walnut Trees of Altenburg* (1948), a mixture of novel and tract, marks his shift to straightforward allegory and to the pursuit of man's dignity not in politics or adventure but in the history of the visual arts.

The principal feature of these novels is a scrutiny of individual initiative and man's power to organize a better world. Against violence, confusion, revolution and torture Malraux creates images of stubborn hope: it is man's fate to have to construct a basis for hope. It would be idle to identify Malraux with any political or religious orthodoxy; he has always managed to keep a little out of step in order to comment generously and honestly. His most constant literary habit (from his early novels to his study of religious art, *The Metamorphosis of the Gods,* 1957) has been to illustrate or indicate secular epiphanies which, he says, give man grounds for hope and a basis for self-respect. Man, in fact, is the creature who can create his own epiphanies through acting in accordance with principles undecreed but inherited from century to century along with the recurring load of human weakness and human need.

"What *is* man?" That is the question substituted at the last moment for "The Eternal Elements of Art," the topic for discussion at the colloquy in *The Walnut Trees of Altenburg.* Walter Berger, the host and moderator, has just learned of his brother's suicide, and his consequent shift to apparent basics is an augury of epiphanies to come. In the same novel German soldiers move forward after a gas attack, only to return, shocked beyond all discipline, each bearing the body of a gassed Russian. Such incidents give man something to hold to: something not very tidy, something he cannot always rely upon, but at any rate something that has always a chance of turning up. And from this Malraux advances to affirm that there *is* continuity of human nature across the ages; man does possess something eternal—something evinced when Katow, in *Man's Fate,* gives to a fellow prisoner the cyanide that would have saved him from his own barbarously cruel execution. Selflessness, like death, is ineluctable: we can no more talk ourselves into the former than we can talk ourselves out of dying. What Malraux calls "the assault of pity" redeems our daily life; the timeless walnut trees, like the voices of silence we discover in painting and sculpture, identify us and stylize what in man is undying. This much, even among the Malraux paradoxes of intellectual adventurer and compassionate aesthete, remains clear.

Art, however, is not subject to the flaws that beset those who attempt to transcend mere humanity through violence, will, self-punishment or political commitment. And Malraux has settled for art. The younger generation of Frenchmen (and perhaps some of his political *confrères*) may find him now rather *passé*, invincibly earnest and visibly misguided; but such vicissitudes are allowed for in Malraux's implied view of his own career. He intends his career to be read as a meaningful sample of human life. The ship captain in *The Royal Way* calls Perken a "mythomaniac," and the same term fits Malraux. Perken, who tries to mask the world from himself, to use it as a mirror, speaks slightingly of Mayrena, king of the Sedangs: "I see him as a player-king, bent on acting his own biography. You Frenchmen usually have a weakness for that sort of man, who prefers giving a fine performance to actual success." If we interpret Malraux thus, we shall not be far wrong.

Malraux has thought most deeply about, has sought action most avidly in, the realm of the mental possibilities between nihilism and the urge to conquer, between fatalism and the longing to be a god. The conqueror, all cosmic initiative and spiritual ardor, ends up devising such a lethal abstraction as Naziism. Hope precedes action; to be any use, action has to be organized, and all organization is a mode of the abstract. Perken fears a death not chosen; Clappique in *Man's Fate,* idling while hostile forces gather, abdicates from choice itself. For action is human—initially; and, initially, so is choice. We are most haunted by what we choose not to do. So it is as futile to try to shape the world to our ideal as to accept the cycle of eternal recurrence.

Such is the theme of *The Conquerors* and *The Royal Way* and, a few privileged moments and beings apart, of the next three novels. Only with the transitional *Walnut Trees* does Malraux begin to reinterpret his sense of "numinous awe," of "frail and humble communion" and post-Renaissance man's sense of power. Neither blind action nor cringing apathy is truly human. Awe outstrips all appearances; communion is not physical; power is to be defined as our response to the demons. And the artist's true job is a demiurgic onslaught on those demons, for he alone can offer, in default of faith, a universal testimony to the nature of the world we inhabit.

This progress of the soul never looked easy. One was always conscious of the screwed-up nerves, the psychic tic and the impulsive sincerity. Needing a fixed law, Malraux needed also a mystery to move about in. He wanted to be a politician and a shaman too. But now, his ambivalences—the aestheticism of action, the commitment to art—have merged. He has given a new twist to his attitude without, however, repudiating *The Voices of Silence.* He still, presumably, safeguards his humanism by condemning and discarding what of human achievement is dross. *The Voices of Silence* embodies art only, the aesthetic core of a humanism; and presumably his old principle survives: all that the humanist needs is sufficient faith, and doubt is no greater than the difference between two successive moments.

But, for the humanist, loss of faith desolates forever; whereas the Christian, however vaguely, has something to look forward to. Humanism, then, is very often desperate, intemperate and contrived, and perhaps this has struck Malraux forcefully since he completed *The Voices of Silence*. He might well be expected to explore misgivings implicit in that book itself, misgivings minimized at the time of writing by resolve and sheer need. For when he wrote about "the art of experiment" which displaces the art that is accepted and "official," he perhaps felt that the denunciation of things created by men should not have spared even art itself. "This victory," he said, "which is that of the individual, begins to seem to us just as hollow as dazzling." We are reminded that an art which studies itself for too long may die of boredom. And a bored art, an art which cannot offer or receive, is just as undesirable and corrupt as the other form of creativity that has given us methods of making mass war. What is it then in *The Voices of Silence* which appears to have failed Malraux? It is art's evasiveness. Art removes a man from the world of everyday without transporting him to a suitably religious substitute. So it is that Malraux's reversion to politics appears to be a criticism of aesthetic humanism at least, and possibly of humanism in general.

It was tempting to envisage him alone in his "museum without walls," supplied with food and adequate facilities. How long could he stay there? Now we know. And to envisage him so was no mere pretext for frivolity. It was to ask whether there is any point, when you withdraw, in trying to withdraw with the best in your pocket. For his aestheticism seemed essentially one of hermetic self-consolation. It had, apparently, no outward movement. It offered, apparently, nothing but the consolation after the utter defeat. It seemed in itself, like the modern art it took under its wing, narrow in appeal: the disillusioned politician who had been adventurer and soldier was looking after himself at last. But

Malraux at least offered the kind of instrument that might help someone to spiritual regeneration. The trouble is that such an offering and such regeneration can be made to look trivial.

It was all very well to assert in *The Voices of Silence* that the humanist delights in art because works of art remote from one another in space and time are so alike as to prefigure and demand affiliation. It is equally true that neither Phidias nor Rodin constrains the murderer, and that art may soothe the intelligentsia without gratifying the larger public. The life of everyday preempts the attention even of the cultivated mind. Rectifying seems oddly preferable to complaint or evasion, and an effort to cope with life, to make do, is more creative than a retreat into art.

The impressive thing about Malraux's almost mystical abandonment of the West was that he, having known intimately the grind of politics both national and wider, must have had some worldly basis for his views and acts. The aestheticism of a Pater is largely the way of life preferred by a shy personality who is lucky enough to be able to pick and choose. The aestheticism of a Malraux is the gesture of a man weary of public life. When he seceded, the affirmations within his move seemed less important than its negative direction. And now, the *volte-face* looks just as negative. After all, Malraux has been accustomed to re-form his experiences in general terms; he has rarely expected people to compare his conduct with their own and to scrutinize themselves accordingly. It appears now that he has ceased to simplify, has ceased to require an attitude both homogeneous and consistent. Perhaps he is right. Western civilization is perhaps unique for its ability to balance its resignations with a vague hopefulness which, oddly enough, becomes vaguer and stronger while the amount of heartening evidence becomes progressively smaller. The sensitives may default, but they keep on serving.

But whether or not our civilization and our attitudes are paradoxical, the humanist has to ask himself an awkward question: Must humanism have a legend which is complete (like that of orthodox faiths) or one which is always proceeding? If he selects the latter view, he involves himself in another question. He has to face a hypothesis. Only a part of his "institution" or basis of faith is settled. One day, perhaps, he finds that the art and thought being produced in his time are of inferior calibre. Or perhaps he decides that technology is being perverted. Shall he retreat, claiming that his faith is not based on the present modes of the creative impulse? Or shall he choke his aesthetic and moral sensibilities and take whatever he is given? Does he, in fact, narrow his faith or lose it?

It is at such a crisis that the humanist feels deceived. To limit his faith is to be a Malraux; seceding, choosing, evading. Conscience prompts a repudiation that in turn strengthens the search for an established religion. A faith has to be capable of being in the world of everyday and remaining intact. Humanism cannot do this; and the humanist finds that, as his faith has to be narrowed, he needs it all the more.

The consequences of a narrowed humanism are obvious in *The Voices of Silence:* the whole intellectual and aesthetic pursuit becomes increasingly inbred. Over the centuries, as Malraux shows, the element of self-consciousness has come to obsess the artist: he is no longer concerned to seek out the devils and make them tolerable. What he depicts belongs more to himself than to any putative audience. It exists more inside the world of art than inside the real world, the world of everyday best. It enters into humanism as something pale and exclusive. The concepts of dedication, civilized concourse, the fusion of sanctity and magnificence, are the very things the artist distorts. He sees tradition as the possessed past, as actually tamed; and the ideal does not exist even in the serenest and most venerable themes. According to Malraux, "the Calvary plainly did not represent it for Fra Angelico, but—more subtly—neither did the School of Athens quite represent it for Raphael, nor even the Entry of the Crusaders for Delacroix. . . ." The artist has become selfish: "As opposed to representing the world, artists wish to make a different one of it—and not only that—one to suit their own purposes." Art is for the sake of the artist. But the change, says Malraux, has been going on for the last hundred years. The passage continues:

To speak of a modern art of the masses is merely to want to combine the pleasure of an art with that of brotherhood, and play on a word. An art works on the masses only when, in serving their prejudices, it is not distinct from them: when it produces

Virgins and not statues. Although the Byzantine painters did not see passers-by as iconic figures, and although Braque does not see fruit-dishes by fragments, the shapes of Braque are not to twentieth-century France what the forms of Daphne were to Macedonian Byzantium.

This panache of allusion looks like a sublime gamesmanship and even seems to have concealed from Malraux, until very recently, the full import of both his discoveries and his method. All we can add to the suspicion we have that Malraux is obsessed by pure form is the qualification, feeble and trite, that the region of pure form is not necessarily easeful. An art derived from art becomes increasingly exiguous.

But the most disturbing thing in Malraux's account is the way in which art apes ethics. Dilemmas compel us to seek precedents; we need reassurance. We have to apply whatever principle we find to our present dilemma; whereas the art of Malraux seems to be an immersion in precedents. If we have to break out of a dilemma, we cannot moralize indefinitely; but if we have to paint, we can do that without looking at actuality at all. So it is not surprising that Malraux should now have traced to its conclusion his argument about "experiment" and "interrogation." Too often, as the facts gathered in *The Voices of Silence* tell us, art has been evasion; and "experiment" and "interrogation" have not included much attempt by man to put discoveries to worthwhile purposes. Art became an escape from, a protest against, power politics.

So a fugitive art has come to be rationalized into something that can uphold or rebut a philosophical statement. But such an art should therefore be able to withstand the kind of commonsense treatment Camus gives to ideas political and ethical. A fugitive art has as much to do with his concept of *l'homme révolté* as have (to take some of Camus's own examples) Stalin, Rimbaud, Sade, Nietzsche and Napoleon. Life, according to Malraux and Camus and Sartre, is absurd: art is part of the absurdity. In *The Temptation of the West* (1926) what is seen as absurd is the conflict between western man's mind and his emotions; Garine in *The Conquerors* repudiates both society and God. This idea of the absurd is not far from that of Camus: conflict causes nihilism, and drives men into irritable, uncreative revolt. Sartre's view is different: man cannot justify his life, cannot make it seem necessary. And yet art as an irritable and revulsed doodling, as a nose thumbed at the human condition, as an attempt at self-justification, does provide a way through absurdity. Its hermetic nature has to be tested as an example of nihilism and as a footling reason for man's being. The irony is that, although art is eligible, it is unsocial: it too easily loses sight of the mundane but suppressed hopes that persuade Camus (and the political Malraux) to devote themselves to the rights of the individual. Art is not the whole world or even essential to the eradication of mass murder.

But is Malraux in *The Voices of Silence* seeking an affiliation between men (just as he sought affiliation between masterpieces), with art as a solace in the event of failure? Or is he less deliberate, acting on a feeling in the heart as the source of right? One wonders to what extent he has a sense of the edifice of his own thought; how much is impulse and how much willed? His dilemma is that, for his platform, he has to look to the very creativity, malign or merely miscarried, which compelled him into aestheticism. He has to rethink his eclecticism. For the majority of men, who could not have penetrated to his art, are still divided and sterilized by the politics. And Malraux must know how the complexity of human affairs as well as something intractable in man himself inevitably contorts the straight lines of idealism. Anguish invariably results. But this is an anguish that some men have to undergo continually in order to provide a framework in which such a person as the fugitive Malraux can repose.

By adopting in *The Voices of Silence* the aesthetic position, Malraux conferred upon it those tragic meanings whose absence until then ensured its almost complete discredit. By abandoning the same position, he increased both the tragic meaning and the discredit: he had lived his way through a phase; and he has now, it would seem, relinquished the search for absolutes. His attitude to his own ambivalence has changed: he remains ambivalent, both committed and unconverted, without trying to obliterate the one in favor of the other. False absolutes no longer tempt him: his attitude is mixed, tastefully unheroic, far from idolatry, pertly amateurish and altogether his own fault. It brings to mind the old questions about his poses and positions. Is there not, between the man who is apart and the man of parts, a man of mere fragments? But then, we cannot gauge the coherence of his personality, although we have to decide whether his new commitment makes him a complete man or merely augments a list of delusions. *The Temptation of the West* offers perceptions of renewed relevance, both ominous and heartening:

The development of oneself which aims at the conquest of power is sustained, not by an abiding conviction, but by a kind of opportunism, by a constant adaptation, or by the acceptance of a party dogma. . . . The wish to be differentiated from others cannot be founded on illusion alone. . . .

When "constant adaptation" goes hand in hand with "the wish to be differentiated," perhaps we should reach for our Hobbes. It is not so much a question of whether Malraux is sincere; we would like to know whether he thinks sincerity important.

To reach for Hobbes is to condemn Malraux, perhaps rightly. But we are also obliged to affiliate him with Heidegger, whose phenomenology he seems to have vindicated. We do not know objects or even ourselves, says Heidegger; all we know is phenomena which are the transitory products of interacting unknowns. Whether we see Malraux as predisposed to action or to art, we can at least recognize yet another effort by him to authenticate his existence by alliance with a cause. Perhaps more bewildered than ever by the flux of life, he remains essentially without serenity. Avid for both self-definition and meditation, he dreams of both, chooses neither and contents himself with a temporary identity by being useful to others. He should not be beyond our sympathy. To humanize to the full is his aim, as ever. But there are times when a man's own problems override his recommendations to readers. Life twists all formulas, even private ones, and even beyond public explanation. Malraux, in widening himself, is trimming his ideals, is demonstrating the humanist paradox: to be immersed in life may entail losing not only our illusions of control, perspective and unity, but even self-control and the abilities to manage and assess. Malraux may pay his price. The way from absolutes to compromise may well end in disintegration of a useless but heroic kind. But Malraux is concerned now with gesture, not proof; and one's abiding impression is of a torrential, morbid, complicating, humane person, always unquiet, yet strong enough to transcend an accelerating dismay.

The Voices of Silence emphasizes, time and again, that the art of Picasso or Braque is anarchic in so far as it eschews the world as we know it. Modern art, says Malraux, "refuses" the world by exploring the extent to which the world can be distorted:

Our civilization is one on its own . . . separate from all but the Greek, by virtue of the primacy which we accord to interrogation. In this interrogation, our sciences have found their awful power. And our art too has become an interrogation of the world.

Such interrogation stems from an impulse to be individual, to be original, to find out, to master and explain. This is the impulse which, as early in his career as 1921, Malraux analyzed, found in no way ambivalent, and then denounced as absurd. Ling, the young Chinese travelling through Europe, writes in one of the letters which make up *The Temptation of the West:*

Our universe is not, like yours, under the sway of the law of cause and effect; or, more exactly, that law, which we do recognize and which disdains what cannot be justified, has no power there. An inexplicable action is, to us, the effect of an unknown cause only because it is engendered in a life of which we know nothing.

Again, from Paris:

Europeans are tired of themselves, of their waning individualism, of their excitement. . . . Capable of doing anything to the point of sacrifice, but sickened by the lust for action which perverts their race, they would like to seek beneath the actions of men a more profound reason for being.

The verb is *chercher.* For the European (and for the American) the cause of being has to be sought out. If such a thing were to come easily, descending on a man as it were by grace, he would feel cheated. That is the flaw in the Westerner, his difference from the Oriental. Action obsesses him. He is haunted by the notion that all things are explicable. The Westerner does not accept: he is deficient in apathy. Even two devastating wars have not shaken completely his faith in humans and progress. The system develops, as does a convention in painting, a life of its own. The exception, the thinker, can settle his personal fate without troubling the system. He can leave. But this is bound to prove unsatisfying; for his concern, with regard to rejection, is that all individuals, or a decisive majority, should reject. To persuade them to do this, he must enrich the system's literature. If he takes office to attract attention, he must sustain the system he is intending to discredit. Yet if he tries to wreck its smooth functioning, he is quickly displaced. He finds that the inaugural spirits have been rash; the sustaining spirits, short-sighted or foolish; and those who think as he does, ineffectual.

It is an attitude of search for something fixed where all is moving. It is what prompts Pater to study times of upheaval and change, times when a civilization seems to change its character: Aurelian Rome, the Renaissance, and what he sees as the seed of the Renaissance, in the twelfth century. Similarly, Malraux is fascinated by China's turmoil under European influence; [1] by the Spanish revolution. Both men, it seems, hope to fix upon something lasting during processes of breakup and resettlement; almost as if they should study a sea-change. They do not seek the faultily regular, the splendidly null, but merely something which, by appealing to the emotions and conscience of a sensitive person, helps that person to tolerate life in the system of which he is part. They are trying to legitimize Western civilization. What they find appears to be the creative impulse in so far as its consequences are not affected by such an idea as history or by such a decay as that of a civilization. And their eyes are not merely backward-looking: "que tels tableaux de jadis soient chargés de poésie moderne, que Piero di Cosimo soit un frère de Chirico. . . ." Pater turns to

[1] For less dogmatic treatment of the effects which Western civilization has had on the Orient, see *Le Bouddha vivant* (1927) of Paul Morand. An article which T. E. Lawrence published in *The Round Table* for September, 1920, entitled "The Changing East," is at once less rhapsodical and more shrewdly dogmatic than Malraux's version of the same theme in *The Temptation of the West*.

Rossetti; he lauds Blake. Malraux juxtaposes a head by Picasso with one from Sumeria of the third millenium: they embody in the same style the same quality of feeling. Here, says Malraux, was something perdurable, something almost divine.

Pater had looked at as much of oriental culture as he had been able to without making journeys to the Orient. His conclusions about it have been confirmed by Malraux. First, Pater spots a difference which has come to obsess Malraux:

In oriental thought there is a vague conception of life everywhere, but no true appreciation of itself by the mind, no knowledge of the distinction of man's nature: in its consciousness of itself, humanity is still confused with the fantastic, indeterminate life of the animal and vegetable world.

This is the inchoate state of which Malraux so often speaks. It is a state not of nirvana but of existence without predicate: "In Greek thought, on the other hand, the 'lordship of the soul' is recognized." It has been, declares Malraux, a consistently European habit to ramify and celebrate that predicate into all kinds of individuality and self-consciousness. To Ling, in *The Temptation of the West,* the habit seems unnatural:

To assert oneself in the world lived in by all, is to set oneself apart, to establish a difference between things of the same kind.

It is absurd enough to exalt man above other created things; but Europeans refine absurdity to the point of trying to outdo one another in enterprise and originality:

The oriental mind, on the contrary, sets no great store by man in his own right. . . .

The service of our mind is to reveal clearly our fragmentary nature and to develop, from this, our sense of the universe; not like scientists reconstructing fossilized animals from a few remains, but rather as reading a name on a map conjures up landscapes strewn with giant creepers. For the highest point of beauty in a mature civilization is an earnest inattention to the self. . . . You want a world that is coherent; you devise it. . . .[1]

---

[1] Hence, ironically enough for Malraux, communist China's odd mixture of Western initiative and oriental "inattention to the self." It is the perfect recipe for totalitarianism.

Such was Malraux's version of a mode of thought largely inaccessible to Europeans. Twenty-five years later he emerged with an attempt to adapt the oriental attitude to a European situation. Ling had said, "To seek and flee oneself is just as stupid. . . ." And this statement is exactly the basis of Malraux's attempt.

It is no use trying to ignore our awareness of ourselves or of what we have done. He is firm about that. He knows that scavengers after solace cannot be choosers. He knows too that any last-stand philosophy must involve its author in reckless self-deceptions, and must seem, to disinterested observers, factitious and naive. The unself-consciousness of the East is to be given to the self-conscious West not only by selecting and combining what, in the arts of the West, is so instinctively done as to be unwittingly human, but also by identifying through analogies between their arts Western man and his Eastern counterpart. In this way might be gleaned a hope that Europe has not gone too far. But the comment might be made that such proposals have more to do with consolation than with efficacy. That is precisely the point. For the mere fact of having discovered something on which to base a proposal can assuage the mind that is distraught.

The advantages of seeing human achievement in such wide contexts are several. First, the excessive grandeur of certain individual achievements is merged into the grandeur of the tradition. Second, the tradition thus established gives reverberations to the minor achievement. And third, to compose such a tradition is a satisfactory way of emancipating one's self from the immediate present. What is pernicious loses importance; what is good attracts strength from the distance. This way the contemplative mind finds consolation; it shares an oriental repose infused with dignity. So does the humanist move towards the kind of religion he needs:

We have learned that if death cannot force genius into silence, it is not because genius thwarts death by perpetuating the same initial language, but because genius enjoins a language which is perpetually being modified, sometimes forgotten, like an echo which would answer the centuries' voices in their succession. . . .
At the heart of the centuries, a remote masque of singing and

dancing appears solemnly in the light; before us, the upturned face of vast designs whispers in the shadow which it fills.

It is not simply art which compels awe. It is not genius. It is what underlies these things; it is man's urge to assert himself nobly in art. And no metaphysical talk about the continuity or not of civilization will discredit or support the view which reveres this urge and its results as the divine in man and as the divine's manifestations. This urge was implanted by no force or being of which we know. So we stop short of speculation and assume that the urge was self-engendered in man. As with destiny, we dispense with the concept because all our acts are destined. To cheat destiny is to follow destiny, because the cheating is destined. So with divinity. It may exist around and within us; it may enmesh us like destiny. But if we never know it, we discard the concept in favor of its tangible version in art. And we keep the attributes which we had called divine. That is one attitude; the agnostic has no worthwhile alternative:

How could an agnostic civilization help making recourse to what outstripped it and often ennobled it?

The first universal artistic culture, which is doubtless going to transform the modern art that led it this far, is not an encroachment, but one of the supreme victories of the West.

None of this has to be proved. Its sufficient justification is in the emotional needs of Western man. The noblest humanism must start and end in the world of nature. Sensation can be refined but never to the point at which it dispenses with nature, for then it has to be explained in terms of an existence in which the humanist cannot believe. That the agnostic who is a humanist should have to discipline himself in this way is part of man's fate. The agnostic who turns to art must turn also to consider his fate. The agnostic who cannot turn to art (the experience most likely to dispel his lack of attitude towards belief) has simply to watch the flux of phenomena. And in so watching, he might become passively aware of his fate. On the other hand, when a Malraux probes into the fund of art, he encounters active refusals of fate which, at the same time as bringing forcefully home to him the concept of fate, bestow a magic which renders that concept supportable.

As for the agnostics who cannot find a consolation, still less a belief, they belong with Garine of *The Conquerors,* the valiant fugitive who escapes into enterprises which bring him nearer than anything to the oblivion he craves. He is the type of man who finds in politics or war or religion or love only an anodyne. He needs a milieu of the spirit, a dimension conferring dignity and perhaps even meaning. He cannot join himself with the universe. Rather, he inherits a barren tradition of disdaining the cosmos. His only nirvana is violence; and even that, with its brief oblivions, brings him nothing of the comfort bestowed by those works of art which are more human than humanity:

. . . the art of the New Hebrides partners Rimbaud just as faithfully as Greco-Buddhist art goes with St.-John Perse.

Such moments as these intoxicate with a feeling of community. The moment of personal exultation becomes a similar moment in prehistory. It is not for a man to explain the consolations of company or the uplift given by sympathy, by "undergoing together." No doubt tradition and the human need of it are grounded on the feeling of powerlessness which a man experiences when he is alone. The same is true of an age which, like the present one, is obsessed with a terrifying feeling of uniqueness. For this age, it is perhaps reassuring to study the record of atrocities which occurred during the Thirty Years' War: we are not unique in our depravity. But history is poor comfort. What we need most is a sense of belonging to an order of nobleness; and it is here that art assists. For the forms of art suggest a history which is not true history, but one through which humanity is nourished. It is better to discern the attempt to make order from chaos than to occupy our minds with the artist's inevitable failure.

It is easy enough to set up an ethic of attentiveness, as if to say: Whatever we have made we must never forget. But men who start a perpetual motion fight shy of ideas of inevitability. They disclaim responsibility and yet refuse to admit their powerlessness. Even the serious artist, determined to compel a good from what seems worst, is likely to take himself too seriously and become too extreme to be supportable. And, in the last resort, each man will suffer as much as he can, or wants, and will then seek his own particular kind of lotus.

One of the curious incidents of Malraux's attempt to build a humanism of art is that he, as a modern man who favors nonrepresentational art, is prompted immediately to explore the art of the primitives:

The fact remains that our anxious epoch wishes to see in the arts of savages not only the expression of another world, but still that of those monsters of the deep which psychoanalysis catches with nets, and politics and war with dynamite.

The masks and heads of the Ba-Luba in the Belgian Congo are carved not to master what was visible but to depict a force—ancestral, divine, malicious—which could be revered only if given visible form. In other words, a religion embodies itself in images. Those carved masks and heads give their beholders a perverted thrill merely by giving horror a face, by capturing inscrutability in a visible form more inscrutable than the power had been before. But, as Malraux emphasizes and as we know, the human psyche demands these forms. If we must live in the presence of what is frightful, we have at least the compensation of indulging our morbid curiosity. As Malraux says: "Art does not revive dead societies, but the ideal or compensatory images they formed of themselves." Religion and the thrill must come together. What is so often termed morbid curiosity accounts for a good deal of primitive art; the urge to commemorate, for an amount which is smaller.

Such art, *"moyen de possession,"* is religious and communal. So it is not altogether surprising that the art of this century, an art which experiments with itself and must in consequence distort the usual world, not only finds a model in primitive art but in so doing gathers to itself something of that art's religious spirit. Similar distortions are sought out among the art of the Middle Ages, and a similar religious spirit is passed on. But this religiosity cannot exist in the void; it is pressed upon the subject matter, which is the medium; it is pressed upon the role of the artist. And in this way art comes to glorify itself. But Malraux should explain:

This art is not a god; it is an absolute; but this absolute has its fanatics and martyrs, and is no abstraction.

Or again:

It is not a religion, but a faith. It is not a sacred thing, but the negation of an impure world.

Such is the consummation of the strivings of Pater. Such is, in fact, the complete and logical outcome of the art-for-art's-sake pattern of thought. Here, more fanatical, perhaps more justified, is the triumph of the aesthetic clique. It is something very much like solipsism:

In Russia, Picasso could not depict Stalin except in a style which denied that of all his pictures, *Guernica* included. For the modern artist, to address himself genuinely to the masses is to convert himself, to change absolutes. Holy art, religious art, demand a community—whose death or dispersal is sufficient to compel them into a sea-change. The artist has found his community composed of those like himself, whose numbers are, moreover, always on the increase; and, as modern art grows, so does its indifference towards conserving the domain of the art which guided it from Sumer as far as the break-up of Christianity: the expression of living or dead gods, of the Testaments or of the Acropolis, of the Chinese mountains and cathedrals, those of Angkor and Elephanta, the painter of the Pietà of Villeneuve and those of the frescoes at Nara, Michelangelo, Titian, Rubens, Rembrandt, tie men to the universe; and even Goya, who flings them a gift of darkness. Does our art tend now to communicate nothing but the split of conscience, which gave it birth?

We see what perturbs him: not any vague suspicion that the artist has reduced his public; not any cock-and-bull rumor that the Renaissance counterpart of Picasso enthralled the masses; but that the artist in general has exchanged one spiritual community for another. He has become so attached to his art that he can attach it to nothing but art. Picasso's paintings are so much his own that they cannot owe allegiance or even lip service to anyone or anything else. Whereas, say, Michelangelo profited from allegiance to a community not of Christian persons but of the Christian feeling which they diffused, Picasso can profit only from a community of the sentiments of artists. And Picasso, in consequence, loses the ineffable power conferred by the spirituality of legend: his lines stop where he terminates them and cannot be projected into any interesting world save that of art. Malraux does for Picasso what can be done; but *The Voices of Silence* proves only that it is better for the artist, as distinguished from the connoisseur, never to be wholly an artist. For, as we see from the disquiet of Malraux, the contributions of Picasso are often not to humanity at all. To contribute to humanity is not the same thing as to contribute to what Malraux has distilled from previous contributions. It must be discouraging for Malraux to find that his own eclectic principle is also the principle of Picasso's practice. And it is for this reason that Malraux seems half-inclined to reprove Picasso.

Malraux is troubled too by the exclusiveness of his own form of consolation. The larger public, as he knows, will have to get on with the world as it is, *impur* or not. This fact leads Malraux to see Picasso's attitude to art as being too intimately related to his own. In seeing this, he interprets himself correctly, but misjudges Picasso who has been landed in a near-philosophical position largely by his having felt obliged to indulge in a good deal of technical experiment. Malraux is right to consider the philosophical implications of such a position, but not to assume that they have necessarily developed from a philosophical starting point. I elaborate this point only to reveal the anxiety of Malraux who seems rightly to reprove Picasso and his like for having taken the wrong road, but to adduce the wrong reasons for the error of their way. But Malraux must be aware of how close is his own attitude to the attitudes struck by the aesthetes of the so-called decadence. He must be even more sensitively aware of how his own attitude differs from those others. And if the apparent ancestry of his attitude involves him in some fretful tergiversations *(il n'est pas une religion mais il est une foi; cet art n'est pas un dieu, c'est un absolu)*, he deserves the advantage of having his own views bluntly juxtaposed with those to which they seem unfortunately akin.

Any attempt to summarize him must consider the polarities of action and contemplation. On the one hand, Claude Mauriac suggests in his *André Malraux ou Le Mal du héros* (1946) that "Perhaps even the intelligence can attain its ultimate perfection only in action and pre-eminently so in the sphere of combat; that is to say, confronted with the extreme form of what rejects it." On the other hand we have Malraux himself, writing on Goya (*Saturn*, 1950):

The Italian discovery, hackneyed as it may have become as a result of praise and imitation, was that Art is one of the most powerful forces for adjusting the world, a kingly domain where man escapes from the human state to reach another where he is at one with the gods. . . . Goya discovered that if the Italian style can make men into figures of divinity, it is art itself which makes the artist a rival of the gods.

But perhaps the most significant utterance, for this context at least, is another from the essay on Goya: "I have said elsewhere that for an agnostic a possible definition of the devil is that which in man aims to destroy him." Man only comes to terms with the world by "blinding himself with childishness": thus Malraux's interpretation of Goya's message.

We have to decide which of the twin devils within man—the childishness destructive or the childishness constructive—destroys him the more. The alternatives are war and escapism, the wild twins who are often confused with each other when men speak of the "art" of war and the "conflict" within the imagination. Both arise in Goya's series called *The House of the Deaf Man*. The cruellest challenge of all is that which man sets himself: to come to terms with the irremediable without destroying harmonies already achieved, or conferred, by nature. Malraux's response to this challenge is well described in his own words on Goya: ". . . his work is full of confused alternations between spectacle, recollection, and the obscure passion of which this recollection becomes sometimes the outward expression." There is a self-induced deafness of the Hemingway dumb ox; it recurs in twentieth-century literature as the artist's version of an actual experience such as we find described earlier in *House of the Deaf Man,* Dostoevsky's *Recollections of the House of the Dead* and Byron's *The Prisoner of Chillon.* There is, to use the condition metaphorically, deafness inflicted, deafness chosen and deafness toyed with as a convenient literary idea. All appear in Malraux's work. Call the condition what we will—blindness, insensitivity, escapism—it is, in the phrase he takes from Goya, his *idioma universal.* And not, of course, his alone.

"In life and painting I can quite well dispense with God. But, suffering as I am, I cannot dispense with *something greater than myself,* something that is my whole life: *the power of creating.*" This, the epigraph to *The Metamorphosis of the Gods,* is van Gogh, and the phrases I have italicized suggest, although obliquely, Malraux's main purpose in compiling yet another sumptuous album *à thèse.* As in *The Voices of Silence* Malraux the idiosyncratic nympholept muffles himself in excited impersonality; but the commentary is highly individual, and familiar Malraux obsessions turn up regularly. In fact it is at times difficult not to feel that one is reading a clever parody in which the old concepts of the adventurer-philosopher have been yoked by violence to the bland allusions of the religious aesthete: "In the last holy place of Persia, Behistun, we sense the same virile fraternity as on the high cliffs of Tagetus." It is time Malraux heeded the dangers of mannerism and, without falling into the deliberately dull prose advocated by puritans who can't write any other kind themselves, ensured that his rhetorical cataloguing did not confound the reader or make him snigger. This lavish attempt to illustrate "something greater" than ourselves, and to collate illustrations of it from Mycenae to Giotto, suffers not so much from the effort to be encyclopaedic (although the theme is vast) as from a Marlowe-like addiction to resonant naming: "In the world where Caesar met Cleopatra, 'Roma' did not replace Athena, nor did Caligula's horse replace consuls or gods." It becomes increasingly difficult to detach Malraux the serious writer from the image of the excommunicated hierophant who offers to let the groundlings in on the arcana.

In *The Metamorphosis of the Gods* Malraux has a more

substantial and more complex thesis to argue than in *The Voices of Silence* or, for that matter, in the general sections of *Saturn*. He argues that "For a long while art has ceased to mean what it once meant in the ancient East, in Christendom, in 'Medieval' Asia and America, even in Greece. . . . What those people for whom art exists . . . have in common is not their refinement or eclecticism but their recognition of the mysterious power which (transcends) history by means that are not those of beauty." This power has nothing to do with the world of appearances; it is not necessarily God but somehow "something else"—"the relationship between the tidal rhythms of human life and a power that governs or transcends it." This is the metaphysics of a highly emotional writer: when he is happy he is an earth-ecstatic; otherwise he resents the remoteness of the governing power and observes that "Even Vishnu only belongs to a higher cycle of appearance." Either way he wants ecstasy, which comes from opening oneself to the "oldest man-made forms" in the Imaginary Museum. Such forms, says Malraux, compose an art not an end in itself, an art which rejects the evidence of the senses in order to reveal "a supra-real world existing here and now." In other words, he is once again extolling imagination as a religious force. It is imagination that fills the void, makes the incomprehensible locally visible, supplies a repertory of gripping rather than delighting images and so frees man from the chaos of his beginnings and the status of animal. All religion is imagination, in fact: gods familiarized by long reverence are no less the products of imagination than, say, the deities invented by William Blake. Both sets of gods begin as arbitrary inventions. The difference is (as the book's two-hundred-odd plates magnificently reveal) that the imagination can keep on modifying and re-portraying well-established gods without fear of demolishing, whereas the man who invents his private pantheon is too daunted by his own arbitrariness.

All the same, Malraux's own pantheon is no-one else's, just as his comparisons, combinations and suggested affinities are unique. He is presenting a faith but no dogma: His responses are less formal than atmospheric; he speaks of "numinous dusk" and "the silken susurration" of the desert:

A stridency of chaffering weaves through the clamor of motor-horns across the rain-swept dusk, and all the electricity of India is ablaze . . . and once more the measured baying of the horn calls down the Vedic night to shroud alike the sleep of the sacred cows and the shrill modernity of chromium.

This exemplifies his atmospheric agnosticism better than any list of transformed or combined deities. In fact the arguing in the book is almost absent-minded, as if it didn't matter anyway: I don't think it does. At one point Malraux explains that "The maker of Zoser sought to endow a Pharoah with eternity; Vermeer did not try to eternize a maidservant." But, we read, "was not Vermeer also trying to withdraw *something* from time?" Well, does Vermeer fit or not? What exactly is the difference between "eternizing" and "withdrawing" something from time? If there is no difference, Malraux is merely offering the old idea of *ars longa*. If they are not the same, then how does Vermeer's maidservant exemplify a metamorphosed god? Malraux seems to try getting just about everything into his religion—an understandable enough impulse provided we aren't supposed to be concentrating on gods (or on the sacred, which comes into being after the divine has been perceived). Nor is it illuminating or even enlighteningly rash to say that "The greatest artists created the forms of their gods but the gods accepted them only if men recognized them as such." Whatever that means, how does Malraux know? *The Metamorphosis of the Gods* abounds in such fancies, as well as in lacunae and rhapsodies.

The consecutive accounts of how the Olympians declined into civic deities, how the theatrical supplanted the divine from the end of the fourth century until the decline of Rome, how Byzantium replaced gesturing statues with static figures, how Christian mosaics resumed late Antiquity through the medium of the illuminated book, and how sacred art responded to the transition from faith to "communion" and then private worship—until "For the first time a Christian artist dared to pit the images of his dreams against those of the world of God," with the nymphs and the angels level-pegging—all this is dazzling, told with gracious enthusiasm in an idiom more colloquial than is usual for Malraux. But surely there is something specious about an argument that runs: sacred art defies the evidence of the senses; so does the art of Picasso and Braque; therefore nonrepresentational art is the most religious. The true Malraux shows, I think, in the section called "The Divine": "For Greece,' he says, "the sacred in its full sense did not exist, but neither did the wholly 'profane'; since immanent in every form of life was a spark of the divine enhancing it." "The Greeks," he continues, "set up against the hierarchy of the Absolute the prestige of the imaginary. . . ." "The sacred is replaced by the sublime, the supernatural by the marvelous, and Destiny itself by tragedy."

The Metamorphosis of the Gods embodies the humanism of a pantheistic aesthete who, in his turn, deposes the beautiful for the arresting. Even so, you have to be able to *see* these things in order to get anything from them; so no wonder Malraux speaks of "a fragile art of daylight." In the long run it is obsessions that count, not art; and they too, as well as all forms of religious experience, must come eventually under the heading of imagination. Only courage—especially to admit how much is no more than imagined—is not illusory. This is a brave book, exposing art's limits but alerting us to art's forgotten uses. "*All* sacred arts are intended," according to Malraux, "to appeal to the simple in heart, and none is illusionistic." Then why the wealth of complex exposition? The simple in heart will go on getting what they have always got without the intercession of a Malraux. On the other hand, every agnostic wants to be his own demiurge. This book shows him how, if he doesn't know already.

Oddly enough the book shows more of a human nature than of gods. It shows especially well the vast human appetite for irrelevance, the urge to temper god-portraiture with cute or excruciating details. A Pharaoh sitting cross-legged (holding his ankle like a little boy) somehow mitigates the sense of awe, somehow stops things from becoming too abstract. The veins on one prophet's hands are prominent enough to bring him into the world of everyday. Another prophet has a vacuous smile; nothing is more realistic than the ropes around the dying Christ's head in Perpignan Cathedral. A Naumberg "Christ before Pilate" fills the background with Brueghel faces. A Goya might have done the gibbering smugness of the candidates appearing for the Last Judgment in a detail from Bamberg Cathedral. In the Autun "Stephen Stoned" the process looks innocuous; one thinks of snowballs. "The Cappadocians" from Vézelay is pure Klee: bizarre, cavorting, ghostly. An Isaac, being sacrificed, holds down his right arm with his left in a gesture of terrifying, childish resolve. A complacent angel hovers; the priest with the sword half-grins, half-scowls. The Saint-Omer "Andromeda" shows her hemmed in with toenails. A ninth-century "Crucifixion" shows two torturers: one offers a drink with his lips pursed in sinister concentration; his long moustaches droop, and he seems to be holding his breath; the other, just about to prod with his spear, has a thoughtful, wistful face. In an eighth-century "Christ and St. Mennas" Christ puts a friendly arm round the saint's shoulder. Everyone in "The Parting of Abraham and Lot" in Santa Maria Maggiore has a wide-eyed spellbound look; each just manages to dare to look at the others, but it is all done with sideways glances. It is a picture of the most intense realism.

The diet, we might assume, had to be diluted; gods are stiff fare in themselves. And in the last analysis *The Metamorphosis of the Gods* tells us more about man than about gods; more about man's inexorable urge to familiarize the divine than about his capacity for worship. This is no doubt part of Malraux's intention. But how interesting it is to find so many pictures of men in religious situations, and so few of gods either in majesty or intervening in human affairs. One is obliged to conclude that man likes to get his gods settled and fixed, made remote by his own hand. Or, as Malraux points out, to show extra virtuosity in painting what does not exist: "Italy was to paint Venus because she does not exist." And to bring Venus into being is both an act of apostasy and a celebration of a world we wish we possessed wholly. She, to use Malraux's own terms, is a scar carved on a world we did not make.

I have tried Malraux, as it were, against a variety of interpretations, none of which seems to fit him quite. Perhaps he is too protean. The Malraux of recent years—renowned for his capacity for extempore lectures when people expected only a brief comment from the Ministre d'État Chargé des Affaires Culturelles—is still the same man who in 1959 appointed Camus to the directorship of the new state theater. It was Camus who said that man, in order to be man, must refuse to try to be God; it was Malraux who in *Man's Fate* observed that man's dream is to be God. And now there is only Malraux to talk of such things. He talks from a very great height, ranging far and wide over the history of art, history itself and the "world situation."

There is something godlike, and certainly sibylline, about this. Addressing the Anglo-American Press Association in Paris in 1964 he said he had not changed his position: throughout time, the same things dominated and characterized humanity; until, that is, the machine arrived, creating leisure and multiplying dreams. He spoke apocalyptically of the realm of sex and the realm of blood, noting in modern man "a great domain of nocturnal darkness" against which the only remaining weapon was culture. (The Venus de Milo must therefore grace the Tokyo Olympic Games, by courtesy of the French government.) Behind such an assertion, there is Malraux's abiding view that mechanical processes of reproduction have made all of art available to all of us and that now is the time to attempt a redefinition of man and of his culture. But while art has unified the world in this sense, politically the world is less integrated than ever: "the century's dream has turned out to be nothing but the drama of nations." The problem, he said, was to reconcile the reality of nations with the hope of justice; and, he added rather wanly, the destiny of the world is settled by "hard realities," not by good intentions. The only possibility he could see of "fraternity" (it is one of his favorite words) was in the "fraternal" elements of the great religions. For the first time in this century, he said, there is a "domain" in which fraternity is possible; and that will be through a continuance of the reconciliations already taking place between the major religions.

So he is still trying for his world view; not, now, through carving what Santayana called important initials on the map and through political action; and not wholly, as seemed the case a few years ago, through art; but through something based on the kind of sense talked centuries ago by Lord Herbert of Cherbury, hinted at by the Positivists, and revealed through the comparisons of *The Metamorphosis of the Gods*. Culture and religion are now firmly related in Malraux, and he has intensified his thinking about world or European unity. Not that he expects religions to lose their special characteristics; he expects, rather, the community of men to acknowledge the common faith underlying the differences between the major public religions. Notice, it is not religion to be attained through fraternity, but fraternity through religion. The end is significant and entirely deducible from his early writings. Malraux still has faith in man, as Camus had; and one imagines that the Cold War, in which Sartre has tried to play a part without being named as an actor and has been an actor without playing any part very clearly, has made Malraux grateful for a century in which there is very little *religious* persecution. Now, he seems to think, the oneness that men have shown in their art through the ages can extend to the level of faith as well. It is a nice (in both senses) extension of himself to project the voices of silence back into cathedrals, chapels, synagogues, temples and shrines. In a way he is making, all over again, the journey back to Angkor Vat, followed now by Jean Genet who also speaks of fraternity and the genius of Rembrandt. Camus, the Algerian pagan who in *The Fall* sketched his own clown and martyr—"a tragic comedian"—and in 1946 said that during his youth (the crisis of 1929; Hitler; Ethiopia; Spain, Munich; the War and Occupation) "The world of culture was beautiful, but it was not real," would have been glad. Malraux, like Eliot, has a wide conception of culture. It is one which, provided there is communication (as the Christian existentialists are always stressing), will make for peace against ideologies that claim control over all of human life.

Knowing the Worst

*I*T may seem bizarre and even tendentious to bring Simone Weil, T. S. Eliot and Graham Greene together under the heading of "action." There are, however, satisfactory reasons for doing so inasmuch as all three happen to be converts of an extraordinary kind who have, in their respective ways, gone beyond what the orthodox might think a seemly mandate. Simone Weil, a Jewess who in 1940 began to practice Roman Catholicism without ever being baptized, was continually drawn, both before and after her "conversion," to the proletariat, with whom she identified profoundly and with whom she took her place in manual labor. She also, of course, went to the Spanish Civil War and made herself awkwardly useful there. Her mysticism contrasts oddly with her socialism and gives her something of the aspect, mutatis mutandis, of the worker-priest. In some ways she is more orthodox than the average believer and in others more outlandish than many heretics.

T. S. Eliot became an Anglican in 1927 but, for all his profession of Anglo-Catholicism, steered carefully away from Catholicism proper. I concentrate here on his plays, and just one facet of them, because, it seems to me, he achieved in them a truly catholic spirituality that recalls F. H. Bradley's "one psychical totality" and makes a generous invitation to the spiritual capacity of everyone. (Of his poems, only Four Quartets achieves the same kind of thing.) From a position which is much more complex than it looks and which is much more tolerant and outgoing than that presented in his early prose writings, Eliot meets Camus in expressing a horror not so much of death as of living a completely negative life. As

F. R. Leavis points out, The Family Reunion *presents a Christian position without invoking Christian dogma and manages to be positive without being dogmatic. The "Reunion" is surely something along the lines of Malraux's recently proposed spiritual "fraternity" and the method of the plays is exactly what Leavis finds in the poems: "a technique for sincerity" which transcends orthodox conceptual frameworks and reaches the "illumination" or spiritual quiver that has to be the basis of any doxy, heretical or otherwise. I include Eliot, then, because he comes toward people of all sorts and conditions, and through the theater with all its connotations of entertainment, relaxation and catholicity.*

Graham Greene too has gone beyond dogma in presenting highly readable accounts of spiritual crisis through his own kind of geographical odyssey. Converted to Catholicism in 1926 (the official occasion of which was his marriage to a Catholic), he has said that he is a Catholic with an intellectual if not an emotional belief in Catholic dogma. He has worn his faith with a quiet, reticent, undemonstrative air. Sometimes his faith has vanished beneath the relentless world-traveller's accounts of Mexico, Vietnam, Sierra Leone, Cuba, Kenya and the Congo, not to mention central Europe, and the mobsters, gunmen, outlaws and spies who sustain the traffic in physical evil in Greene-land. The sinner, for Greene, is at the center of Christianity, and the human spirit in all its contradictions is what he concentrates on to the exclusion of overt preaching. Here, then, are three converts who also act heretically from within the established faith. Their deviations have as much to reveal to us as have the more obvious ones of the writers already discussed.

Simone Weil

To Simone Weil ethical wisdom was a mode of the sacred, an impersonal regimen of the sublime. "Everything that is impersonal in man," she said, "is sacred, and only that." The individual's private and intact identity she valued, but only because "the personal is opposed to the impersonal. . . . There can be a transition from one to the other." And because the collective prevents an individual from operating in his own right, she denied the collective any sacred value, stressing that the individual himself is worthwhile only in so far as he transcends himself in moving towards the Good.

These views serve to introduce her unsparing, antiromantic attitude to religion; an attitude all the more surprising when we consider the highly subjective nature of the many agnostics who have held views similar to her own. She cuts self-indulgence to the minimum; they often regard it as a good in itself. Her "transcendent Good" transcends what she calls "gravity": that is, all the mechanical, physical forces which make us what we are in this world. Exactly what we are, we do not know: for her, that is of little concern, for identity is what we transcend in penetrating to the Good. As she saw it, the developing edifice of one's own thought brought into being standards, concepts and attitudes which begged the main question. "Privileges are by definition inequitable; base because they are not worth being desired." "The Greeks did not have the concept of rights. They had no word to express it. They were satisfied with the term justice." Her anathema is the prescribed, the legislated. In fact she often seems to commend whatever is inarticulate or inchoate. The power of thought is supreme; but she finds it a dangerous power, productive of illusions and fantasy-worlds. "People suppose that thinking does not pledge them," she said, "but it alone pledges us." Her thinking is not towards an adjustment with life, but towards the void, which is life stripped of its familiars, of liberal and muddled tolerance, of exact and narrow prescription, of science, "progress," arts and personality. She proposes a purely metaphysical moment distilled from a synthesis of all the "gravity" there is.

But she does at least presuppose a synthesis, a sustained affiliation of the similar. (And in this affiliation she often includes questionable analogies—witness her Christian interpretation of Sophocles's *Antigone*.) But the value of her synthesis consists not in itself but in its role as a preliminary apparatus: once she has integrated what she knows, she puts the lot to the crucible. What Malraux in *The Voices of Silence* elicits from art alone, she seeks in all modes of life and then extolls not as a marvel of affinity but for its ground in impersonality. Her method is severe, almost manic; it is capricious and obtuse. (She turns Plato into a lukewarm creature addicted to half-truths: he was not *really* an advocate of slavery; he really wanted to proscribe only those arts which were decadent.) But one of the fascinations of her method is the way she strengthens epigram with anecdote. In the severest sense she keeps her feet on the ground. She shows a practical mind which commands equally the abstract and the palpable. Her attention to the destruction of cities, to the torture chamber, as to the everyday whim towards evil, was no less resolute than was that of Camus. Similarly her passionate attention to religions other than Christianity prevented her from becoming an orthodox Christian. Here it was that her bent for elimination failed her. She extracted too much of what she needed from too many places. Instead, she recommended that men should study "the science of religions," sensing that the weight of synthesis made worthwhile the lack of one recommended, unquestioned way.

It is of course difficult to "summarize" her thought: her *Notebooks* (1956) abound in contradictions; consistency of definition was always slightly beneath her. But in fairness it should be said that in her fundamental paradox—elimination by an attempt to experience everything, with herself the raw material of experiment—she is undeniably human. That is enough to rebut the rather too easy criticism that those who are not happy propound ascetic views which do not bear on the art of living. She may not ever have been happy; but there is no doubt that she sought the good life with avidity and staggering selflessness.

Yet her avidity was in some ways blind, and her selflessness was never so thoroughgoing as to rule out her *bêtes noires.* Jews, Ancient Romans, the Catholic *Church* were all anathema to her; only the Ancient Egyptians won her approval. The Jews, she said, had no religious insight; the Catholic Church was not to be disassociated from its Roman past; Aquinas she found the merest Christian; Maritain was system-bound. But the Egyptians had both religious illumination and religious sense, as she purported to demonstrate by quoting from *The Book of the Dead.* She was really an old-fashioned Gnostic, contending that "The Scriptures themselves contain the most clear proof that long before the time of Christ, at the dawn of prehistoric times, there was a revelation superior to that of Israel." (Perhaps Hellenistic gospel-writers had sifted out and eliminated Gnostic elements in the sayings of Jesus.) Her pantheism, which would see God in a grain of sand, recalls Blake and seems to find its justification in some of the sayings recently published as *The Gospel According to Thomas;* for instance: "I am the Light that is above them all, I am the All, the All came forth from me and the All attained to me. Cleave a piece of wood, I am there; lift up the stone and you will find me there." Other sayings in this Gospel deprecate almsgiving, fasting and even prayer; what is recommended instead is esoteric spiritual knowledge—gnostic privacy. Thus attentiveness is substituted for observances, the private (almost solipsistic) experience for the system or the institutional community. We are not very far here from John Locke's theme, *The Reasonableness of Christianity as Delivered in the Scriptures* (1695):

"The hour cometh, when ye shall neither in this mountain, nor yet at Jerusalem, worship the Father: but the true worshippers, shall worship the Father both in spirit and truth; for the Father seeketh such to worship." To be worshipped in spirit and in truth, with application of mind and sincerity of heart, was what God henceforth only required. Magnificent temples, and confinement to certain places, were now no longer necessary for his worship, which by a pure heart might be performed anywhere.

Locke, quoting what Jesus said to the Woman of Samaria, augurs the heresy of Simone Weil. Such efforts to dis-institutionalize religion come from intellectuals frequently; and it is no use objecting that such efforts are unhistorical and willful. Gnostic religion is not for the majority; it is simply the creed of a few religiously-minded individualists who, when they criticize (as she did) the Church, are attacking not its imperfections but, in so far as they are themselves concerned, the principle of imperfection itself. As Simone Weil argued, an intuition of perfection is preferable to any institution; hence her reverence for "pre-Christian intuitions" and any form of heresy. Plato and the Egyptian philosopher Ipuwer influenced her considerably. When she admitted that the Church held, nevertheless, "an incorruptible core of truth," she was being fair without backing down. She was careful to distinguish faith from "social idolatry"; she insisted upon the role of the intellect in the formation of faith—even to the extent (and this is surely minority religion at its bleakest) of construing God's aloofness or absence as the best possible earnest of God's presence. God, she stressed, is not formal in the sense that a Church is; God is not to be sought out, hunted up, flushed from hiding; God is free to appear or not to appear: "We are incapable of progressing vertically. We cannot take a step towards the heavens. God crosses the universe and comes to us." Man must wait, must not predetermine the kind of experience that will attest to God's presence. All preconceptions are part of "gravity," which is the force that draws us away from God—like Wordsworth's "the heavy and the weary weight of all this unintelligible world."

But of course we have to populate the void with such things as systems, myths and rites. The difficulty is to be continually able to distinguish our own concoctions from a glimmer of the divine, or at least to be ready to see even in our concoctions an element not of our own devising. This second mode of "waiting" she renounced: we must, she said, discard even the concepts of past and future; we must live in the moment, in which we are nothing or (in both senses) *next* to nothing. Just as creation by God was an act entailing God's withdrawal from us thereafter, so God's grace is attracted toward us only when we are empty and null. We are to "fall upwards"; for "God can only be present in creation under the form of absence." Rather than bewail the existence of this corrupt world, we should seek to make ourselves nothing. It is no use wishing that we could wipe out the old creation in which we have to live, and then start again: there is no communal way back into Eden. Instead, we must (and we cannot do more than choose the occasion) empty ourselves, open ourselves: a shell full of sand cannot capture the sea's noise. Once open we can learn "to love purely," for so to do is "to consent to distance, it is to adore the distance between ourselves and that which we love." For "love is not consolation, it is light."

But we have always to reconcile ourselves to a work in which the divine and the beautiful will be usually at a distance from us; the universe is mechanical, the beautiful is frail; and faith will never be cozy even when we have it. Why we exist, and why we are afflicted, are questions having no comforting answers. "In the beauty of the world, rude necessity becomes an object of love. . . . Christ proposed the docility of matter to us as a model when he told us to consider the lilies of the field which neither toil nor spin." She counsels us to be stoical.

It is less easy to follow her explanation and justification of suffering. God, she says, tore himself apart in order to create; all true creation is self-loss; and God "denies Himself for our sakes in order to give us the possibility of denying ourselves for Him." Her anthropomorphic conception of God is relentless and often, it seems, falls over backwards in order to vindicate His apparent absurdity. In fact all that we know of God is, according to Simone Weil, the absurd and the beautiful. But she does at least see beauty in surprising places; like an eighteenth-century deist she finds a marvel in death's intensely personal method—seeking out each one of us in turn. There, she contends, is a sufficient demonstration of God's presence and guiding hand. She continually stresses the law of necessity that governs matter, pointing out that we are, in our own materiality, subject to the same law. "Affliction," she says, "is a marvel of divine technique." Such is the rationalization of Father Paneloux in Camus's *The Plague;*

such is the attitude that Rieux in the same novel cannot comprehend.

The human assignment, she says, is twofold: to wait patiently (*en hypomenê*) and to attempt humility. "A patience capable of thus wearying God proceeds from an infinite humility." At the same time we have duties towards our fellows: the subtitle of *The Need for Roots* (1952) (*Prelude to a Declaration of Duties towards Mankind*) makes that much clear. Yet human solidarity and fraternity must come not through idolatry of society—"the Great Beast"—but through restoring to each individual the sense of being "in place." In other words she wants hierarchy and tradition, not the promise of "equality" or of a "new order." With everyone firmly aware of his place and function, there is a community of equality in respecting one's "roots." We are not far here from the Platonic notion of virtue: that is, efficiency in performing an assigned function. Society is made for man; it is one means of preventing him from drifting, but it must not be allowed to unsettle him with impractical promises of indefinite "progress."

She could be both practical and mystical; her prolegomena to a reformed French polity, in *The Need for Roots,* is balanced by her lucid mysticism. But her social concern is natural and down-to-earth; her mysticism is unelaborated: she had an illumination but continued to regard it, as well as accounts of other mystical experiences, as noumenal—not to be talked about. She counsels a wise passiveness to such an extent as to minimize all personal individuality. But not utterly so; for she was always suspicious of absolutes and extremes. No matter how passive one should be, there is always provision in her thought for a touch of scepticism; no matter how resigned one should be, there is always an opening left for initiative in the form of a mystical leap or of charity to others. Above all she speaks to, and for, the spiritually displaced, offering a way but no guarantee. Her own way was complex: she could put national pride before any ideology; yet she could scoff at mystical utterance while disparaging the arid lucidity of Aristotle and Aquinas. Resolved to study suffering and to put it to some purpose, she worked manually in the Renault factory and on Gustave Thibon's farm. And she read endlessly.

To what extent, then, did she achieve a synthesis? The question is inapt. She took her stand on a stoical patience: she thought that life was neither the One nor the Many, but a constantly changing unity which no system or synthesis can describe. She received two epiphanies without seeking them; and they are, in their respective ways, no more astonishing or less subjective than the epiphanies we find in the lives of humanists who remained unconverted. Visiting a small village in Portugal, she watched the patronal festival:

It was the evening and there was a full moon. It was by the sea. The wives of the fishermen were going in procession to make a tour of all the ships, carrying candles and singing what must certainly be very ancient hymns of a heart-rending sadness. Nothing can give any idea of it. . . . There the conviction was suddenly borne in on me that Christianity is pre-eminently the religion of slaves, that slaves cannot help belonging to it, and I among others.

This passage from *Waiting on God* (1951) closely resembles the sudden illuminations to be found in the novels of Camus and Malraux. How much is autosuggestion and how much "given," there is no point in asking. The experience suits the person, is enough in the circumstances.

Her second illumination, in the chapel of Santa Maria degli Angeli in Assisi, came shortly afterwards. Suddenly she felt spiritually overpowered; from then on she entered churches and went to mass, but only in bemused curiosity. Eventually, spiritually and mentally tautened by recurrent migraine, she found "a pure and perfect joy in the unimaginable beauty of the chanting and the words." In some way she discovered how to shed her bodily self and, with it, pain. Introduced to the poems of George Herbert she took to reciting them; and while reciting the one called "Love" "Christ came down and took," she says, "possession of me." Often in physical pain, she considered that she had discovered "the possibility of divine love in the midst of affliction." Affliction as "a marvel of divine technique" had succeeded. We cannot say that she "interpreted" her experience in only one of several possible ways, for the experience itself was in interpretation. Oddly enough, her churchgoing seems to have been the merest adjunct to her faith, although her second illumination occurred in a chapel. She seems to have remained a spiritual anarchist to the end, her faith being strong enough to need no bolstering by communal worship or holy places. Her whole life, in fact, was an attempt to enlarge the concept of holiness. Understandably, then, her writings are mainly philosophical and concerned with *situations,* not people. When she wanted to deal with people she went out and met them rather than explore them in novels. Fundamentally she was interested in outlines; and, like Camus, she sometimes let an abstract concern separate her somewhat from the quality of individuals. In this she shows up the French existentiatlists for what they are—which, by virtue of her immersion in practical life, she was not: defter at explaining situations and dilemmas than at defining how men can remedy them. We are becoming increasingly familiar, in our modern reading, with the view that life is something "done to" man, allowed to happen to him by the *deus absconditus.* Action, even charity, have become miraculous, the objects of cults. We have been shifted from man as a potent character to man as a submissive spectator. But, then, in an era in which action and control—human initiative in the controlling of nature—have recoiled on us devastatingly, perhaps there is reason for a time of contemplation. Simone Weil's distinction is that, writing in a time of nihilism, she found a positive value in affliction, and hope of virtue in being active. For her, even man's cosmic loneliness had its merits. Her "wait" was a form of public service.

"I can make efforts to discover truths, but when I have them before me," she said in *Gravity and Grace* (1952), "they exist and I (i.e. my ideas) do not count." Towards herself she allowed no undue charity; she denied herself inordinately and in fact starved herself to death. Towards God she was hardheaded: no comforting illusions; and even her anthropomorphism is meant to be comfortless except to the resolute realist. She brings to mind, from the *Bhagavad Gita,* Arjuna's plea: "Forgive us, O Home of the Universe, that we have dared to call you 'Friend.' " But with her awareness of God's otherness went an insatiable interest in, and care for, people. She went out and about, a passionate humanitarian, and bewildering because she combined colossal charity with pigheaded logic. The reason for her paradoxicality is not far to seek: she recommended passive emptiness so that grace might have a chance to arrive; but she wanted at the same time to know and alleviate the human lot. This combination of self-denial (in all its senses) and relentless charity tried her considerably. Her attitude to free will was necessarily ambivalent: on the cosmic plane it was pointless; in daily life it had to be exercised as much as possible, but according to charity. However, unlike the atheist-existentialists she constructed no self-comforting theories about action and self-determination; and, unlike the Christian existentialists, she did not seek to fill a void with otherworldly solace. Certainly she was aware of what Evelyn Underhill calls ". . . a passive purification, a stage of helpless misery, in which the self does nothing, but lets Life have its way with her [the self]." But as well as a passive side she had its antithesis, which Evelyn Underhill expresses in words that have particular force when we apply them to Simone Weil:

Others, with Suso and the virile mystics of the German school, have experienced it (the dark night of the soul) rather as a period of strenuous activity and moral conflict directed to that total self-abandonment which is the essential preparation of the unitive life.

We cannot miss the strenuous, "virile" quality of Simone Weil's mysticism, or fail to see how it differs from the strenuous conceptualizing of the existentialists, atheistic or Christian. For her, little of that theoretical default, that compensatory logomachy over such words as "essence" and "commitment." She lacked the existentialists' agonized sense of the arbitrary, their fear of dilemmas, their inability to dismiss alternatives, their fondness for exploring those alternatives in fiction. The existentialists suffocate themselves with possibility; she utterly rejected the life that is theory and the life that is lamentation and the life that is impotent myth. It is one thing to combine few theories and a seeming disregard for individuals with a passionate charity of conduct. It is quite another to assert, as the existentialists do, that the only goodness is goodness done, and then to elaborate casuistries about good or bad intentions. The difference between those two combinations is the measure of her superiority over the scholiasts of ethics. She knew which combination she preferred.

Such an odd combination of masochism and *affabulation* (fantasticating a mystical experience) is bound to provoke, even in the most open-minded of us, a few harsh misgivings about frustrated spinsters, algolagnia and hatred of the good old flesh. And it is possible to read Simone Weil's account of Christ in person ("Sometimes we stretched out on the floor of the *mansarde* and the softness of the sun came down upon me") in almost the same way as we would one of Moravia's studies in adolescent eroticism. Irreverent as it may be to say it, she had a crush on Jesus. Yet, of course, as Gustave Thibon and others noted, she winced away from physical embrace—at least until the day she forced herself to declare with rather dotty braggadocio, "I like being kissed by men with moustaches. It stings!" Remove the sting and the kiss is nothing for Simone Weil. After she had told friends about actually being kissed by a coal trimmer in Barcelona, she burst into tears when one of them asked if the man was drunk. In fact she, the tireless intelligence who beat Simone de Beauvoir into second place in the École Normale entrance examination, belonged to her own version of the human condition. Frustrated, pain-wracked, ill-at-ease as a woman, disconsolate at being human, she was reassured only by extra suffering and convinced only by what she thought God had told her. It is no wonder she became a kind of amateur saint and a successful suicide.

Yet in many ways she was one of the most admirable, worthy, fascinating bluestockings who have ever lived. Jacques Cabaud, the author of the definitive biography, does especially well by her commitments—those relentless and sometimes hectically inept self-expenditures—and, what is essential, her personality and the minutiae of her behavior. He gives us the Red Virgin, as her fellow students called her, in the raw. Or, to put it more respectfully, the naked quirks of (another nickname) the Categorical Imperative in Skirts. Even divinity's iron maiden lived among the everyday.

First, then, we have Simone Weil the deliberate. What else can we do, however uneasy or inferior we feel, but admire her passionate, sometimes maladroit devotion to the working class, her intense and unsectarian religious zeal, her capacity for self-denial, her gift for converting pain into something wholly fruitful, her brilliant disruptive mind, her painstakingly trenchant prose, her audacity in teaching the young, her almost peasant simplicity in aphorism, her refusal to defer to evil wherever she found it, her will, her guts, her crabbed truthfulness? We admire, but with a hunch that much of it amounts to a frenetic displacement of womanhood. Something crackpot emerges alongside what is her evident genius and her almost pernicious goodness. I find myself reading her essays, commentaries and jottings and having to reassure myself that such utterances as "To the degree to which affliction is hideous, so is its true expression supremely beautiful" and "Father, in the name of Christ, grant me this: That I may be like a total paralytic" did come from a human being. It was just like her to extoll pain and desiderate a living death. Like most thinkers of her type, she was determined to make life somehow make sense even if she had to claim black is white and, through a method essentially that of paradox, reap constant harvest from what is unalterably barren.

Not that we don't respect the person—whether writer, say, or doctor—who uses himself as raw material. We do. But Simone Weil, ostensibly on the side of life to the extent of justifying all of it, was really on the side of death; and her achievement, such as it is, implies the abandonment of the last, inalienable human privilege: the privilege of saying, "I loathe such and such a part of being human—say, the small child with cancer of the clitoris, the child born deformed, the ugly and hardly quellable agony in which many people die, the obvious lack of divine justice—and I will not, much as it might be comfortable to be able to do it, involve myself in schoolmen's casuistries just to praise a pattern I did not invent." Camus, in *The Plague,* has put that point of view for all of us.

At root, it seems to me, someone who falls over backwards to justify the ways of God to man (as Simone Weil did) is doing something personal and private and romantic which is meaningless to the rest of us who go on impotently refusing to condone. All told, she was more concerned with perfecting God's geometry than with confronting the human lot. A determined enough mind, like hers, can eventually prove that a child's laughter is a piece of evil and that, because pain is not bad and degrading and impersonal, we should all be lining up for our ration of cancer or arthritis. Some English public-schoolboys, after forced habituation to sodomy, can take to nothing else. I find something monstrous in Simone Weil, something that doesn't respect an ordinary human joy.

So then, not looking for warts or wens but to make her seem less of a right-minded monster, I fastened avidly on the details of her womanhood. Mr. Cabaud's patient, authoritative and impartial biography supplies a vivid picture, keeping this girl-saint down to earth and revealing in fact what a nuisance and an unstreamlined, amusing busybody she could be. The photographs mutely record the decline from her second year, when she was chubby-cheeked, with curly black hair the color of her almond-shaped eyes—a pensive, cute doll—to thirty-four, when she starved herself to death in order to share the sufferings of the French. Her face in 1936 (at 27) is handsome, firm, full-mouthed and rather appealing, and in the uniform of *Confederación Nacional del Trabajo* she looks like an Arab youth dressed up for a baggy-trousered prank. But five years later she has an expression of intent vacuity. She has become the headmistress type, owl-eyed through excessive perusal, her expression an odd blend of hennish timidity and impatient pity. And there is a general look of—well: dryness. A sad little gallery of snaps indeed.

Mr. Cabaud sought out and questioned those who knew her, and they have remembered well. Astute and tomboyish, she chain-smoked and even rolled her own cigarettes. Because she did this carelessly she often had shreds of tobacco in her mouth. She wore large horn-rimmed spectacles for myopia, walked awkwardly in a forward lean, preferred clothes of masculine cut and low-heeled shoes. She "had a sharp, restless glance" and spoke in a staccato monotone, aspirating almost all her *h*'s. She played women's rugby and would return from the fray covered with mud and bruises; and it was on her return from a game in 1930 that she had by far the worst attack, up to then, of her migraines (later attributed to sinusitis) . But she pressed on, studying with "Alain" at the École Normale and thriving on a certain amount of notoriety.

Among Mr. Cabaud's action shots these are the best: Simone Weil picking plums in the country and getting stranded on a high wall; hiding herself and her cigarette behind a Russian newspaper at staff meetings in school; on paydays at the Renault works treating herself to a packet of cigarettes and some stewed fruit; digging potatoes for ten hours a day; insisting on carrying bundles of thistles in the wheatfields; helping (?) Marcel Lecarpentier on his thirty-foot, eight-ton fishing boat and the plumber she pertly nicknamed "Robinet"; exclaiming over the photo of some brawny tough, "That's my kind of man!"; giving away so much of her schoolteacher's salary that she went a whole winter without heat; burning herself while welding; asking a peasant if she might drive his plough and at once overturning it; scalding herself with oil while cooking for the CNT in Spain; aiming her rifle at an aeroplane that dropped a small bomb; neglecting to wash hands before milking cows; refusing a cream cheese because Indo-Chinese children were starving; actually becoming a member of a *résistance* group which was a German trap; and, later, on her way to New York by way of Morocco, handing Gustave Thibon her notebooks on the station platform in Marseilles with a kind of absent-minded abruptness; thanking Father Perrin, her spiritual mentor, for never humiliating her; wandering in Harlem and attending a Baptist church there every Sunday ("I'm the only white person in the church") ; studying folklore and quantum theory at the New York public library; asking Simone Deitz, who acceded, "Would you like to be my friend?"

We badly needed these glimpses of that indefatigably groping spirit who said "Pain and peril are indispensable to my mental make-up." Her life, as Mr. Cabaud says, was a series of phases colored by successive friendships. But, of course, God alone was the constant inimical friend of the woman who saw herself, with more than a little wilful melodrama, as "a misshapen piece which God cut out so badly."

She returns to Europe, playing volleyball on the way over and even dressing up on one occasion as a ghost. Finally she discovers a haven, during the thick of the air raids, at 31 Portland Road, London, and lives on black coffee, coughs all the time, refuses to look after herself or be looked after, strews papers all over her room, commends the good humor of the British, the pubs, the police system, wanders regularly into Hyde Park and even elects to sleep out in the rain in the grounds of a convent. She tries to learn to drive and deliberately upsets herself and Simone Deitz from their boat into the Serpentine. She sets herself a Benjamin Franklin-Jay Gatsby type of regimen: "avoid all loss of time . . . sleep on the floor or on a table in order to limit the hours of sleep to four or five. . . ." Desperately eager to be parachuted into France, she occupies herself with the English metaphysical poets, her work for the Free French Ministry of the Interior, and the composition of *The Need for Roots*. At last, too weak to lift a fork, and refusing a pneumothorax as well as deciding against baptism, she is moved from the Middlesex Hospital to Ashford. The death certificate said "Cardiac failure due to myocardial degeneration of the heart muscles due to starvation and pulmonary tuberculosis. The deceased did kill and slay herself by refusing to eat whilst the balance of her mind was disturbed." Perhaps, though, her mind's disturbance balanced for the first time. The Certificate of Burial reads, "Conducted own service—Catholic—French Refugee—Depth: 6 feet."

What we make of her—this Jewess, born a stoic and brought up an agnostic, who gravitated to the godhead by using her magnificent brain to construct what George Herbert in her favorite stanza calls "a full consent"—depends on how far skepticism erodes our tolerance of experiences so private they cannot be appraised at all. Whereas the "system" of Teilhard de Chardin seems an inane wish-fulfillment garbed as optimism, Simone Weil's embraces the pain of being—not just bureaucracy (it *"always* betrays") or war (never a means of liberation) or humiliation (the worker enslaved to a mass-producing machine) or force ("it makes a man a thing"), but man's biological, chemical and metaphysical state—and she seems a Cleopatra, hugging the asp. Understandably her best books (*Gravity and Grace, Waiting for God, The Need for Roots*) constantly shock us with their sustained, oblique obviousness. "The existence," she writes, "of a

Thomistic current in contemporary Christianity makes a bond of complicity—among many others, unfortunately—between the Nazis and their adversaries." Or take this: "The desire for gold is not made of gold, whereas the desire for good is itself a good." Or this: "If a man were alone in the universe he would possess no rights at all, but he would have obligations." She always believed the resolute simpleton could match the genius, truth for truth, and there is plenty of evidence that she found her own very French, very Jewish intellect something of an embarrassment and even a torture. Her few poems are bad, her play *Venise sauvée* is fustian, and much of her voluminous journalism (listed in Mr. Cabaud's excellent bibliography) has not worn well.

It was Trotsky who contemptuously alluded to her "new cause—the defence of her personality against society," and it is true that she always maintained a barrier between herself and friendship, just as she maintained one between herself and the Church. She cannot, could not, always be reached. She was too busy reconciling poles expressed in these two statements:

We wish to uphold not the collectivity but the individual as the supreme value.

[we] owe our respect to a collectivity, of whatever kind—country, family or any other—not for itself, but because it is food for a certain number of human souls.

And when she was not doing that she was pursuing her own *ascesis*, asking to become as defective "as an old man in his dotage" and, like Samuel Beckett, linking up with "the poor, and the maimed, and the halt, and the blind." When she died, "Alain" would not believe it. "It's not true," he said, "surely she will come back!" Simone Weil herself said: "If there is something in afterlife, I shall come back. If I don't come back, it will mean that there is nothing." Which, really, is the endgame to beat all.

T. S. Eliot

Mental intolerance and spiritual generosity mix oddly in T. S. Eliot, the former dominating his prose writings up to about 1930 and the latter becoming evident with *Ash-Wednesday* (1930). I want to explore this contrast, first making what are by now routine retorts to an intolerance he outgrew in his last years and then considering how Eliot the dramatist has captured an audience commensurate with that gained by Arnold, whom in his early days Eliot chided with the almost forensic jollity that people habitually reserve for people whose ideas tempt them. (Eliot the former disciple of Babbitt took some time to get humanism out of his system, and Arnold served as a useful whipping boy.) On the one hand we have the doctrinal Eliot who in the prewar years used his affiliation to a large religious orthodoxy as a licence for being censorious. He denounced the unfit to an audience that was no doubt fit though few. On the other hand (and here the hands overlap without clasping) we have the playwright, contemporary with Noel Coward, who managed to transmute Coward material into something liturgical for the London stage and thereby appealed to a large public audience. I propose, in fact, a neophyte's progress in which increasing security of faith (plus some worldly success) enabled Eliot to discard severity for benignity and which, I think, brought to the fore Eliot the romantic who was always there in disguise, meditating an exposure of the heart.

In his essay on Arnold and Pater in *Selected Essays* (1932) Eliot links Arnold with Charles Eliot Norton, observes how, in the nineteenth century, art, religion, literature and ethics had grown apart from one another, and then complains that various thinkers attempted to effect new syntheses but, in so doing, only contrived to confuse religion with morals, with art, with philosophy or science. The syntheses, Eliot contends, were just as harmful as the original severances. He does not say precisely why they were harmful, but he almost certainly means that they promoted muddle, inwardness and emotional laxity. He is objecting not so much to the attempt to produce a synthesis as to the imperfect nature of the result. It sounds like sense, but is it? Surely no synthesis, not even that of Rome, is perfect. And Eliot's criticism of Arnold, Pater and others comes with reduced force from the holder of that notorious, much misunderstood and eventually retracted triangular position: classicist in literature, royalist in politics and Anglo-Catholic in religion. What kind of a synthesis, one wonders, was this? What kind of synthesis is Anglo-Catholicism itself? To know exactly is, presumably, to incapacitate oneself for the task of judging. For one can know exactly only when one is persuaded: a celebrant, a member, a devotee. I am none of these, so what I say has to be said from the outside, so to speak. But, even from the outside, it is clear that Eliot is not logical and not fair in disdaining religion become morals or art or what have you: for people with no mystical or miraculous experience approved by a religious orthodoxy, such "trespassing" religion might serve as a lifebelt. T. H. Huxley didn't fare too badly with religion become morals; it helped him to survive while coping with religion become science. As for religion become art, it would be hard to say where Catholicism ends and art begins, whereas Protestantism is clearer in its philistinism—as objections to the purchase, out of church funds, of elegant candlesticks make plain. Surely Eliot is not arguing for Protestantism because it does not confuse religion with art. And as for religion become science or philosophy, who is to say *what* religion has to be? Is the standard what religion has been previously? If so, it is too narrow a standard for a world that has advanced (whether it *should* have done so or not) from bleeding as a remedy to antibiotics, from Ptolemy to Einstein, from primitive animism to primitive Anglo-Catholicism.

One is struck by Eliot's indifference to those people not in the same position as himself; or, rather, by the indifference of Eliot the doctrinaire who sticks by the social and civic principles of his elected church. He objects to Catholicism (the undilute variety) as "American" and "democratic"; he objects to what he calls "the living death" of modern technological civilization, even to the extent of having to admit that D. H. Lawrence was on the right lines for the wrong reasons; and, in his most magistrally condescending manner, he objects to the fumbling, sometimes hectic and desperate attempts of such as Arnold, Pater, Blake, Hardy, Irving Babbitt and Norman Foerster, to construct their own systems or faiths: to open an account with whatever spiritual funds they have. Eliot resents their choice of bank and resents too any pence that are not "piaculative." But what is most remarkable about this phase of the man who wrote *Four Quartets* is his lack of charity toward Jews and the working class. In *After Strange Gods* (1934) he held that "reasons of race and religion" combine to make any large number of free-thinking Jews "undesirable" and that any spirit "of excessive tolerance" was to be "deprecated." Now, there is no reason why a man should tolerate everything; many of the people most worth knowing and respecting are intolerant in some ways. Men are no more perfect than systems. But the question about Jews, even now, after the mid-century, is not that they be tolerated but that they be allowed to go unpersecuted: to make the point, one has only to cite the anti-Semitic practices of modern Russia.[1] Simply, Eliot had not caught up with the times, and his attitude to oppressed peoples was far from that of such an ungushing humanitarian as Camus.

About the working classes (mostly the English) he was similarly out-of-date. He was patronizing about motorbikes, sexuality, slang and the Anglo-Saxon capacity (which he found rather proletarian) for "diluting" orthodox religion. One can discern here the influence of Julien Benda, Charles Maurras and Wyndham Lewis. Eliot was no liberal, it goes without saying; yet he had a liberal side which, when he wrote prose, disappeared entirely but which like a reversible mirror swung into place when he wrote poems and plays. One of his explanations was that in his

---

[1] See, for example, the anti-Semite Ukrainian booklet by T. K. Kichko, *Judaism Unmasked* (1957), published by the Ukrainian Academy of Science. This text, owing a good deal to the infamous Czarist anti-Semite Shmakov, explains that synagogues are centers of swindling activities and includes cartoons of the type printed in *Der Stuermer* under the Nazis. It is worth adding too that the secret police, the KGB, a body with a long tradition of anti-Semitism, "cleans up" in its own traditional way, preferring to make examples of Jews whenever it can.

prose a man occupies himself with "ideals," whereas "in the writing of verse one can only deal with actuality." It is an odd distinction. Presumably, prose has no bearing on actuality, and poetry (or verse) has none on ideals. What, one wonders (this in prose), is *The Republic* or *Paradise Lost?* The distinction comes, of course, from Eliot the proseman and therefore embodies a craving to separate genres in much the same way as the Victorians he pummels separated the higher activities of the human spirit in their time. It is confusing and it helps to create a false picture of Eliot himself who was surely the last man to promote the Barthian severance which, implementing to the full the eschatology of the New Testament, keeps secular and divine clearly apart. The truth is, of course, that Eliot the man of ideals is Eliot the extremist who punished his own weaknesses in others and who, perforce, misrepresented Eliot the romantic poet who dealt in both ideals and actuality. Eliot the prose-executioner, I feel, is only one of the masks that Eliot the poet assumed. Behind the shirt stuffed with stern, narrow tracts there throbbed a dreamer's heart.

Let us go back a moment. Poetry, we feel, should come from the whole of a man, not just from one side. The intolerance that suffuses a man's critical prose is likely to get into his poems; in fact, if it does not get into them, the poems are likely to lack weight and edge. Eliot seems to have realized this, for in *The Idea of a Christian Society* (1939), he discarded his rigid separation of prose and verse, as well as his pawnbroking distinction between the orthodox and the rest—in short, dichotomies of all kinds—and said that the complexity of modern life made it imperative not to separate the life of the Spirit from the life of the World or Christian from non-Christian. What happened was this: Eliot the poet corrected Eliot the doctrinaire, to some extent dismissing him as an excrescence; it was not merely Eliot the doctrinaire trying to do the best he could for Eliot the poet. Not that Eliot's performance since then was what we might call liberal; it was not, but he could no longer be found having a knock at Arnold and Pater for their fuss about culture (in their definition so much narrower than in Eliot's), at the whimsy in Yeats, the libertinism in Blake and Lawrence, and the muddle in such American humanists as Paul Elmer More and Norman Foerster. The Eliot who rejoiced over F. H. Bradley's sarcastic repudiations of Arnold never quite died; but Bradley, we should remember, wanted a full-blooded God, none of the Arch-Mathematician, none of the "best self," none of that "Eternal not ourselves," none of that "heart even as mine, behind the vain show of things." And, in one sense, Eliot always wanted the sort of God that Bradley wanted: no substitutes, but the real thing; not appearances but reality. Where someone such as Arnold coyly holds out a hand to the infinite, hoping God will grasp it, Eliot prefers Bradley's dictum "That the glory of this world in the end is appearance leaves the world more glorious, if we feel it is a show of some fuller splendour." This is the mood of *Ash-Wednesday* and very much the mood of the young Eliot who wrote his Harvard doctoral thesis on Bradley. Of course there are no guarantees to private mysticism; if there are any guarantees to be made, then it is the job of theology to provide them.

On the one hand, then, we have the early Eliot who wants no half-measures, no substitutes and no lies; this is the Eliot who constantly in his major poems left a door open for divine illumination. On the other hand we have the Eliot who, beginning uncharitably and sternly with prose onslaughts on the wildest of the heretics and mystagogues, tempered his doctrines until he was dogmatic only about such empirical matters as church procedure, public morality and the role of an elite. This is not to say that Eliot completely integrated himself; he did not. His sensibility, like that of any intelligent, sensitive and (in the widest sense) religious modern man, remained somewhat split: there are rifts here and there, areas in which the theological is imperfectly articulated with the intuitive, and the ethical with these. But he came to respect the variety of religious experience; and this, I feel, makes him rather more than a doctrinaire. His disciplines are for himself and for those who agree with him theologically, whereas his poetry and his plays are undenominationally open to anyone who wishes to find, or find expressed, religious intuitions of all kinds. In this, unlike Mauriac or Bernanos, he leaves room for the humanist to approach him, even to approach his intuition of God. For, after all, humanists are like diviners exploring land said to hold water, and most of them find life worth living for the occasional illuminations it offers, whether the illuminations come on the moral and social plane or on one that is mystical and poetic.

Eliot, in fact, achieved, although more long-windedly, the kind of equilbrium he commended in Simone Weil who, as well as joining her lot with that of ordinary people, also cared fiercely about her right to solitude and individuality. Wrongly finding her position paradoxical, Eliot reveals his own dualistic history: on the level of doctrine or proposition, Simone Weil's double stance does seem self-contradictory, whereas on the level of common sense and common experience—whether of peasants or industrial workers, whether of blue or white collar, whether of collar clerical or lay—it is no more than a reflection of life itself, of life's mixed quality. Hers was a single fulfillment with two faces, and with both faces turned (sometimes irritably, and why not?) to the best in man. And Eliot, sensible of his own contradictions, calls her paradoxical when he means she is versatile. She achieved a synthesis, an integration, without losing sight of the extremes she had to confront and combine; and, not being a poet, or even a prose poet, she had to accomplish this on a doctrinal level that represents only one-half, and the narrower half, of Eliot.

But, notice, Eliot does put his finger on the vital thing in Simone Weil, and his Preface to the translation of *The Need for Roots* shows him fighting a philosophical predisposition that detests blur and muddle and suspects synthesis as something lax. He wants to think that such a fusion, such a synthesis, as she achieved is not a mode of self-deception and that paradox is a legitimate way of handling the world in both words and action. His strivings, for which one cannot help feeling a good deal of respect, led him eventually to the drama and thus to a large public. In *The Cocktail Party* (1950) Reilly tells Celia there are two ways only: one is that of "common routine," and the other

. . . is unknown, and so requires faith—
The kind of faith that issues from despair.
The destination cannot be described;
You will know very little until you get there;
You will journey blind. But the way leads towards possession
Of what you have sought for in the wrong place.

The people who accept "common routine" have apparently had a vision of some kind; but "they cease to regret it." Why? Perhaps because its original painful or ravishing impact has become an evident good or because it has been allowed to fade out altogether. Either it sustains or it dies away; and some people, such as Celia, need more. So—if we discount people who reject the idea of vision and do not find vision forcing itself upon them—there are four ways of developing one's life, of making it worth living: (1) hoping for vision even though you do not receive it, (2) hoping and receiving, (3) receiving and living by vision's strength, and (4) receiving it, living by it, but eventually choosing Celia's way. Those people in (1) cannot be blamed for not being in (2) : there is no compelling vision to arrive and we are only too eager to deceive ourselves. Those in (2) cannot be blamed for not knowing what to make of vision in their everyday undertakings—how to use it, apply it. And those in (3) , who do know how to live by it, cannot be blamed for not being Celias, who act out of sheer dissatisfaction or (as the theologians say) are called. (It is worth noting here that Eliot's proposal of a clerisy, some of whom are agnostics, seemed designed to cater to the problems created by the idea of vision: the spiritual skiddings and longings, the tedium and the frustration, the nihilism and, sometimes, the demented enthusiasm men can imagine themselves into. Just as it is the role of a clerisy to assist people to keep their heads—to behave with spiritual sanity—so it is that of church ritual to assist them to a communal privacy. And Eliot's plays, as I see them, discharge something of the work of ritual: they give unorthodox mystics a place in which to relate their vision to other visions, and to those who have had no vision—or epiphany; I am using the words interchangeably—they offer a provoking mimesis. In a sense, then, Eliot's plays work as Eliot's projected clerisy does, and at the same task.)

There is, of course, no universal paradigm of the relations between public and private faith. But Eliot, in his donnish way, provided some clues to the nature of moments of intense, seemingly mystical, private experience and in so doing related his own writing to that of literary contemporaries with whom, in nearly

164

every other respect, he was at odds. To read him and then return to other authors, and especially to their more mystical passages, is to see more in both and to enrich one's own life in incalculable ways.

The variety is amazing. Pater's concern with seeking the "highest quality" of our moments, conducts us (if we wish) to Arnold, awaiting *Vernunft* (inspiration) to flash in supplement of *Verstand* (understanding of the sort Bradley thought "cold and ghost-like"). Yeats has a cosmic vision all of his own, and invents a cosmology to tether it down; he also plays cuckoo in the nest of any willing clairvoyant. All the same, Eliot can teach us to respect Yeats's moments of vision and perhaps even to relate them to moments of our own, if we have any. From Eliot's account of "moments in and out of time" we may return to Rilke's *Duino Elegies* and more confidently distinguish the severe, religious eloquence of his late "Angel" images from the rather glibly reported accessibility of the early one. Along similar lines we might recall and reconsider Lawrence's abrupt, atavistic communions with nature and his rapt sexual congress; or the moments in Pound's *Cantos* when the immanent god Dionysus erupts into the daily world and transforms sailors into dolphins, masts into vines; or St.-Exupéry's fitful mystique of flight or Malraux's overhearing the voices of silence in an echo of a long-dead artist's manner; or Gide's sensual rapture, fondling pebbles in a stream, or Alissa's searing insights in *Strait is the Gate;* or Hemingway's secular, sexual and bucolic ecstasies—"what we have instead of God"; or Cummings's childlike visions of the magic in ordinary things—the balloon-man and gravensteins; or the harsh pantheism of Camus's story, "The Adulteress" in *Exile and the Kingdom,* in which the wife surrenders to the landscape; or Wittgenstein's moments of revelation—provoking "deep notational needs." Such epiphanies as these serve to renew the spirit and re-establish one's personal momentum. And such, surely, are the moments in Eliot's own poetry—moments which have almost become our own property because they express for us, or give to us, experiences transcending the events of everyday: the pool, "filled with water out of sunlight"; the winter lightning, the laughter in the garden, the trilling wire in the blood, and Agatha's visionary moment in *The Family Reunion* (1939):

I only looked through the little door
When the sun was shining on the rose-garden:
And heard in the distance tiny voices
And then a black raven flew over.

It is not, I think, a matter of saying what such experiences, read about or actually undergone, can "mean"; it is rather a matter of making ourselves aware, of realizing as much as we can of the ineffable or mysterious in our world. The first epigraph to *Four Quartets* is especially meaningful here; it is Heraclitus's "The law of things is a law of the universal; but most men live as though they had a wisdom of their own." Usually, the only way in which a man can approach the universal is through the courage and the will to explore which his own wisdom gives him. But the great appeal of Eliot's epiphanic poetry is its universality. These revered and elated instants never presented too sectarian a point of view: he saw to that from the beginning of his career, and he fixed upon concepts—say, "vibration of delight Without desire"—with which most of us are familiar and which we can compare with the humdrum quality of most moments of our lives.

For such a natural mystic as Wordsworth the problem of communication is single: if he does not simplify into fairly concrete or exact terms his experience remains incommunicable; if he simplifies too much, what he communicates appears far from exceptional. Eliot, I think, has a double problem: he has not only to simplify but also to present his experience on a generalized level, and he does both superbly. His non-doctrinal rendering of intense epiphany clarifies two things. First, it demonstrates the *symbolic* significance of his church, its spiritual meaning as atmosphere, edifice, tradition, fund of mystery, community, table of signs and point of departure. Second, it reveals the considerable extent to which all systems, museums without walls, "beloved republics" of love and Paterian "Houses Beautiful" are substitute churches. There is no reason to suppose that the sudden or gradual illuminations of the agnostic or the unpledged differ greatly from those of the believer, or are less fortifying. The difficulty for the orthodox believer is to see all edifices and illuminations as reflections of the same thing. Efficacy in one's personal spiritual life is the criterion, and not position in some hierarchy of epiphanies. This is why Eliot's plays, making the mystical speakable, make his noblest gestures, for they relate private intuitions to public conduct in a subtle, unprejudiced way that has to be seen as a capital feat of charitable responsibility. Read in private, or taken at speed in the theater, they are a long way from the prescriptive Eliot of the early essays (these especially) and closer to the problems of morality than almost any of the poems.

The terminology is religious but never excludes. *Murder in the Cathedral* (1935) makes the point that, just as martyrdom entails an unfoolish attitude to the idea of God, so does it also require intelligent appraisal by the general public. Martyrdom is the supreme reminder of God's interest in man (or of what is most divine in man), but it is hard to remind the un-attending, the unthinking, of anything at all. The hollow men will never have martyrs for they are incapable of creating their share of the individual-public interaction that martyrdom is. What is mundane and what is otherworldly cannot be fused without the assent and interest of the mass of men; and that is why Eliot's plays open doors to so many kinds of spiritual experience. Better a gallimaufry than a few doted-on labels. As Eliot said in an article, "Religious Drama: Medieval and Modern,"

. . . a religious play, to be good, must not be purely religious. If it is, it is simply doing something that the liturgy does better; and the religious play is not a substitute for liturgical observance and ceremonial, but something different. It is a combination of religious with ordinary dramatic interest.

Or again, in the essay called "Poetry and Drama": ". . . the audience should find, at the moment of awareness that it is hearing poetry, that it is saying to itself: '*I* could talk in poetry too!'" The original and the humdrum are to be fused: Harry in

The Family Reunion exclaims "O that awful privacy of the insane mind! Now I can live in public." And, of course, he can then go on to decide:

> What would destroy me will be life for John,
> I am responsible for him.

His responsibility is to atone. But such a perception needs to be put convincingly in the idiom of everyday, not in the idiom of *The Family Reunion*, which is very much that of Eliot's major poems.

With *The Cocktail Party* language and doctrine coincide: arcana are stated, not analyzed; and not the least of the arcana is the responsibility of getting to know oneself:

> . . . finding out
> What you really are. What you really feel.
> What you really are among other people.
> Most of the time we take ourselves for granted . . .

And, because our identity is never fixed, we are supposed to find reassurance in any plain, valid generalization—such as the above: hence the vast emotional claims of folk-saws, runes, proverbs and mottoes. We might have had an illumination, but illuminations often disappear beneath the dull facts of diurnal managing:

> They may remember
> The vision they have had, but they cease to regret it,
> Maintain themselves by the common routine,
> Learn to avoid excessive expectation,
> Become tolerant of themselves and others,
> Giving and taking, in the usual actions
> What there is to give and take. They do not repine;
> Are contented with the morning that separates
> And with the evening that brings together
> For casual talk before the fire. . . .

Such a passage may earn Eliot the title of hierophant of the humdrum; but he is at least being realistic, discharging *that* responsibility without invoking sectarian or remote myth. There are some (Harry, Celia) who have to prefer a lonely going-away to a cozy domesticity; the deciding factor is responsibility; and where there is no clear vocation, it is always attention to others that prevails. Mrs. Buzzard in *The Confidential Clerk* (1955) knows that

> We all of us have to adapt ourselves
> To the wish that is granted. . . .

And Lady Elizabeth declares, "Claude, we've got to try to understand our children." Such an assertion seems more congruous in this play because the characters are more of a piece: there is little of the romantic, heroic cult of election that we find in the preceding plays. Eliot is not only down-to-earth here; he is also dealing in meekness such as Colby's, diffident through reverence for his as yet undeveloped powers and thankful for a promise he himself did not create.

But meekness and tameness can go only so far; and the next play, *The Elder Statesman* (1959), makes the inevitable recourse to melodrama. Dramatic exigency has to be met. We have travelled from Beckett's martyrdom, down from the sublime to the quotidian impact of the spiritually elect. A financier finds he has to fuse private and public selves; an elder statesman recognizes his real self; the skeletons are tipped out of the cupboards, the facts of life prevail, the E. M. Forster idea of "only connect" becomes a minor version of the saint's obligation to serve the mass of man, and order is always imposed whether it brings serenity or meek hebetude.

It may be that Eliot's plays fatally attract the half-educated and the ill-educated, whose sophistication rejects simplicity of statement; who must always be searching for hidden meanings. So much for the commentator who introduces Greek myth and Greek drama into his search for meanings hidden, meanings too obvious to be noticed by sophisticates, and meanings special to the Christian. Eliot paid close attention to his Greek models, just as his interpreters must to his writings on culture, the Christian community and the nature of "Guardians." But the matter of Greece is of small living import in the lives of most of us; and it is possible to find Eliot's plays moving and inspiriting without hunting up archetypes or, for that matter, accepting Christian metaphysics.

We must not let extraneous matter cloud our apprehension of the plays or invoke Greek precedents for what is palpably the modern human condition or overwork Eliot's assertion that "we have today a culture which is mainly negative, but which, so far as it is positive, is still Christian." Bound up with this assertion is Eliot's view that to possess considerable intellect is not necessarily to possess understanding, any more than to possess understanding makes one "a better Christian." We have to be careful not to overapply his statements of motive, or to intellectualize anything that strikes us as too obvious for him to say. The fact is that Eliot's plays seek to make a perception of the obvious and the trite into a fructifying experience. No dramatist has so ingeniously resisted the temptation to present life as intenser than it is. In an Eliot play the imagery is everything that is not primarily devoted to the maintenance of syntax; banal hyperbole ("I've loved you from the beginning of the world," says Monica in *The Elder Statesman*) is offered as an emblem of spiritual simplicity. It may be that Eliot is essentially concerned with the heartening influence of the spiritually elect: they restore to us such elementary concepts as "presence" and communication; by their very nature, by their enigmatic departures and abstentions, they sustain people who have to live among daily banalities, who believe all that they want to believe, who have assumed fake identities but who are yet capable of managing "a vibration of delight Without desire."

All living is sacrifice; all sacrifice is community; and all men have to find a way between their longing for ecstasy and their need to survive. Worlds coexist within *this* world. And the plays present, in a language which both flaunts its artificiality and puts on the artlessness of daily speech, a spirituality for Everyman. Eliot, the poet who cunningly evolved religious terms apt for unbelievers, gave way to an Eliot even more ambitious: the dramatist who devises myths both emotionally satisfying and innocent of dogmatic theatricality. He is the only arcane poet who, having made precise his own awareness of momentary illuminations, coined an idiom as appropriate for secular or noninstitutionalized ecstasy as for the humble, crabbed explanations of a Celia. In this idiom a moment can indeed seem momentous.

Eliot's characters (Sweeney excepted) are often no more than talking metaphors, but they have to be so for the presentation of such apparently pallid themes as the complexity of the commonplace, the magic inferrable from sordid particulars, the gamut from mere involvement—through Gomez's "I have a gift for friendship"—into unselfish love, the comfort possible for two people communing unpretentiously on the same dull level: Eeldrop and Appleplex, for instance, or Edward and Lavinia resurgent. The Lady Elizabeths, the self-redeemed ex-floaters, are significant in Eliot's version of low-gear stoicism—much more significant than "Trunk, and horn, tusk and hoof, in odd places." Eliot's are not Gothic plays or overtly spectacular; they are meditations in mime. They present a diligent case for charity as well as communicating an agonizing sense of identity as a flux that has to be reported on, allowed for, daily. One must eventually relate the Eliot of that well-known observation in the essay on Marston's *Sophonisba*—"we perceive a pattern behind the pattern into which the characters deliberately involve themselves; the kind of pattern which we perceive in our own lives only at rare moments of inattention and detachment, drowsing in sunlight"—to this: "What poetry should do in the theatre is a kind of humble shadow or analogy of the Incarnation. . . ." Eliot offers the idea of intuitive humility; and it is a rich idea, for it embraces both the possibility of a similar rapture in lonely self-colloquy and the possibility of a similar rapture in humble recourse to companionship. In the last analysis it is to humility that Eliot directs our minds; humility is incumbent upon us. Even with it we are vulnerable, feeble and precarious creatures; without it, however, we affront the dignity of all created men.

Strangely enough, the plays of Eliot the Anglo-Catholic are less dogmatic than those of Arthur Miller the agnostic or those of Brecht the Marxist. Eliot's dogma is for himself while his plays move toward a highest common factor of spirituality. In the long run, he implies, it is experience that counts, not the label we put on it. One might invoke Colby's words in *The Confidential Clerk:* "Walking down an alley/I should become aware of someone walking with me"; Lucasta tells him she knows what he means even though, as he says, he can think of no other way of putting what he feels. And I think we know too. It is a matter of our finding, in language which would otherwise seem disappointingly bare, an intimate feeling of our own expressed without esoteric imagery. Eliot's images are invitations, not mystical or doctrinal scalps. To the physicist, entropy is the measure of the unavailability of any system's energy for conversion into practical work. For Eliot, there is an entropy of the spirit: he relies on the presence in us of experience not readily articulated or applied. And his plays proceed by offering patterns, each of them fitted with clues and a few mild images, into which we accomodate our own version of the ineffable. If his plays were more sectarian, we should be much less welcome in them.

Miller and Brecht, on the other hand, provide wads of theory or propaganda as if they are afraid the plays in their own right are not enough. Where Eliot—amazingly when we remember his early prose writings—strips the doctrinal scaffolding away, they try to reinforce. Where Eliot invites us to contribute the full gamut of our feelings, especially of the mystical or intuitive sort, they keep us strictly to the dramatic convention that prevents us from forgetting we are no more than spectators. Eliot's plays—to resume the metaphor I took from physics—are highly modifiable by the spectator or reader; theirs are not. With him we go through our own private performance, which is really an exercise in the art of human graciousness, unaided by such dogma as Miller's introduction to his *Collected Plays* or Brecht's long commentaries to plays which, some of them, he regards in any event as "lessons." I relate this expansive generosity of Eliot's, this near-permissiveness, to his gradually widened view of culture: a view which excludes nothing that people do. And it seems to me a triumph of spiritual flexibility for him to have settled his own religious position and then have to set about writing plays that invite everyone in. They are not models of compression or of intensity; they are meant to be performed and, most of all, "assisted at." Only a self-righteous drear would damn them for their essentially functional quality and only someone truly without hope could find them blank. They are not, I think, plays to be studied intensively, for they throw us back on our own resources at the same time as demonstrating how communication is possible between those for whom

God is present and those for whom God is absent or unknowable. Religious dispute, so often, is nothing more than an argument about the choice of terms.

In his pamphlet on George Herbert, Eliot distinguished between Herbert's congregation—composed of a few rural parishioners—and that of Donne, which was large. It is tempting to see Eliot assuming the role of Donne, but without dogma, while at the same time emphasizing that Herbert's *The Temple* is "a document of interest to all those who are curious to understand their fellow men; and as such I regard it as a more important document than all of Donne's *religious* poems taken together." That, surely, is worth construing as Eliot distinguishing between arcana and demotic performances, cherishing the former and being modest about the latter. Donne he finds a poet of intellect, Herbert of sensibility. And, oddly enough, it is a feat of intellect that we find in the plays, helping to make his religious sensibility available to a large audience. We should be glad that Eliot had both the intellect and the sensibility, for neither without the other would have made him the accessibly religious writer he became and remained.

Graham Greene

"I suppose," a Dutch priest wrote to Graham Greene after reading *The Power and the Glory* (1940), "that even if you are not a Catholic, you are not too hostile to us." The rather grateful tentativeness of that says a considerable amount about Greene and reminds us of the dictionary example of oxymoron: "Faith unfaithful kept him falsely true." There are welcome ambivalences in Greene, welcome because what he has to say is not necessarily doctrinal and what he believes is not necessarily the most important thing he says. Decked out as thrillers, spy stories and even in some instances as "entertainments," Greene's novels, as everyone says, are parables about wasted or damned spirituality. The trappings are means of getting us interested and also, perhaps, of introducing us to his own kind of invisible limbo, the region in which Greene can exercize the right of the artist to be "disloyal" to any institution, whether religious or political. He described *A Burnt-Out Case* (1961), for example, as "an attempt to give dramatic expression to various types of belief, half-belief and non-belief." This is why he has on many occasions scandalized the representatives of orthodoxy—but only, it should be pointed out, because he has chosen to present the full spiritual spectrum of his obsessive fictional world instead of fixing on the few routine cases. He is not simply a general practitioner and not solely a specialist. He has always felt more or less equally the attraction of the world's surfaces and that of metaphysical delving. He is drawn to, and writes about, the shallow as well as the deep. It is perhaps an uncomfortable position, for some readers blurring his "message" and for others making too much concession to heterodoxy. But then, Greene is not Mauriac (who applies the methods of a Jane Austen to his chosen region of the Landes) and he is not Bernanos (whose sulphuric vision often disregards circumstantial particulars). Where Mauriac deals with a small gallery of characters in a small region and Bernanos conducts us on a dynamic tour of hell that we begin through a small hole in another small region's crust, Greene spreads himself, seeking like an explorer (as he has explained) to "fill in the map" in the same way as he would "fill in the character or features of a human being." In other words his Catholicism is adventurous and private, not, like that of Mauriac, repeatedly affirmed in public and certain in its local habitation and name. Not that Mauriac fails to explore his small cast and his restricted subjects; he does all of this. But Greene speaks, I feel, to those who are rootless and restless, the floaters and the gracehopers, and he does it so well because he writes as a man writing to all men and therefore conveys a sense of security and worldly-wide wisdom. The reader can entrust his mind to Greene without feeling he might suddenly be shot out of the novel as a trespasser or beguiled into a faith he does not really understand. Greene gives, in short, the same kind of licence as Simone Weil and the later Eliot.

In Greene's novels two varieties of love are put in conflict: it is an old game, in which the lover resorts to the mystic's figures of speech and the mystic to those of the lover. Greene argues the spirit against the secular not to make converts but rather to illustrate and realize the power of love, human or divine. In *Brighton Rock* (1938) there is, as down a stick of seaside rock, a legend running through. Pinkie defies the norms of the society he was born into: he marries to save his neck and then plans to murder his wife. It is not enough for him to have achieved power through the protection racket; it is too little and yet too much for the man who, as a child, witnessed his parents' love-making. It is the violence which cuts him and drives him into a career of crime and murder. But Pinkie is no stereotype; far from it, he is the compound misfit who brings together different worlds. As well as being a destroyed teenager, a small-time crook, a lapsed Catholic and a slum kid, he is groping baffled humanity writ small. So the novel can be a document of psychology, a thriller, a religious enterprise and a sociological study. At the end he remembers fragments of the liturgy (he is a person of fragments) and for the first time is connected with something which dwarfs him without terrifying him. But it is no use reading the novel with an eye to progress of the spirit or some such abstraction. We have to meet it on the level of the thriller if we are to experience without self-consciousness the spiritual current which is antithetical to the paraphernalia of gangsterdom. And it is not going too far to include Greene in that tradition of romantic mixture that we conveniently identify with Shakespeare. Without making his work heterogeneous, without resorting to bathos, shock, contrast, discordance and incongruity, Greene could not achieve the dialectic he does.

Mauriac's comment that Greene tries to make religion too difficult merely exemplifies the point further: Greene sets spirituality in the midst of a bewildering, complex, heedless, mind-numbing world. And he plies spirit there without many labels, without any overt calling-to-order such as one might expect from a writer who has behind him the robust, assertive tradition of English Catholicism. This is just as well. A Mauriac can write his Catholicism technically and not leave behind the average vocabulary of Catholic French readers; he can also speak out with a certain freedom in a country where Catholicism has little competition. Greene, on the other hand, cannot afford to be technical (English taste always runs to amateurism, anyway) ; and lest he be called upon to define and redefine his position, he declares it hardly at all. So Mauriac can take a great deal for granted, can reveal all the shades of his doubts as "flux and reflux around a central rock." Greene can take little for granted and, while presenting his own flux and reflux, suppress the rock. It is not surprising, then, that Mauriac says "The work of an English Catholic novelist always gives me a sense of being lost" and that Greene seems to have no preconceptions beyond corrupt nature and an omnipotent Grace. He finds something surreptitious about Greene while Greene finds him, in turn, too stringent and possessed of too acute a conscience. Mauriac relaxes cerebrally; Greene works things out by straining into melodrama.

In other words, Greene, deprived of an uninterrupted Christian tradition, is somewhat in the position of those—Blake, Yeats, Hardy, Lawrence, Pound—who invent their own systems. It is a position which makes, as Eliot said, for excitement, confusion, strain and depletion. But if we consider Greene's characteristic fiction, we can understand why. Greene-land is international, seedy, obsessive, packed with types, picaresque and melodramatic in the Jacobean way. In the midst of it are those who sin (not always against God) and symbolize the difficulty of being devout at all. Greene, it is true, makes religion difficult because he does not separate it from the large world and cannot, as a Frenchman can, extract it through abstractions. Greene is nothing if not empirical. As he has said, in *Journey without Maps* (1936), "centuries of cerebration" have caused so much unhappiness that he feels he would like to go back and see where, how and why man went astray. The typical Greene "hero" has, therefore, a great deal in common with the adventurer-heroes of Malraux and heads for the same kind of territory. He is similarly obsessed with surrender and self-destruction and feels the same need to actualize abstract ideas, which means that he re-creates the jungles of Indo-China or Africa to express his own prejudices and needs. Greene, like Malraux, seeks a continuing identity of man; and his work, like Malraux's, assembles many instances toward an act of induction. Greene has always been interested in humanity as a category, and that is why he has created his own brand of categorical characters (less cluttered with minutiae than Mauriac's) : he writes about, and rewrites about, what interests him most. Hence his picaresque pilgrimage of a literary career, whereas Mauriac seems to mark time on the same piece of sand.

The Power and the Glory exemplifies the paradoxical Greene still further. His Mexican priest on the run from the local authority enacts many of the varieties of unintelligible terror. A good priest would not, presumably, have been on the run. Or—it is the type of question Greene breeds in our minds—would he? The flight here is both physical and spiritual; the priest is both man and soul. If he had been entirely either (and either would be inhuman) he would have been less interesting to the average reader, but we should remember Greene's admitted predilection for eliciting the human from the apparently inhuman. The same remark applies also to the remoteness of God and the inaccessibility of our fellowmen. There is a sense in which Greene's novels tug what is human, or divine, from the reader himself: the books conduct an exercise upon him and make him stretch, strain, wonder and puzzle. We are meant to live ambiguously while experiencing *The Power and the Glory*. Greene is on both sides, both the whiskey-priest's and the police lieutenant's. Both men embody a discipline and both confront us with modified extremes. Greene (the man who rebuked the Cardinal-Archbishop of Paris for refusing Christian burial to Colette) is closer to enraged compassion than to lip-serving piety. He has never forgotten playing Russian roulette: the empty chamber always evoked its opposite, and the empty man (say even the empty priest) always evokes his opposite too. And Greene's recurrent images or motifs—of adjacent and conflicting worlds, of self-inflicted ordeals, and spiritual shabbiness—recall a great deal of his boyhood. In the opening chapter of *The Lawless Roads* (1939) he recalls the door which separated his parents' quarters from the school of which his father was headmaster. On the one side, security, the amenities of home; on the other, the public-school jungle and the obstacle race of growing up in public. It is the type of dichotomy he never transcends, and that is why he makes so wide an appeal without misrepresenting or abandoning either side of his concern.

It emerges most of all, and in its perhaps most moving form, in his suspicion that spirituality is inimical to human aspiration. In one sense, man's faith is not his own until he has investigated God for himself as best he can; but as soon as he eschews lip service or popular piety for introspection and meditation he imperils the very possibility of faith. Faith in fact is too much of an assumption, too much of a leap, for any but the most inert or desperate mind. And Greene, more melodramatically than anyone (it *is* a melodramatic theme) has demonstrated for skeptics the befuddlement of believers. The rigmaroles of heresy—nothingness, absurdity, condemnation to freedom, agony of choice, secular mystiques and substitute temples, inner checks and blood consciousness—all appear in his novels minus metaphorical color but with, as it were, God's caboose attached to the train. God appears to Minty who sneaks into a Lutheran church in Stockholm. Scobie hides a broken rosary in his desk. Sarah's prayer in *The End of the Affair* (1951) is granted. But God's general absence is not construed (as by Simone Weil) as certain evidence of presence. The dichotomy persists. Scobie loves God, but no-one else; the priest in *The Potting Shed* (1957) loves his nephew only to lose faith in God. Saints, like humanists, define themselves. And their serenity is no greater. Bendrix in *The End of the Affair* gains nothing from the gradual burgeoning of his religious sensibility, and Father Rank, in the epilogue to *The Heart of the Matter* (1948), warns Mrs. Scobie: ". . . don't imagine you—or I—know a thing about God's mercy." It takes a human irrationality to justify a divine irrationality.

The End of the Affair perhaps pushed the reader's credulity too far. When an obsessive jealousy is dispersed by divine subterfuge, even the devout are apt to wonder. And Greene's next novel, *Loser Take All* (1955), reads like a book produced absentmindedly. But *The Quiet American* (1956) found him back on a less wilful road, again probing the soul's own resources while God remains decently disguised in the machinery. Greene called *Our Man in Havana* (1958) a "fairy-story," ironically remarking his return to surfaces. Obviously he had wondered whether to materialize the mystical and thus distort it, or to leave us baffled with what looked like an amusing spy fantasy just right for reading on a train to Istanbul.

A Burnt-Out Case gives us a revulsed man of the world, empty of ambition and love, bored even by his fame as an architect, and voluntarily entering a leper colony on a tributary of the Congo. "The Congo," Greene says in his preface, "is a region of the mind," evoking Conrad's own observation of the "fascination of the abomination." Querry is not punishing himself so much as acknowledging his membership in humanity. He adds himself on, whereas parts of the lepers' members deaden and fall off. Rycker, the small-time businessman, tries to see him as a saint in the making but also spots him as *the* Querry. It is Rycker who sends for Parkinson, the journalist, so that another Schweitzer can be announced to the world with the right degree of panache. But Querry is too far gone to care: like his servant, Deo Gratias, he is a burnt-out case. He has achieved his cure by losing all that can be eaten away. He has no ties now and perhaps he seeks a return to prerational, prehuman innocence. When he spends a night in the jungle comforting Deo Gratias, he listens to ramblings about "Pendele" and "a dance at a friend's house, a young man with a shiny simple face, going to Mass on Sunday with the family, falling asleep in a single bed perhaps." Perhaps, Querry amusedly thinks, this is what he himself wants: the two of them overlap in their longings. The priests of the leproserie are childlike creatures, preoccupied with carpentering and dynamos; when Querry tells Rycker's child-wife about himself he does it through a fairy story in which he figures as a jeweller. He cannot feel pain or pleasure: the night he spends with Mrs. Rycker is innocent. She herself is Innocence just as Parkinson is Corruption. And Querry, designing his rudimentary extra hospital, what is he? A little bit the spoiled saint, a great deal the successful failure.

This novel re-presents the argument of *The Heart of the Matter:* "Here you could love human beings nearly as God loved them, knowing the worst." Querry, like Scobie, feels no responsibility to the beautiful, the intelligent and the graceful. Leprophilia is the extremist answer to such a view as Yusef expresses: "The way is not to care a damn, Major Scobie. . . ." Everyone in *A Burnt-Out Case* cares his damn; but Querry has eliminated not just his own aesthetic standards but his character and his personality. He may look utterly empty until we realize that there is a great deal of impersonal compassion in him. No labels or names. He becomes aware of others' suffering in an almost theoretical way; he does not share their pain as physical pain but (as in the anaesthesia which is a side effect of leprosy) notes the fact of it. In Hemingway when the character numbs himself to pain he also numbs his power to formulate it mentally; but in Querry the unfelt fact provokes a kind of sleepwalking reflex. Greene keeps on using his mind, not only about compassion and worldliness but also about the problems the mind can never solve, problems which the mind creates in order to stay human.

Greene's symbolism (leprosy; the hospital being the riverboat's last stop; the road almost, but not quite, overwhelmed by the jungle) simplifies, as does the violence in thrillers. Such a simplification or dilution gives the reader more opportunity to read himself into the novel; no heavily stressed idiosyncrasies get in the way of his own. Greene's triumph is that he has always contrived to make the simplifications of the thriller condemn themselves. For the main agony is in the constructions, not the destructions, which the mind achieves while seeking to answer an examination none can pass. And Querry, hardly described at all, is Everyman without approximating to the least common denominators of humanity. He is an *un*common denominator, outstandingly available to all of us.

Among Greene's statements concerning art and fiction there is one which clarifies not just his practice and his development but the whole basis of his art. "Creative art," he says, "seems to remain a function of the religious mind." Notice the word "remain." He is talking about immutable things: let the artist experiment as much as he likes, let him deny and obfuscate, misrepresent and concoct—the result is always the same, and that is a celebration of the gift of life. In this, Greene is close to the much less detailed, much less ingeniously expounded reverence for life of Dylan Thomas. In the long run it is not argument that persuades but some interaction of sentiment. Thomas makes no claims to understand life, but he enthusiastically expresses his awe and love of vitality. Greene, never slow to speak out against or to ignore institutional regimen, knows no more than Thomas, but he does not hesitate to describe even murder as a religious subject. In fact, as he has said, the English novel has suffered for a long time from the loss of the "religious sense." As well as opposing "Infinite Love" and human love to allegations that our world is absurd, he achieves "a reverent openness before life" that enables him to write of anything with dignity and force. It is not a matter of asking questions and of getting answers; it is a matter of affirmation, whether of the commonplace or of the exotic worlds he has taken from gangsterdom and such remote corners as Vietnam and the Congo. And this, I suggest, is why Greene appeals to many readers who are not only not Catholics but not even Christians. In his work the sense of life overpowers any doctrinal recommendations he has in mind; and this, moreover, without gilding the image of the modern world, which Greene does not hesitate to reveal as sordid, ugly and degenerate. Querry, the hero-surrogate of *A Burnt-Out Case,* amounts to an affirmation that is firm without being glib, all-encompassing without grandiosity, and humble without mealy-mouthed pietism. As his name suggests, he is both a man on the run and a query: he is pursued by his past in the persons of Rycker, Parkinson and Father Thomas, and he is also pursued in his spiritual pilgrimage-adventure by his own inquiring, interrogating mind. Querry is his own quarry; his quest is for himself—for a self uncluttered by reputation, admiration and the public image behind which no-one has ever seen. He wins our sympathy through an act of self-abnegation which evokes Mauriac's "kiss to the leper." Querry stays out the night in the jungle with the trapped, injured and demoralized Deo Gratias. It is a secular epiphany. It marks the beginning of Querry's own cure, a cure which ends with the words "I think I'm cured of pretty well everything, even disgust" which he says just before his death. And this death of vanity prompts Doctor Colin to say, after the physical Querry has died, "He'd learned to serve other people, you see, and to laugh." Even a Positivist could not resent that, and Greene is careful throughout the novel to make the reader himself engage in the same "creative sickness" as himself: that is, "to fill in the character or features of a human being" in the same way as an explorer feels driven to fill in a map. While writing this novel, Greene thought of Querry only as X, a *terra incognita* of a character whose "meaning" depends upon ourselves the readers. The variable here is the adventurer, the pilgrim, not the setting or the adventure.

Greene is, then, a man who writes the same novel all the time: he supplies us with a pattern, and to read him entire is to participate to an increasing extent in the fleshing and blooding of his characters. He shares the skepticism of the Apostle Thomas, who had to "see the marks of the nails"; and he caters to a similar attitude in his reader, relying on the old human craving "to see for myself." Greene's reader sees for himself by entering into the novel as a companion-creator to the novelist, and is therefore at liberty to modify, say, the Congo or Querry within the limits established by Greene's own modifications and openings. Not that any of Greene's novels is a do-it-yourself kit. I am just saying that he appeals on a level not militantly theological. He came to the serious, religious novel *via* an early enthusiasm for Marjorie Bowen's *The Viper of Milan* and he has paid tribute to the adventure stories of John Buchan, Rider Haggard, Anthony Hope and Percy F. Westerman. His work derives something from these authors but also, as T. S. Eliot has said, from the fantasy tradition of Stevenson, Chesterton and Waugh. And it is this kind of fantasy that Greene refurbishes into nightmare adventure with fantastic trappings similar to those we find in the plays of Ford, Tourneur and Webster, in all of whom Greene has more than once expressed his interest. It is helpful too to remember that epiphany, revelation, grace (or whatever we choose to call sudden moments of vision or illumination) does not come on time like a train or pop up like a slice of bread from a toaster: there is no predicting and no planning. The moment itself is sudden and melodramatic, and Greene makes the most of this quality. Horror too is melodramatic, and Greene assents to Bossuet's "One must go as far as horror to truly know oneself." But the most vital drama or melodrama of all follows upon his "duty" as a writer, and that is "to roam experimentally through any human mind" and "to draw his own likeness to any human being." This is no mere *tourisme* or feat of malleable face. It is the literary version of the priest's pastoral care. Greene tries to communicate the drama of his own faith delving deep into himself. It is not a proselytizing gesture but, like the kiss to the leper, an affirmation of human consanguinity and a sacrament of awareness.

It is also an attempt to awaken us spiritually, to do for us what Africa did for him (as for Hemingway) with its "religious fascination." Africa, Greene has said, "offers the European an opportunity of living continuously in the presence of the super-natural. The secret societies, as it were, sacramentalize the whole of life." And when he explains that he went to Liberia in 1935 to penetrate beneath the "cerebral" veneer of modern culture, he is implying also, I think, that his concern is always to penetrate beneath conceptual surfaces—not only those of reason but also those of theology. Hence his heresy. In *A Sense of Reality* (1963) he even likens theological explanations' impact on mystery and faith to that of cyanide on a butterfly and presents a fictional Catholic writer who declares that if he went back to the Sacra-ments he would lose what little belief remained to him. We are all in the position of the Greene doctor who, after refusing to be charitable to a patient, realizes suddenly that the world is absurd (he has just helped to make it so) and that there is no difference between his doom-to-come and that of his patient. That, I think, is as good a summary-image as we shall find. Greene is continually stressing the togetherness of men and the omnipresence of mystery. The two belong together and inform each other. Greene is an artist, not an apologist, and it is not hard or humiliating to follow him into those dark and secret areas of the spirit which he, more than any English novelist writing now, has made his theme. At times he may even go too far, as when in "A Visit to Morin," he relates the discovery of God to the finding of an old tin chamber pot. (Tin pot; tin drum. Greene and Grass come together in unlikely ways while creating their respective versions of what Conrad called "a weary pilgrimage amongst hints for nightmares.")

For some readers, Greene may be too melodramatic, Eliot the dramatist too tame, Simone Weil too abstract. We cannot have everything, even if we share their faith. But, underlying the words of each of the three, there is a resolve to promote awareness in the most active and least doctrinal way, not so much arguing as trying to express the inescapable mystery of life in which it is impossible not to participate. We may not be able to assent to their opposition of faith to the absurdity, nothingness and secular action proposed by Camus, Sartre and Malraux, but we would be the losers if we allowed what is no more than a theological difference to discourage us from interesting ourselves in them while they interest themselves in us. That leaning toward us is *their* mode of action, in some ways not much more spectacular than the bookish divining practiced by the Myth Critics but certainly something we can respond to without anticipating the objection that we want all the magic of faith without faith's discipline. First and last it is not discipline or label that counts; it is awareness, and the eclectic has every right to shop around, especially where he is welcomed without demands being made of him. The "square hyena" that haunts Eliot's Beckett belongs to all of us and can no more be theologized away than it can be dismissed with a wave of the heretical arm.

Morin, the aging Catholic novelist, has not only offended orthodox Catholics and pleased the liberal ones; he has even pleased Protestants and non-Christians. The last group have valued him for a freely speculative mind which operates on premises that the non-Christian can apprehend imaginatively. This is the kind of communicative Christianity that Sartre finds lacking in Mauriac's *The End of the Night* (1935). Mauriac, Sartre claims, has chosen divine omniscience and omnipotence and denies his characters freedom. He is demanding that the novelist should not exercise his creative liberty over the fictional world he has brought into being: in other words, he wants an illusion within an illusion. After all, the characters must do what the author decides; no-one else will tell them what to do. This is a quibble on Sartre's part. What is more interesting is his demand for the accommodation of the reader who might not share the writer's religious persuasions. Sartre's complaint voices among other things the feeling that even doctrinal writers should offer the agnostic reader some imaginative purchase on their work. It is a fair request, but it cannot be insisted upon. Finally we have to judge by some such standard as Marcel and Jaspers have applied. I mean the desirability of, on the one hand, a work's remaining open (not just an enclosing, mechanical medium for faith) and, on the other, its communicating in an unpossessive way an imaginative truth which both author and reader strive jointly to apprehend in the most intimate way possible. In this respect, it seems to me, the three authors I have just discussed are more open, more outgoing, than Sartre ever is (except perhaps in *The Devil and the Good God*) and as appealing imaginatively as Camus and Malraux at their best.

A New World

*S*antayana once said he was Catholic in everything but faith, and his paradox typifies him. He meant, of course, that the faith was the least thing since, as he said, Catholicism was paganism spiritualized and religion was "valid poetry" infused into common life. He was Catholic, then, in all that mattered; or so he thought. He had a habit of turning things inside out to make a witticism only to find his heart was not on the side of his verbal triumph. And this habit, as one might disingenuously predict from his early writings, caught up with him at the very end. It was the part of his scholar-gypsy role that came to him too easily and—unlike his urbane bachelordom and his wry hyperboles about the ways of people everywhere—got him into metaphysical trouble.

Born in Spain and brought to Cambridge, Massachusetts at the age of nine, he was always restless. A poet and mystic, he was also an uneasy materialist. Detached and aloof, he countered his scepticism with an "animal faith" that ripened and intensified until his last years, which he spent in nihilistic anticlimax. He had the Victorian itch to get things tidied up: his five-volume compendium, The Life of Reason: or the Phases of Human Progress (*1905–6*), and his four-volume survey of The Realms of Being (*1927–40*) consort oddly with his claim to be "an ignorant man" only setting down what anyone could know if he wondered for a time. There is no doubt of his anxiety for cosmic reassurance or of his fear that, in the long run, spiritual dryness and hopeless verbalizing might afflict someone as unappeased and peregrine as himself. Firmly in this world, he was not fulfilled by it; but groping to transcend it, he found his mind objecting.

Religion, he said, is not "truer" than perception or science.

The following discussion, mostly concerning one book of essays he published in 1900, presents him as a figure who thought his paradoxicality enriched his life and that his twin attitudes—an ingenuous, not-quite-at-grips fervor for modern materialism and a passion for pre-empting epiphany so that, if it came, he could call it poetry—strengthened each other rather than cancelled each other out. His odd view of poetry—as something to be applied to previously clarified ideas—betrays his dualistic habits of mind. He feared the medium's becoming dominant; that is, the loss of, the absence of, clear ideas amid verbal froth (which was his view of Shakespeare). Only someone who so passionately wanted to separate the rational from the emotional could have reached the spiritual fiasco of his last years after a lifetime of confident, poised negotiation with limbo. Santayana is the good mind who discerns no virtues in sloppiness; and in his chaste, ascetic way he rejoices when J. M. T. MacTaggart, the Cambridge philosopher, quotes him ("Truth is a dream unless my dream be true") and calls the line philosophical poetry at its best. Berenson detected about him "something philistine," especially about his Catholicism, so-called, and something "without pity and without humanity." It is a harsh verdict, telling us something about Berenson the Jew who was Episcopalian by baptism, and only to be balanced by Santayana on Berenson: "he keeps the old flame alive, but I can't help feeling it was lighted and is kept going by forced draft, by social and intellectual ambition, and by professional pedantry." Where, one wonders, did sweet reason go?

George Santayana

It is easy not to read Santayana: his abstract and magistral titles—*The Sense of Beauty* (1896), *The Life of Reason, Scepticism and Animal Faith* (1923), *Egotism in German Philosophy* (1916)—deter us and suggest a mind too philosophical and too ambitious. Indeed, as Lionel Trilling testified in *A Gathering of Fugitives* (1956), his generation found Santayana culpable in the line from Pater, and underestimated his robust, uncynical disillusion. (Pater, in fact, for all his sense of the actual, had not the kind of sensibility which would embrace the glamorous, raucous American myth.) But Santayana, contrary to the supposition of many who relegate him without reading him even in part, applauded the increase of industrialism, the painful maieutics which brought into being a tradition of America. And his detachment, his way of preserving his personality without despising the hubbub, is very different from a secession into Brasenose. For he wanted a non-Europeanized America; he never overrated the power or the importance of the arts; he rebuked Boston gentility and Boston inclusiveness. At the same time he knew the role and power of what might be called a spiritual attitude. To him, whatever America did was neither inevitably vicious nor divinely sanctioned. His life was devoted to the construction and advocacy of a complex attitude; and one complex enough to limit idealism without impairing the promised and proceeding amelioration of material life. Admitting resignation early, he yet valued endeavor. Extracting sweetness and light from the life around him, he yet avoided being either a metaphysical crank or a sybarite.

But what he needed above all was the compensation of optional withdrawal: not from virile fraternity to pensive isolation, but to do what in their respective ways Pater, Arnold and Ruskin had all attempted. He wanted to get things clear, and to do this he had to free his mind from distraction. For, in a country without long traditions, if you dissent from something not yet a *fait accompli,* the illusion persists that the plan of action can be changed by sheer animadversion or that a new integration is needed.

Santayana exemplifies a paradox common in American thought—conscience says that material benefit is not enough, yet that withdrawal of any sort entails a culpable disdain of material progress. On the surface, that is not a paradox, but a misunderstanding of withdrawal. To Santayana the perplexity of his contemporaries as well as the falsity of American philosophical thought were accounted for by an insufficiently complex outlook. To get things straight, to keep always a very fine sense of the edifice of your own thought, these were essential and quite apart from pleasure or pain, from aestheticism or adventurousness. "The joke of things," said Santayana, "is one at our expense"; and the irony is that his renunciation, in fact a means of accepting things into a continuously coherent mind, came to be disdained as effete escapism. But Santayana's taste for the complex extended also to his prose; so it is perhaps understandable that his doctrines have been misconstrued.

He had above all an acute sense of man's impotence to control the course of civilization. The material world, progressing or not, could at any stage outstrip the ideals which sponsored it, without in fact making a chaos. There was a conflict, so to speak, between brain and brain-child such as transcendentalism could never preclude or conceal. He separated the ideal from the institution, and advocated a lively, developing sense of the material world. In his opinion, transcendentalism was a shady, illogical way of admitting that the world didn't always come up to expectations. What he proposed to substitute was an ideal of integration such that, whatever the world produced, the product could be assimilated without its destroying the coherent identity of an individual: such identity constituting for him the most enduring and most sensible achievement possible in the flux.

It is, of course, high time that we had a thorough book on Santayana and a careful selection from his writings: in other words, something to tempt readers beyond his autobiography, through the sonnets, into such a work as *Interpretations of Poetry and Religion* (1900). Particularly interesting is his response to the American Dream: "I was a teacher of philosophy in the place where philosophy was most modern, most deeply Protestant, most hopefully new!" This comes from *My Host the World* (1953), a book in which Santayana is at his most approachable and most consistent. "You give up everything," he said, "in the form of claims; you receive everything back in the form of a divine presence." That is his final position: a disinterested gratitude. The secular beatitude there is no less profound than the *je ne suis pas heureuse; je suis contente* of La Vallière whom he quotes. After all, his main concern was not with life and nature "running on at full tilt"; that he could and did accept. "It is the spirit that asks to be saved from that insane predicament"; he saves it by opinionless, almost innocent immersion in the flux. And such a move can help us to understand the true irony of American history: that those most alive to what is unworthy are often the least effectual.

Santayana, confronted by a developing way of life, eliminates less than, say, Berenson. That is the difference between an expansive unconcern and a constricting passion. Berenson repudiates all he cannot like. Santayana, in spite of his old-world cynicism, owed something to the divinely determined polity of the Pilgrim Fathers; not so much for what he believed as for the oddly messianic nature of his submissiveness. President Stiles of Yale spoke of "God's American Israel"; but for Santayana, everywhere was a spiritual Israel and all men were chosen. As he saw it, Providence made no special dispensations, and the rapt conviction of a Jefferson could have been adopted equally aptly by any man in any situation. What puzzled Santayana was to see his own undiscriminating attitude being applied so narrowly to one society. His conclusion was that grace is available whenever men need it badly enough to have to secure it by their own means.

That all is respectworthy and can be seen to be so by concentrating on it, is a conviction he never lost. The effort of concentration is an act of sympathy which in turn assists people to new perception—in short, to new definitions of the poetic and, indeed, of any prized quality. Of course, the ostrich may be said to be concentrating when he buries his head. But when a man looks for solace, for grace, he moves outside the realm of responsibility.

The spectator is participant, but can renounce or condone what-ever he wishes. That is Santayana's defense: the world is an eloquence, could we but hear it. Beyond that, talk of responsi-bility amounts only to a man's vague feeling that he must witness as much as he can when all is manifest divinity. His witness may be denounced as Neo-Platonic; but he may well communicate in his writing that insight into cosmic order for the lack of which so many ambitious modern novels and poems become incoherent and perverse. The mind needs order; and better a factitious order than none at all, even if some obvious facts have to be rejected in consequence.

Having proposed the world's eloquence in fairly vague terms, Santayana is free to explore it in terms that blur the arbitrary but clear labels of everyday usage. *Interpretations of Poetry and Religion* will serve as an example. The essay topics range from Homeric Hymns to Emerson and Browning; there are some shrewd inquiries into "The Dissolution of Paganism," "Platonic Love in Some Italian Poets," and "The Absence of Religion in Shakespeare." The most fascinating essays concern "Understand-ing, Imagination and Mysticism," "The Elements and Function of Poetry" and, key to the collection, "The Poetry of Christian Dogma." Santayana's general idea is that "religion and poetry are identical in essence, and differ merely in the way in which they are attached to practical affairs. Poetry is called religion when it intervenes in life, and religion, when it merely supervenes upon life, is seen to be nothing but poetry." He adds that neither religion nor poetry deals with matters of fact; both concern themselves with what he calls "the ideal," and their dignity lies in their "ideal adequacy." Exactly where supervening develops into intervening he never says; and one cannot help feeling that sometimes he is merely playing with words—devising a spurious identity in order to create nothing more than a new dualism. But we are supposed to concentrate not upon what distinguishes poetry from religion but upon what they have in common. About his "ideal," to which both aspire, he is rather clearer:

Its [religion's] function is . . . to draw from reality materials for an image of that ideal to which reality ought to conform, and to make us citizens, by anticipation, in the world we crave.

Poetry's function is identical. But both forms of expression endanger themselves: religion when it presumes to deal in facts or laws, poetry when it indulges in "an unmeaning play of fancy without relevance to the ideals and purposes of life." Which almost seems to be the same as saying that poetry is not poetry when it is escapist; and that is just. For what Santayana intends is a poetry that will do duty for religion, and a religion that will do its own duty properly. We seem near, throughout Santayana's writings, to a poetry that meets the agnostic's craving for spiritual rapture and a religion that introduces the philistine to aesthetic delight. In other words, he seems to propose a redistribution of familiar, set elements, but to no ultimate gain: the agnostic, regarding poetry as religion, effaces some of his literary demands; and the philistine confuses religion's trappings with its meaning. In the abstract, Santayana is impressive. But when his ideas are forced down into the shuffle of everyday living, his ideal poetry appears portentous and his ideal religion mere allegory.

He is particularly vague about what he calls "facts":

The expedient [he says] of recognizing facts as facts and accepting ideals as ideals,—and this is all we propose,—although apparently simple enough, seems to elude the normal power of discrimination.

It has eluded a good many with more than normal power of discrimination: Santayana knew enough of philosophy to deter him from being so sweeping. But his argument proceeds by assertion instead of demonstration; he is trying to effect a spiritual merger in terms of absolutes. There are, he says, those who "have a sense for reality" and those with "a sense for ideals, but mad." It often seems that he thinks his own ideals ideal but those of any opponent to be mere "facts"—which is, of course, to belittle them. He nowhere suggests that all ideals are "psychic facts." In other words he is attempting a reconciliation of ideas, but only an incomplete one. And his absolutes are pretence: not complete versions of the realm of fact or of ideals, but selections according to his own whim. The selections he dresses up and presents as twin emanations from the imagination. Out of the window go, right at the beginning, both the possible historicity of Christianity and all unphilosophical poetry. Santayana seems to have been over-influenced by what he calls the "liberal school that attempts to fortify religion by minimizing its expression, both theoretic and devotional . . ." For he cannot see the difference between a devout interest in historical fact—in sifting evidence—and a destructive pedantry. "Mythology," he contends, "cannot become science by being reduced in bulk, but it may cease, as a mythology, to be worth having." True, but such a study as Frank Morison's *Who Moved the Stone?* assembles and reviews the "facts" of the Christ story to provide a consistent version of what happened. Nothing is more fascinating than the historical provenance of a "miracle." And if some elements conflict and some have to be discarded, that is not to reduce a mythology's bulk. The same would be true of the investigation of the Dead Sea Scrolls. In neither instance is piety degraded to the level of a quiz; in neither does the mythology "cease . . . to be worth having." Santayana wants no fact-finder to clip his religion's wings, and he overstates his case. He is really concerned to protect the metaphorical nature of religious statements. The odd thing is that, anxious as he is that mythology should not be mistaken for science or history, he makes religion and poetry overlap considerably, the one insuring the other.

The overlap is the imagined ideal. Like Tocqueville, he thinks poetry's function is to lead men towards ideals of both personal character and eventual heaven; and he believes that a retributive justice weeds people out according to their degree of attention to those ideals. By a leap of the imagination men can orientate themselves both morally and cosmically. But imagination alone will not always suffice; a degree of discipline must come first:

. . . the respect exacted by an establishment is limited and external, and not greater than its traditional forms probably deserve, as normal expressions of human feeling and apt symbols of moral truth.

This view is similar to Swift's formula of rational Christianity aimed at unregenerate man. But Santayana does not share Swift's preference for church discipline and for social suitability before self-discipline and private ecstasy. Not too anxious to tie down his religion in institutions, he prefers the vague region of religio-poetry. So he talks of "a reasonable deference" to authority in the same sentence as he recommends a mind "inwardly and happily free; the conscience . . . not intimidated, the imagination . . . not tied up." And, if we are to judge from the pace of Santayana's exposition, the transit from the disciplines of traditional forms to a vision of the ideal is swift and smooth:

All observation is observation of brute fact, all discipline is mere repression, until these facts digested and this discipline embodied in humane impulses become the starting-point for a creative movement of the imagination. . . .

But of course the imagination misleads us: Santayana should have recalled his Montaigne on that; and fifteenth-century art, as Sir Kenneth Clark points out in his book on Leonardo, "aspired to be a branch of knowledge." For Santayana no use of the imagination is corrupt, no feat of the imagination can be a fact. He tends to work things out too neatly: he is a Procrustes of piety. Proposing always a reverent attention to a world of essences, he reminds one of the Eskimo who, living in a world only sparsely populated and far from crammed with objects, evolves several names for snow (according to its type and condition) and for the polar bear at its successive stages of growth. On the surface he seems to advocate such a minute attention to everything: actually he thins out his world and attends exhaustively only to what he fancies. Like the Eskimo, he imposes his own terminology on the "facts" remaining. He does not always play fair with the evidence: "Only as conditions of these human activities (society, religion, art) can the facts of nature and history become morally intelligible or practically important." If he is disdaining useless knowledge and recommending the pragmatic, then he is talking sensibly. But he is doing more: he has no time for the category of "information," just as he has little tolerance for lyrical poetry. He finds no use for either human curiosity or directionless joy. Not that one would wish him so pragmatic; he simply is so, and indeed simply so. He is a relentless purpose-hunter, applying dogma to modes of expression and modes of mental exercise which are ends in themselves. In other words his is a hectoring aesthetic, an almost ferocious evasion of the Pater tradition.

Had Santayana not lived so long in America, would his views have been different? Would the fascinations of mere fact (as in our empirical way we must term them) and the elations of joy for joy's sake have won a kinder reception from him? Perhaps so; one recalls David Riesman's exposure of the conformity cult. Santayana is really trying to make everything respectable and purposive; and this is the legacy of the divine polity of the early settlers as well as of the philosophy of William James. There is more than a bit of the ethical busybody in this, for example:

This human life is not merely animal and passionate. The best and keenest part of it consists in that very gift of creation and government which, together with all the transcendental functions of his own mind, man has significantly attributed to God as his highest ideal.

A little further on he comes right into the open:

In comparison with . . . apathetic naturalism, all the errors and follies of religion are worthy of indulgent sympathy, since they represent an effort, however misguided, to interpret and to use the materials of experience for moral ends, and to measure the value of reality by its relation to the ideal.

No sooner have we noticed a thing than Santayana is moving it away towards some goal. Of course, neither dogma nor sensuality has the full answer to questions about how to live. Santayana overesteems dogma, is too afraid of sensuality in its own right. All the odder, then, that he should have been thought one of Pater's heirs. Irwin Edman, one of his most distinguished pupils, admired Pater; and Edman's own pupils (as Lionel Trilling has noted) tended to lump Pater, Santayana and Edman together into a "genteel tradition whose dominant trait was the 'perfection of rottenness.' " But Santayana was no effete escapist—as his severe views on aesthetic experience demonstrate. In fact he was always pushing forward to some kind of civic vigor which made no more of the arts than they merited from a pioneer nation. Santayana was much less of an aesthete than even William James. Reading him nowadays is like poring over a vast expansion of Homer's description, at the close of *The Odyssey*, of the Shield of Achilles: the moral imagination of art—or, in Santayana's own words, "the moral function of the imagination and the poetic nature of religion." If Homer was no aesthete, neither was this ungenteel American philosopher.

In the essay, "The Poetry of Christian Dogma," Santayana explains that Neo-Platonism and Christianity arose from the same conditions: "weariness and disgust with the life of nature, decay of political virtue, desire for some personal and supernatural good." He goes on to outline the notion of paradise; both systems had it in common:

It was necessary to point to *some sphere of refuge* and of *healthful resort,* where the ignominies and the frivolities of this world might be forgotten, and where the hunger of a heart left empty by its corroding passions might be finally satisfied. (my italics)

Arcadia is the man-made heaven, *the* heaven, and it is on earth, but very rarely down to it. Neither Neo-Platonism nor Christianity offered an Arcadia, however; the former was too abstract, suffering from what Santayana calls "the hypostasis of abstractions"; and the latter was not man-made. The one's principle was dialectic—a cold road to quietness—and the other's was love. But, Santayana carefully explains, the one's mythological machinery —especially as represented by the great dialogues interpreted by such as Plotinus (the modish Bergson of his day)—"formed the starting-point of the new revelation." For all that, Neo-Platonism was based on a dichotomy whose social side (current superstitions, fasts and penances, marvels and fears) "had no necessary relation to that metaphysical system." So Christianity could take over not only the social end (which the metaphysics left vague and apart) but also the Neo-Platonic categories, vocabulary and speculative method:

Paganism was a religion, but was discarded because it was not supernatural: Neo-Platonism could not be maintained because it was not a religion. Christianity was both.

See how Santayana fastens upon the dynamic—much in the

manner of an apologist for the American Way. A case in point is that of Philo Judaeus, a Neo-Platonist Jew: powerless in his duality. Yet, says Santayana, he failed "because of the inadequacy of his religion," which was national. What was needed was an imaginative generalization from the life of each one of us: the idea of purposive suffering. And the Crucifixion gave suffering an interpretation; it gave each man an opportunity to associate himself with godhead and regeneration.

We notice once again Santayana's liking for value, aim and general purposiveness. Christianity, as he sees it, not only makes the Hebraic international (which Judaism was not) but also bears on our present and future; and for one reason only. It gives us "Christ and him crucified." The Crucifixion is a powerful image which does not need to be empirically real: it sets man in the center of the world, and enables him to live out his life in terms of justified suffering. In other words, every man's life becomes a pendant to the Crucifixion. Christianity is a story, not a cosmology; it puts, not facts, but "values" into man's hands; not causes but results:

The facts were nothing until they became symbols; and nothing could turn them into symbols except an eager imagination on the watch for all that might embody its dreams.

As Santayana sees it, Christianity illustrates the futility of "fact" and the paramountcy of "values." That is, it proffers no undirected thrill, satisfies no aimless curiosity, but goes so far as to supply both direction and interpretation before fact. Whatever we bring to it, it evaluates and transforms. We are not to build up a religion from facts; we are to ignore the facts because the religion—the attitude of mind—is already there.

No wonder that Santayana speaks of "an eager imagination on the watch"; for this is creative and evolutionary religion—a kind of *poiesis* we might expect from Bergson or Croce or any other thinker who claims to be non-Procrustean. Santayana makes his point clear by full repetitions. He presents the idea of Christ as "something spiritual, something poetical":

What literal meaning could there be in saying that one man or one God died for the sake of each and every other individual?

By what effective causal principle could their salvation be thought to necessitate his death, or his death to make possible their salvation? By an *hysteron proteron* natural to the imagination; for in truth the matter is reversed.

How far is this from merely seeing what we want to see? Or from autosuggestion? A fair distance, it seems; for Santayana presents the "ideal" as a guiding and restraining influence. "Men could 'believe in' his [Christ's] death, because it was a figure and premonition of the burden of their experience." In other words, the Form or the Ideal of the Crucifixion is there all the time; we have premonitions of it; we grope towards it and perfect it as what today might be called an archetypal pattern. Santayana is a genuine Platonist. He deals with "the intuition of ideals" rather than the "multiplication of phenomena."

The Oriental mind, Santayana goes on to say, has no middle: it vacillates between the senses and mysticism. But Christianity deals in "eternal essences, forms" suspended above the flux which are the guides and goals of an immortal soul. The test imposed is that of trying to live according to the best light we have: that is, the Ideal. And it is a test, not a mere acquiescence in the operations of benign Nature:

It may be thought, for instance, that what is regular or necessary or universal is therefore right and good; thus a dazed contemplation of the actual may take the place of the determination of the ideal.

Both optimism and mysticism hamper the effort to live morally. We must attend to the world in all its mixture of good and evil. We must be hopeful without illusions and independent without rebellion: for Christianity offers rewards. After all, if everyone is ultimately saved, "there is nothing truly momentous about alternative events: all paths lead more or less circuitously to the same end." It is interesting to see this Maritain-like argument used for the demolition of facile determinism, but used in a context so vaguely religious-poetic. (Actually Santayana's role for the imagination is not much different from that proposed by Maritain for "creative intuition.")

So far, then, Santayana is fairly consistent although rather mystifying: his intuitions seem consonant with one another. By using our imaginations we shall discover the ideal of the moral life. We must do nothing without enlightened purpose. Mysticism "is not an imaginative construction at all but a renunciation or confusion of our faculties." Similarly, lyrical poetry is a slack indulgence, an evasion of moral responsibility. And there will indeed be a last judgment of how far we have applied our own intuitions of the Ideal. To use the imagination is to attest to God's presence; and we cannot complain that we are set a task for which we are not given the tools. Self-redemption *is* possible.

But before we assume that Santayana is a conventional Christian we must consider his views on two subjects: church regimen and the theory of poetry. For both of these hinder him—more than he ever seems to realize. Christianity, he says, ought to be an eternal religion:

But it may forfeit that privilege by entangling itself with a particular acount of matters of fact, matters irrelevant to its ideal significance, and further by intrenching itself, by virtue of that entanglement, in an inadequate regimen or a too narrow imaginative development, thus putting its ideal authority in jeopardy by opposing it to other intuitions and practices no less religious than its own.

That is the typical statement of the intellectual theist: he reserves the right to approach God in his own way; he will evolve his own system, his own creed, his own unceremonial piety. In that way he will not jeopardize his faith by subjecting it to the regimens devised for the "vulgar":

What the religion of the vulgar adds to the poet's is simply *the inertia of their limited apprehension,* which takes literally what he meant ideally, and degrades into a false extension of this world on its own level what in his mind was a true interpretation of it upon a moral place. (my italics)

He wants, not "inertia," but something both dynamic and private: something more like poetry than like institutional religion. He reminds one of the condescending snobbery of the aesthetes. Once again, we notice, a degree of apartness is as essential to the intellectual as a degree of orientation.

So, having fended off the institutional requirements of organized religion, Santayana has to look to "poetry" for an uncommon amount of guidance. But how much guidance or, for that matter, constraint, discipline, "belonging" and "system" can poetry give? It is all very well for Santayana to recommend his "higher plane" of "significant imagination" where poetry offers a "significant fiction." This is certainly to supply what Maritain calls "the supersubstantial nourishment of man"; but what happens to poetry as a result? It becomes, says Santayana, unfrivolous. We end where we began: with didactic poetry and merely aesthetic religion. This poetry "is metrical and euphuistic discourse, expressing thought which is both sensuous and ideal." It is supposed to give a glimpse of the divine; yet it cannot (within Santayana's limits) celebrate a sudden consciousness of God's presence. Exclamation is out. So is poetry that reports. In fact Santayana goes so far as to lump exclamatory, documentary and atavistic poetry together under the label of "barbarism." True, he never shirked raucous, expanding America; but he would not at any price admit it into the sacred province of poetry. For the data of democracy cannot do duty for a religion: what in one of his sonnets he calls "the soul's invincible surmise" precludes muddle, whether secular or spiritual. The poetry of democracy (as Tocqueville had prophesied) was confused, too factual, too apt to show "imagination" at its wildest:

There is clearly some analogy between a mass of images without structure and the notion of an absolute democracy. Whitman, inclined by his genius and habits to see life without relief or organization, believed that his inclination in this respect corresponded with the spirit of his age and country, and that Nature and society, at least in the United States, were being constituted after the fashion of his own mind. Being the poet of the average man, he wished all men to be specimens of that average, and being the poet of a fluid Nature, he believed that Nature was or should be a formless flux.

The drift here is obvious. Men who evolve their own precarious cosmologies fear nothing more than confusion, flux and chaos. Santayana's own spirituality is formless, concocted out of the worst of both a supervening religion and an intervening poetry.

But what could he expect? He tries to mix Platonism and pragmatism to produce a cosmology from which, for their formlessness and lack of tendentiousness, ecstasy and "facts" are banned. His entelechy is meant to arrive in spite of the absence of these things. How ironic it is that his view excludes the expression of the very joy it is supposed to make available.

In 1887 he wrote to a friend "That the idea of demanding that things should be worth doing is a human impertinence" and that there is little in the world that is good. It sounds bleak and Santayana never quite abandoned that position. To read him attentively (not a fashionable activity) is to learn that we live in an alien, soulless, material universe that has no attitude to us one way or another (an interesting anticipation of the view underlying the French "new novel"). For Santayana, no divine polity and no sentimentality either; his naturalism was not romantic, he said in 1951, as Goethe's and Bergson's were, and he was not—whatever Columbia University professors read into his *Idea of Christ in the Gospels* (1946) —a theist. In short, he is bracing, not least because he acknowledges that the small amount of good in this world is irreducible. The odd thing about him is that his empirical account of the facts is not quite impersonal (he is no mere reporter) but comes essentially from a temperament which distrusted the American mystique of materialism and preferred Europe, where people knew what was what and didn't confuse matter with spirit.

Compared with him, Irving Babbitt, who sought for "a standard above temperament" and averted his gaze from so much he did not like (democracy included) seems less worldly, a more run-of-the-mill university professor. Where Santayana is the reluctant naturalist noting *things* are not spiritual, Babbitt is the academician noting *people* and their spiritual potential. (Santayana, one feels, tended even in the generosity of his friendships to regard people impersonally as the most amusing bits of the alien, material universe.) Babbitt, right through, wants to develop character, sustain traditional humanist values and promote a new kind of self-discipline. He is more bookish than Santayana, less *blasé*, just as antiromantic. But for all his stern academicism, he seems more humane than either Santayana or another humanist, Paul Elmer More, who once said property rights are more important than the human right to life and claimed that Anglicanism is not a compromise but a "direction." The obloquy Babbitt and More attracted, for various reasons, from John Dewey (whom they reviled, too), Mencken, Van Wyck Brooks, Kenneth Burke, Edmund Wilson, Louis Mumford and Granville Hicks, only serves to remind us that American humanism in general is bedevilled by the following complication: it takes root in democracy but must be neither plebeian nor socialistic and must certainly not be mandarin or genteel. Humanism, it seems, is almost impossible in America where material progress is part of the national romance whereas in Europe such progress is relished because it feels nice.

On Myth and Modernity

Babbitt, Dewey and More, each in his own way resorting to reason, expects to find actuality rational and then damns mystique because it isn't rational enough to serve as a substitute. Now that Leftist conviction and the New Criticism have had their day, various individualists such as Jacques Barzun, Lionel Trilling and David Riesman have turned criticism into an affair of agonized individuality with the critic searching around to identify with some kind of communal sentiment. In the process they have given humanism, the American kind, a new twist and have brought matters of unorthodox religion into the exegetical arena. This is both good and bad, depending on the works under discussion, but it can at least be said that these isolated, socially-minded figures stand on their own feet and speak to us without the *préjugés* of such converts as Allen Tate and W. H. Auden. The Myth critics, on the other hand, have found their metaphor for community in the sub-religion of myth and pattern where Aristotle and anthropology meet, while another group, the Beats, who share some of the same problems, have made a community out of being marginal.

I want next to discuss these three postludes to the humanism of Babbitt and More. It is worth noting that the literary flavor of all this has something in common with the humanism of Norman Foerster who, less rigid than Babbitt, less confused than More, looked back to the "dignity and gentility of other days" and was responsible for instituting courses in creative writing at the University of Iowa. Santayana and Dewey, the naturalists, stand apart from all this: unyielding, stern men with clear ideas about matter and fact, about ideals, liberalism and faith. Had they been alive now they would not have flinched away from the new vulgarity; Santayana would have nodded wryly and thought a bit more about essences, Avila or sonnets, and Dewey would have taken it in his stride, regarding it as a new mandate. The others find in it an existential struggle, as Trilling says, "not to live, but to be," and an almost religious crisis to be settled by some sense of public role (Trilling), by transcendence (Myth criticism) or by opting out altogether (the Beats). The American fear is the fear of possibility, the fear which tears thinking people between respecting what comes about because it is American and reserving the option of despising it should it be crass.

The humanist tradition in literature has always based itself on man's special qualities: on reason, inventiveness and sensibility. So it is natural that many rational, creative and cultivated persons should base their faith on the existence of that tradition itself, even to the extent of setting it up as a substitute religion. In this way the humane person of some taste can associate himself with a generalized version of civilized experience; he may come eventually to see that version as a kind of myth—essentially fictitious in that it does not portray the whole of life, but also undeniably impressive as a saga to live by.

The trouble is that, in the present age, with reason and inventiveness apparently adapted more than ever before to the ends of power politics, the humanist is forced back upon his sensibility—perhaps the least outward-going of the civilized qualities. In this way a new aestheticism has arisen which consists in substituting the second-hand for the first-hand: an acute version of literature's usual method. Meditation comes to be not so much a means of making wiser contact with reality as an end in itself; a comforting *huis clos* of speculation. Literature, and the whole burgeoning critical industry it supports, are tending to lose touch and to arrange themselves into a self-contained discipline such as Classics or Philosophy. In other words writers, critics and professors are manipulating their subject—once a casual effort to live vicariously—into one of the "humanities." It has, inevitably perhaps, become the staple *vade mecum* of baffled humanists who expect it to guide or console them while they grapple with the liberal dilemma: how to prevent nationality, position, creed and moods from deluding you about morals. This dilemma is fearsome, for it demands self-definition without reference to circumstances and yet requires a political answer.

So it is that the aestheticism of extremes—literature as a

mode of complete living, life as essentially a subject matter, philosophy as Boethian consolation, theory as conduct, literary criticism as myth and faith—gives rise to and makes worse a situation in which the liberal mind is constantly recoiling. The more a man sees of life, the less he dares to think about it; the less he thinks, the more he finds himself returning to it for sensual escape; and the more he escapes, the more he is inclined to feel the lure and guilt of the contemplative life. Exacerbated sensibility turns in upon itself and conquers its fear of life's possibilities by devising theories.

We might notice in passing how developments on the literary scene since 1930 send us back to scrutinize the original meaning of such words as *myth* (a highly meaningful fiction) and *theory* (from *theoreo*—"to behold, contemplate"). Myth criticism and atheistic existentialism are the typical products of a period in which cultivated minds instinctively resort to supreme fictions and spectatorial anguish. It is the loneliest crowd of all that puts up fiction and theory as barricades; our time sees a maximum of intelligence combined with a minimum of effective power. The Myth critics are not evading life, but merely seeking to interpret it in the widest sense: to relate literature in its most general aspect to the major findings of such other specialized studies and disciplines as anthropology, economics and sociology. They perhaps consider the texture of literature too little; but, then, exegetes have made themselves a substantial summer. What the Myth critics do propose is that excellent chimera, the synthesis of each speciality's main conclusions. Probably such a synthesis, in its envisioned completeness, amounts to disregarding the turmoil and detail of everyday life. But we should remember that this is the humane mind taking stock, devising a syllabus for self-respect, and even devising its new version of *literae humaniores*. All knowledge is basically a means of control. The problem is to combine high mental standards with wide range: man at his best without man at his second-rate. And that seems to be the concern underlying Jacques Barzun's jeremiad, *The House of Intellect* (1959).

Barzun is antidemocratic. He fears for the trained mind in a world crammed with middlebrow sciolists, canting intellectuals, affluent artists and diluting mass media. Intellect's near relatives are undermining the family, are extending it too much. Intellect has too many relatives. This is all very well; Barzun makes a convincing later version of Julien Benda: he has the same austerity and mordancy; he also has Benda's notion of Intellect as the conspiracy of a clerisy. Barzun, it is true, is anxious to notice Intellect in its operations in "the law, the state, machinery and trade." But what does this imply? It looks like Intellect's own brand of philistinism and resembles an Oxford attitude in which "Greats" is merely hard rusks for the mental teeth of men destined for the ruling class. Intellect *per se* is all right; and it is tolerable to the extent that it is exercized by public administrators. But perhaps even they are "administraitors" too. For this is the aristocratic conception of the Intellect: stern, unsoppy, unsloppy, strenuous, snobbish, official, callisthenic. Its perfect outlet is ten three-hour papers in five days; those who manifest it are regarded as hurdlers; they are not so much educated as in possession of a sharp instrument which they wield in public office or in the mental empyrean. With the arts this Intellect has no truck.

Barzun is no philistine; but he does like to play at being the savant among the frauds. And his own myth of Intellect is very English, very French. It comes into being at a time when English is becoming in America, and even in England, the main unspecialized discipline in universities. English is not a training for the ruling class: it has no prestige and no snob appeal. It is essentially the Classics of the democracies and is more of a taste-testing and taste-developing subject than Oxford's "Greats" ever could be. It is, if anything fixed, the subject for future teachers. But how far does it resemble Barzun's Intellect, "an establishment requiring appurtenances and prescribing conventions." Not much. Barzun, an historian, is being unhistorical: a brahminism that wishes to conserve Intellect for use by savants and the manipulators of public power is out of date in a society which, astonishingly enough, manages to persuade Barzun to appear in solemn synod, with Messrs. Auden and Trilling, advertising books. When the brahmins are the best salesmen, surely things aren't as bad as Barzun, for one, would make out. The "scuttling" of Intellect seems to be another way of phrasing its liberation from snobbish, dotty, proud possessors. At any rate, Barzun's House of Intellect is his compensatory gesture; as far as one can see, except for a few minds in a few laboratories and a few bookstacks, Intellect is nowhere near as esoteric as he thinks. The truth seems to be that he is longing for the French tradition of the unaffianced, trigger-happy mind: a pastoral idyll of pure cerebrality such as Voltaire might in some ways seem to embody. But if Intellect is in jeopardy, if the old ancestral homes are being opened to the public, then surely Intellect must be forthcoming. And surely it already is. The works of Wright Mills, Galbraith and Riesman, not to mention Oppenheimer's Reith Lectures and some high-quality paperback originals, may not be arcana, but are certainly not scuttlings. But then, Barzun's velleity for a detached Intellect (that is, detached from Art, Science and Philanthropy, but manfully behind law, state and business!) corresponds to a rather less intolerant intellectual pride on the part of his academic contemporaries. Control, which is the illusion all intellectuals need, is inseparable from detachment. Or rather, there is no control; it is the illusion that entails being detached.[1]

What is fascinating in the work of the Myth critics is the fact that, perfectly aware of the inevitably aesthetic nature of any theory, they have sought to establish a code of the polymath. If extreme aestheticism is blinkered sensibility, their own tincture of aestheticism is simply their concern for coherence. They are more humble than Barzun (or, at least the Barzun who owns the House of Intellect) and more imaginative than, say, such socially-conscious critics as Edmund Wilson and Lionel Trilling. They are less urgently concerned with themselves; Trilling, for instance (as I shall try to show later on), thinks very much in terms of The Situation of The American Intellectual at the Present Day, whereas such a concern, to the true-blue Myth critic, is only a part of a larger theme which entails the compilation of a disci-pline by which an inward-looking man might live richly rather

[1] Mr. Barzun is still detaching himself. *Science, the Glorious Entertain-ment* (1964) is a diatribe against the way machines, gadgets, mass produc-tion, propaganda, etc., ruin everyday life in North America. But he is excel-lent on that chimera, "the two cultures": there is only one culture, he says, and we use the same head for both.

than endlessly explain himself. Of the mythologizing cast of mind apparent in the work of Trilling and Wilson—from *The Liberal Imagination* (1950) and *The Opposing Self* (1955) to *Axel's Castle* (1931) and *The Wound and the Bow* (1941)—it is enough to say two things. First: it is a more desultory, more casual, less Procrustean cast of mind than we find in the professed Myth critics; second: it has some affinity with the characteristically English critical tempers; it is not quite as cozy as the work of Lord David Cecil, or anywhere near as riddling as Leavis is on poetry; but rather like the Leavis of *The Great Tradition* (1948) and certainly in the same sphere of inquiry as Richard Hoggart's and Raymond Williams's investigations of "culture" as both exclusive and inclusive. In short, it is interested in society at large. Both Trilling and Wilson exercise themselves to find out how literature, seen as a corpus of classics, may be *used:* as a discipline or as a theory of conduct or as a secular religion. But their grip on and fondness for social texture (as exemplified in, say, *The Middle of the Journey* [1947] and *Memoirs of Hecate County* [1946] respectively) is stronger than that of the Myth critics, who, taking such concepts as the "dark-light," "innocence-initiation" and "reborn god" archetypes, relate them to a specifically American cast of mind and to the essential nature of American literature itself. And this is all towards discerning the harmony of hidden order, an Arcadian peace, some kind of grand design. The Myth critics seek, as it were, the music of the spheres all over again, but in the literary firmament. So they necessarily stress the merely documentary aspect of literature and become as exclusive as Leavis himself is in the Puritan-moral bias upon which he founds his own "Great Tradition" of the English novel.

The liberal mind, in America, inheriting from Santayana, Babbitt, Dewey and More, evolves a theory of classics, a *logos* of myth, which subtly combines American habits of abstraction (Man versus the Cosmos; the self-helper as Prince; the Divine Experiment—"choice grain sent into this wilderness"; the alien environment pioneered with much trouble and much effort) with the characteristically French habit of the mind-game. And when we say "mind," we should think at once of the universities; for there it has taken refuge. It is the mind, seeking order, which uses myth toward solving what Babbitt in *Rousseau and Romanticism*

(1919) called "The problem of the One and the Many . . . solved only by a right use of illusion." A little further on in the same book, Babbitt went on to state his conviction that "A study of Buddha and Confucius suggests, as does a study of the greater teachers of the Occident, that under its bewildering surface variety human experience falls after all into a few main categories." Such is the perfect brief for the Myth critic, whether or not he sympathizes with Babbitt's own "three levels": "the naturalistic, the humanistic, and the religious." Sufficient to say here that the Myth critics blend both popular tradition and such academic design as that of Babbitt.

I think the persuasions of the Myth critics can be explained socially and historically. A decreasingly open society begins to assume the appearance of an alien continent; and, seclusion within literary disciplines and the university being feasible, the liberal sensibility retreats, passionately eclectic and not a little self-obsessed. As Richard Chase says in *The American Novel and Its Tradition* (1957), American literature usually "pictures human life in a context of unresolved contradictions—contradictions which, for better or for worse, are not absorbed, reconciled, or transcended." Hence the eclecticism of the brahmin-polymaths; thus it is that works obviously archetypal pre-empt literary attention. Reportage has little chance. As Chase says:

Many readers have in recent years formed a distaste for works of literature which are radically involved with the dilemmas of our time and their place and which draw too directly on the reality and the moral contradictions of human experience.

Not that the Myth critics are evasive; if they fail at all it is by virtue of their imaginative response to the truism that literature is the only means we have of living out a part of our lives intelligently. Outside books there are too many obstacles; inside them, perhaps, there are intoxicatingly, dangerously, few. What the Myth critics appear to seek is a kind of philosopher's stone which turns all conflict into golden myth.

On a popular level, the means of self-appraisal and self-understanding are abundant; and it is from a society mythologized in terms of Hidden Persuaders, squatters in the House of Intellect, Organization Men, Status Seekers and the Lonely Crowd, that the Myth critic seeks to emancipate his elected discipline. Not in aversion so much as in an attempt to make truth homogeneous and universal—no less than an existentialist, with his doctrine of essence and existence; and sometimes no more lucidly than a Heidegger, arcane neologisms and all. The avidly interpreting mind emerges in many forms; but, fundamentally, R. W. B. Lewis's *The American Adam* (1955) and *The Picaresque Saint* (1959), the work of the Chicago Aristotelians, of Chase, Fiedler and Young display the same motive, the same view of Myth. The myth they envisage in common is one that enables us to live intelligently in the presence of a suggested pattern. Such a pattern we can invoke in trouble, and use to develop a sense of belonging and identity. Perhaps it is the mythical habit that fosters such phenomena as these: a national American weekly phones people to ask such questions as "What Trends Will Guide Our Culture in the Coming Decade?" Messrs. Auden, Barzun and Trilling gather before the TV cameras to discuss "The Crisis in our Culture." Broadway theatre goes biographical; and plays about Franklin Roosevelt, Gypsy Rose Lee, Fiorello La Guardia and Helen Keller supply badly needed folk heroes: soft-soap Aeneases and unenigmatic Helens. *The Jolson Story* purveyed much the same kind of image. Perhaps in this way people can reassure themselves about the old myth of the open society and, on a much more sophisticated level, console themselves with the charm of a waning folkway, deluding themselves a little that the myth, like Wallace Stevens's jar—"tall and of a port in air,"— is potent:

> The wilderness rose up to it,
> And sprawled around, no longer wild.

But, of course, the wilderness stays wild, yields to no idea of metaphysical order. The jar in all its immaculateness has no public power; its impact is private and romantic. Writing on Jane Austen, Trilling has said that "She perceived the nature of the deep psychological change which accompanied the inception of democratic society. . . . She understood the new necessity of conscious self-definition and self-criticism, of the need to make private judgments of reality. And there is no reality about which the modern person is more uncertain and more anxious than the reality of himself." In an essay on Santayana he suggests that Santayana defined himself in the world by withdrawing from it. He seems to imply that both Jane Austen and Santayana were self-obsessed; and his fecund interpretation of their search for identity suggests that he shares their problems.

Such problems of self-obsession appear to fit the old idea of romanticism: self-regard to the possible detriment of almost everything else. As William Barrett said some years ago in *Partisan Review,* "The American, so far as he is conscious, is engaged everywhere in asking himself who he is, and one sign of our extraordinary self-consciousness as a nation is that we have produced so many books of literary introspection." One way of establishing national identity is to contrive a national epic, such as the Great American Novel with, as hero, the businessman or tough guy. *The Man in the Gray Flannel Suit* (1955) and *The Naked and the Dead* (1948) are contrivances of this type. But, of course, it is only the intellectual who worries deeply about this problem of national or personal identity. And he is hardly the archetypal national hero. So he defines himself in terms of a milieu: the university. Yet it is precisely from the standpoint of that milieu that the novel of epic action looks ingenuous, that the novel of manners looks both desirable and impossible. It is not surprising, then, that American intellectuals have welcomed works of socio-philosophy. Riesman's *The Lonely Crowd* (1950), for example, explains American *homo sapiens* in terms both subtle and reassuring.

The intellectual—especially the one who writes—feels that he owes it to himself not to conform wholly to society. He separates himself the better to observe. Yet he should not abuse his privileged apartness; it should produce a more rigorous perception, not a parade of eccentricity. The trouble is that the American intellectual finds it hard to detach himself from the middle class: success installs him in its admiration and sucks him into its corpus. Nonentity makes him depend on it. So he tends to deal with his craving for apartness by seeking a scheme which confers not only a sense of belonging but also a rationale of standing apart. This he finds in the writings of the socio-philosophers—those American sophists who, unlike the Egyptian priests, the Brahmins and the Druids, are not rooted in a particular culture as guardians of tradition and authority, but are iconoclasts and innovators. (It is interesting to note that the Greek sophists flourished at Athens where democracy was so jealous of the idea of unquestionable authority.) These neosophists propound a *logos;* they make a subject for study out of the intellectual's sense of his own marginality. To formulate is to conquer and possess; and the role of these professional formulators is to fill the gap that the novel cannot. After all, a man reads literature to see whether or not his own feeling of uniqueness has any parallel. And it is because American society, like the Greek, is concerned with what one needs in order to do well as man and citizen that any self-realization in romantic terms seems outlandish. Greek ethics entailed the superficiality of classical literature, as well as its clarity and sanity. Similarly the cult of Success entails a superficiality in American letters and, in the university writers, a vexed and overingenious effort to find something worth erecting into a discipline. In one sense the Myth critics are trying to avoid a Greek superficiality. To them, for instance, the magic of *The Great Gatsby* or *Adventures of Huckleberry Finn* is in the mythic pattern they suggest. But the pursuit of myth can go too far: the pursuit eventually produces an ancillary myth of the pursuer; and one imagines professors giving to baffled students courses on "Our Problems, and How You Will Have Them Too." The solipsist as sophist. The sophist in possession of literature and expanding the *logos* of his situation into a university subject. Babbitt's warnings loom: "Sophistry flourishes, as Socrates saw, on the confused and ambiguous use of general terms"; "The more a word refers to what is above the strictly material level, the more it is subject to the imagination and therefore to sophistication . . . *the imagination itself is governed by words.*" So culture becomes not an atmosphere but an attainment: something defensive and aloof; a retiring, shy kind of humanism; a fringe activity. The crux of the matter is that American intellectuals find themselves in a snobbish position in an unstratified society or rather in a society that fosters snobberies very different from theirs and even classes intellectual snobbery as sour grapes.

In *Democracy in America* Tocqueville said that American religious and political thought never quite separated eternal felicity from prosperity in this world. Santayana took up the same point, maintaining that contentment has to be constructed: it does not arrive as the product of historical destiny. Men define themselves by constructing a coherent world. That is why, when rational, they refuse to accept history as an antinomian catalogue. They have to interpret. Hence those who comment on their own society: Santayana in *The Genteel Tradition at Bay* (1931), Reinhold Niebuhr in *The Irony of American History* (1952), Riesman in *The Lonely Crowd*. Santayana the intellectual advocated the examined life. But he did so only for those who *cannot* achieve self-definition by belonging to a social or religious group. If man were happy as a cypher, there would be nothing to add. For most people, the sense of belonging is enough. It is only those who crave a special coherence of their own (and perhaps try to scrutinize God for themselves) who must detach themselves from the flux in order to construct an edifice of thought.

This is where Trilling, along with other American agnostics like William Carlos Williams, Robert Frost and Wallace Stevens, seems to affiliate himself with such a writer as E. M. Forster. All crave a coherence both cosmic and personal. From the sum of beliefs, myths, mental structures, systems and creeds they try to isolate a single permanent factor valid throughout the world and throughout history; this factor yields a sturdy humanism. In its presence a secure sense of *liberal* identity can be shaped. Two views have to be constructed: public and private; and, of course, whether inchoate or immaculate, each ruffles the other. Trilling, anxious like Santayana to make something out of the flux, is troubled by a need to appear faithful to the American dream and its public. Increased social mobility (now perhaps in decline), the vast slide into agnosticism, the increased speed of technological development, have pressed Trilling into the bare predicament, stripped of familiars, of Santayana's dictum: "It is the spirit that asks to be saved." So it is legitimate to ask at this juncture: to what extent can a definition of one's identity save the spirit?

There is little point in reviving the old disputes on humanism; how *can* it, Maritain asks, ever take the place of orthodox religion? It does because it has to. It seems to work for Trilling—largely through his faith in his own calling. Those arresting titles of his—*The Liberal Imagination, The Opposing Self, The Middle of the Journey*—display the preoccupations they tend to explain away: the preoccupations of (to take two of Trilling's chosen authors) an Arnold and an E. M. Forster; of a lively, analytical and cultivated mind anxious for spiritual aliment, rather exhilarated by Freud the moralist but daunted by the legacy of the early Puritans. In an interview with *The Observer* (London, 29 September 1957) Trilling suggested that "the artist needs to take sides." Of his own case he said: "Ten years ago I was involved in a group of people who felt themselves to be standing together in defense of progressive and idealistic views, in a world that seemed largely in opposition to them. And nowadays, when that situation has become obsolete, I feel rather let down. . . ." In other words, one's identity is best defined in terms of commitment. To maintain a judicial, unattached attitude may be praiseworthy, but is really abortive. As we might expect, then, Trilling has had to seek other means of selffulfillment; and has found it in his vocation as a teacher. Speaking of America he has said:

There's no sophisticated class: none of that inter-action of the social and educational systems that produces a *milieu* in which basic problems are never discussed, simply because it's assumed that everyone is too advanced to need to go back over them. . . . It's largely because the generations don't carry on from one another. As a teacher, I find that every job has to be done again from scratch. You can be confronted with a generation of students, and inoculate them with certain ideas, and then ten years later the equivalent job has to be done all over again.

But, in the absence of a sophisticated class, there does exist something worth tackling instead:

. . . the general tendency of American life is producing a very rapidly multiplying class of people accessible to ideas. The fact that so many people are employed in the higher technology, or have jobs which make it necessary for them to undergo long periods of training in colleges of one kind or another, is bringing into being a very numerous class which, while it isn't educated along traditional lines, is nevertheless taught to think of itself as friendly to ideas.

These, surely, are the usurpers of Barzun's Intellect; there are, as David Riesman has said, too many "intellectual" callings. But humanizing beggars cannot be choosers: in the absence of a sophisticated class, a Trilling has to find what he needs—even at the risk of sanctioning those whom a Barzun finds mountebanks. Trilling's acute awareness makes correspondingly greater his craving for identification. In his own way he inherits something of the old Puritan theory of Providence which has to find every event meaningful in immediate moral terms. One feels that he thinks that "very numerous class . . . friendly to ideas" just had to turn up. These are friends in time of need, indeed. And yet Trilling's outward-looking, receptive attitude seems more sensible and more practical than that of Barzun.

It is possible to polarize the American mind in terms of opportunity and predestination and to see how easily even yet Americans identify choice with providence. Max Weber, in his *The Protestant Ethic and the Spirit of Capitalism* (1920), found good reasons for attributing American diligence, honesty and thrift to what he rather frighteningly called "the intramundane asceticism" of Calvinism. It is not always easy to realize how difficult and how unpleasant it is for Americans to reject the idea that prosperity is the basis of virtue, which is Jeffersonian, or that virtue is the basis of prosperity, which is Puritan. Breadth of opportunity seems to support either principle. You see what you need to see; what you see is destined, and to turn your back on it is to affront the divine element in the experiment. So, not surprisingly, the comforting determinism of the national habit is likely to inflict an agony of choice upon every American intellectual.

I can now pose three questions. First: the special problem of the new-rich and the *arriviste* apart, does the myth of freedom of opportunity tempt thoughtful people to prize too highly not only personal identity but also the need for personal commitment? Second: if a man seeks contentment, must it lie in a devised coherence rather than in an attentive resignation? And third: is not the anguished "existentialism" of American intellectuals likely to precipitate either the end of the status "intellectual" or a resurgence of extreme aestheticism?

Niebuhr is relevant again: "We tried," he says in *The Irony of American History*, "too simply to make sense out of life, striving for harmonies between man and nature and man and society and man and his ultimate destiny, which have provisional but no ultimate validity." There it is, the romantic's Eldorado: ultimate validity. If a man cares as much as that, he is very likely to seek in the body public something to annul his conscience. One wonders whether the new technology is really producing a new audience for the intellectual; the sort of extracurricular class a Trilling needs. One wonders what that putative audience has to do with *The New Yorker*, for instance. After all, the sophisticated audience in England—that which reads, say the *New Statesman*, *Encounter* and *The London Magazine*—is very small. This fact it admits and deplores. But it does not pretend that the new technology is responsible for (and capable of) creating a large new audience "friendly to ideas." Trilling seems in fact to be a romantic along old lines: self-concerned to the occasional detriment of his ability to interpret the society of his time. Hence his extreme concern with identity. Self-definition remains an inward exercise, as he seems to admit; and no amount of attention to the public good or to the democratic conscience is likely to alter the facts. Rather than inventing an illusory new thinking class, the intellectual should consider whether his essential apartness is really the betrayal that it seems. Neither Barzun's pique nor Trilling's worry is unjustified: Barzun wants no prostitution; Trilling wants an audience, even if he has to simplify things for it. But the one goes not far enough toward present-day society; the other too far.

The principal obstacle to such integration tends to be masked by the very word "humanist." For the word has two applications: one who professes the humanities as a subject; and one who takes them as a likely alternative to religion. The two often overlap. Thus, when we call on humanities teachers to throw in their lot with the scientists, a heresy is being

proposed—at least as far as those with a religious attitude to the
humanities are concerned. We should not forget (much as we may
deplore it) that the humanities offer a way of life, a *mimesis* of
actual life. This the sciences do not offer. To many minds the
humanities represent a haven, a solace, an ethic; and the alleged
reluctance of humanities teachers to co-operate is not so much, as
has been suggested, a sign of academic snobbery as a near-religious
gesture: the fear of possibility, the fear of loss or travesty or
indignity or even persecution. Into the bargain exponents of the
humanist disciplines have evolved almost sacerdotal methodol-
ogies that they take very seriously indeed. It is not my concern
here to argue the merits or otherwise of such procedures as those
of the Myth or the New critics, but to suggest that their real
significance has more to do with existentialist philosophy than
with academic curriculum. No doubt a Myth critic wants to make
some kind of a synthesis; but when he brings it off, it is likely to
bear more upon his private anxiety for coherence than upon a
plea for overhaul of curricular oddities. Certainly the exponents
of Myth criticism (using the phrase in its widest sense) offer to
the scientist an aspect of literature that is more generally interesting, on the level of knowledge, than the aspects offered by the
lemon-squeezer school of criticism or by fine-writing panegyrists.
Northrop Frye's *Anatomy of Criticism*, T. R. Henn's *The Apple
and the Spectroscope* (1951) and the more philosophical writings
of I. A. Richards, to cite only a few examples, would seem to
promote the integration of knowledge without, however, quite
yielding the pass to the clicking minds of mathematicians. It may
indeed be that the singularly wide-ranging efforts of a Bronowski,
a Richards, a Riesman, a Russell and a Snow are merely the
polymathic counterpart of Myth criticism; it is all towards restoring *scientia* as a useful general term. There is nothing reprehen-
sible in this. But the literary humanist is naturally wary of any
program that seems to overlook the analysis of texture. That is
one source of reluctance. Another, of course, is academic blinkers.
And another is the religious humanist's fear that his cherished
tradition will crumble when once in the arena with science. The
strange thing is that the ideas the humanist cherishes are, in their
own way, possibly no less dangerous, no less inhumane, than the
scientists' latest experiment in fission.

Take Aldous Huxley's last book, *Literature and Science* (1963). Novelist, belletrist, visionary, polymath and intellectual adventurer, Huxley was well qualified to write his own contribution to the wearisome argument about "the two cultures." Both geographically and culturally, he was a man of several worlds and it is disappointing to find his last book constricted to such jejune matter. It reads like a duty piece. Not that he had to get into the act, either: he was in it long before either Snow or Leavis. And his opening sentence has something of the detachment of the habitué: "Snow or Leavis? The bland scientism of *The Two Cultures* or, violent and ill-mannered, the one-track, moralistic literarism of the Richmond Lecture? If there were no other choice, we should indeed be badly off." A headmaster is writing term reports or commenting on his possible successors. The Balliol hauteur was never more appropriate than to this brilliant, urbane collection of examples. Flick the pages and you hit on *Istigkeit;* "polypeptide chains of amino acids"; "the ripe hips of *Rosa canina"*; bits of French and Italian; Tolstoy, Shakespeare, Emma Bovary, Moll Flanders, the Lisbon earthquake; *haiku* by Basho; Marvell's green shade; "Inflaming transubstantiations" according to Bishop Rovenius; chats with D. H. Lawrence about *Lady Chatterley's Lover; Paradise Lost* as *"Syntax Regained";* Rimbaud on dictionary definitions; Aladdin; Antipater's piece on the water-mill; Jodrell Bank; chemical sprays; nightingales; Indian gymnosophists; blood types (AB peoples in the Balkans) , *satori, samadhi,* and the *Police Gazette.* It is a showy, casual piece of one-way talk by a racing, encyclopedic mind. The whole, slight thing is lucid and free of ponderousness.

Yet the bravura supports a feeble, old-hat argument. The language of literature, says Huxley, is many-valued and ambiguous; that of science is not. Writers, he feels, should make more use of science and technology. He then concedes that the writers who *have* dabbled have come off badly. The consolation, however, is that the science of our time is accurate and will not easily be made obsolete. Thus the writer will not be hitching his waggon to a fading star.

Surely this is wrong. There is already a vast amount of writing that celebrates the technology of our day. It is not all bad writing. One has only to glance, for example, at Arthur O. Lewis

Jr.'s anthology, *Of Men and Machines* (1963), or Paul Ginestier's study, *The Poet and the Machine* (1961). In any case, the discussion rests on a false premise. A work of literature can be "scientific" without mentioning science once; what counts is a recognition by the writer of the climate he is writing in. In this sense, then, Eliot's *Four Quartets* and Günter Grass's *The Tin Drum,* not to mention Durrell's "Alexandria Quartet," acknowledge science and technology just as much as *Brave New World* does. The problem is not one of exposition, but of awareness. The motion picture itself, whatever its theme, is a product of an industrial era. Science is not a new idiom for the writer, a new source of imagery; it is a force that shapes his whole world; not, like literature, through image-making, but through analysis and logic.

One reads Huxley's ninety-nine-page essay with enormous pleasure, but it makes one sad. Sad that his ranging, astute, gracious mind has gone, and because his last offering perpetuates a shallow notion. The two cultures have come about because two different jobs have to be done in appropriately different ways. Overlapping and borrowing there may be, but the writer and the scientist have different aims. The one keeps trying to record the world that the other keeps changing. The two cultures are not opposed and not parallel, but discrete. The scientists get on with their work; so do the humanists. But the latter worry, self-consciously afraid of appearing evasive.

It would be ridiculous to accuse Lionel Trilling of being evasive; but, at the same time, he shows signs of preoccupations which might explain his rather intense attachment to his discipline. Commenting on David Riesman in *A Gathering of Fugitives* (1956) he recalls how surprised he was to discover that Stendhal's Julien Sorel bored intelligent students. To them Sorel represented nothing of their own ambition; he was too self-centered. Instead, they held an ideal of "decent, socially useful cooperative work." "I felt," Trilling says, "like an aging Machiavelli among the massed secretariat of the U.N." In other words, these students were what Riesman would call other-directed. One senses that both Trilling and Riesman dislike something almost priggish, almost sanctimonious in the other-directed: that is, in the conformists, who would rather fit in, get adjusted, than make the world come to heel on *their* terms. Trilling and Riesman have an ideal of the "autonomous" man, neither utterly self-centered nor utterly conformist. It is significant that Riesman's findings came about as the result of research into the social causes of political attitudes; "the political life," says Trilling, "is far more likely to be healthy in a culture in which inner-direction is dominant." It was around 1920, according to Riesman, that children began to be "less impelled to establish the old parental authority within themselves." Parents "were less certain of how to establish it in their children and of whether it ought to be established at all." This observation reminds one of Trilling's own lament that "the generations don't carry on from one another." What is missing is the sense of continuity, of tradition; and the consequence seems to be that the intellectual has to devise his own, usually out of his own discipline, and with a strong sense of himself as a limitedly co-operative person with recourse to a secret coherence. Take Trilling in the essay already quoted from:

The exacerbated sense of others, of oneself in relation to others, does not, it seems, make for the sense of polity.

Writing in the same volume, but in another essay, he says of Riesman's *Individualism Reconsidered* (1954), "There are no characters in his book, only situations." A point well taken: it fits his own unnerving sense of personal malleability amidst clearly seen circumstances. But, as ever, he holds nothing back in describing situations that implicate himself:

In speaking of the diminution of literature's impulse to discover what is going on around us, we must have in mind not only our novelists but also our literary-intellectual class in its totality. So far as our culture generalizes itself and presents itself as an object for consideration and evaluation, it does so chiefly through the medium of our literary intellectuals. The virtues of this class are greater than people now seem to wish to admit, yet I think it is true to say that it seems to find more and more difficulty in believing that there is a significant reality to be found in anything except literature itself and a certain few moral assumptions which modern literature has made peculiarly its own; or in believing that any profession save that of literature is interesting and deserves credence.

It is, he goes on to say, a Riesman who keeps us abreast of ideas in the world. The literary intellectual busies himself with devising an inward pastoral, whether of myth or exegesis, whether of theory or dream. The result is a lack of ironic tolerance, of conflicting claims. Opinion is all one way, and shallow at that: it is enough, to prove one's individuality, to denounce McCarthyism; "it would be difficult," says Trilling, "to discover, in all the many denunciations of conformity that have been uttered, any conception or example of nonconformity that implies more than the holding of a particular set of political opinions." The marginal group stands in danger of being brain-washed by the public notion of a stereotyped nonconformity:

. . . the individual is threatened not only by the tyranny of the powerful but also by what he [Riesman] calls 'the tyranny of the powerless' . . . of beleaguered teachers, liberals, Negroes, women, Jews, intellectuals, and so on. . . .

Perhaps this is what, by way of the university, will be passed on from generation to generation.

What remedy then? What can a university teacher do? He can explain that a civilized attitude is one neither wholly anarchic nor wholly conformist: trite enough, but hard to explain to students who think Julien Sorel uninteresting. Most of them, understandably enough, regard university studies as a route to bread and butter—not in any sense an exercising of the spirit in an effort to emulate what Trilling calls Montaigne's "poetry of individualism." In Montaigne, he says, we find the ideal: a stubborn sense of self and "the catholicity of his awareness and responsiveness." Trilling and Riesman have in mind some idea of moderation: no absolutes. They go through a groping, half-fearful restatement of traditional practice; Trilling, for example, says with consummate and genuine self-consciousness:

. . . one may live a real life apart from the group . . . one may exist as an actual person not only at the center of society but on its margins . . . one's values may be none the less real and valuable because they do not prevail and are even rejected and submerged . . . as a person one has not ceased to exist because one has 'failed.' That this needs to be said suggests the peculiar threat to the individual that our society offers.

This is peculiarly American; a European outsider will show himself and let society get on with the spectacle—take it or leave it. A rigid society has little fear of eccentrics; they abound in England and not as typed eccentrics either. It would not be surprising if, as American society rigidifies and unifies, the stream of self-justifying marginality dries up altogether. For the present, however, the intellectuals and academics resort to a variety of devices in order to justify themselves. The alleged threat to the individual produces delusion as well as default; thought that is about thought and not about physical experience; and—perhaps unhappiest of all—an intellectual quest that integrates knowledge only by detaching it more and more from daily life. This process can end in nothing but a literary algebra swarming with unknown quantities, solipsist patterns and impractical equations. The irony is that, if none of this were true, overzealous administrators and do-gooders would, according to their own lights, be heading toward the same result. The humanities and arts, certainly as creed, possibly as curricular subjects, are all, it seems, grounded on dissent. So, more blatantly, is the mandarin dogma of the Beat Generation.

There is no justifying or dismissing the Beat Generation in a sentence or two: its members, habits and declarations evoke a plethora of earlier versions from St. Alexis, the wealthy Christian turned wandering pauper, to Pico della Mirandola, switching from debauchery to piety by thirty. The Lake Poets, *The Yellow Book,* Dada and almost every defiantly esoteric movement in the arts come justifiably to mind as well as the mores of gypsies, layabouts and hermits. There is, in fact, more precedent for being beat than for believing in "progress"; the Beats cherish no chimerical hopes, political or social; their miscellaneous pieties—Zen, jazz, poverty, snobbery—lead them to no goal. They live in the present, savoring and transcending it. Stern eclectics, they alternate between unchaste monkishness and picaresque saintliness. They seek an adolescent availability that requires a congenial and unvarying setting. Conflict, tension and the middle way do not attract them; secessive self-engrossment does. They are really the first aesthetes to attempt a Coleridgean Pantisocracy on urban terms. Bloomsbury, Mallarmé's *soireés,* the circle of the Countess of Pembroke are quite different: chapels to be visited. The Beats, with the exception of a few who work desultorily at menial jobs, have evolved an ethos of scraping and scrounging, a *vita minima* whose theme is that the aesthetic top is the economic bottom.

The Beats' motives are fairly clear: protest against, rejection of, the affluent society, its mealy-mouthed politicians, its perpetually compromising conscience; its lip service to respectability and the State, its incapacity for ecstasy and honesty. So far so good; but obviously the Beats have oversimplified the phenomena they detest. If the outside world is so thoroughly corrupt and stupid, then surely the Beat ethos cannot be so thoroughly worthy and sensible: the outside world, like the human condition, seeps in. There is a lack of concern with the realm of "ways and means" and down-to-earth realities. There is a preponderance of hedonism, amorality, clannishness, arty-craftiness, irresponsibility; an insufficiency of stoical alertness, of the charity that flourishes far from home, of sheer getting to grips with complexity. If apathy and jazz-worship amount to an affirmation of life, then so does a not too idealistic willingness to remain knitted into the usual social pattern. These Holy Barbarians preach and practice atavism, the *pueblo* way and voluntary poverty against, say, the weekend bohemianism of prosperous copywriters. One can well understand their allusions to Saint Francis of Assisi in explaining the mystique and penury of "disaffiliation." But in Beat communities the lone wolves seem to gather unwittingly and rather pathetically around the few married couples, families and "steady" pairs in their midst. Perhaps the untethered life isn't worth having after all, even when jazz, marijuana and a stultifying slang foster the state of mindlessness. The Beats have more in them of Huck Finn's artless anxiety to light out than of the will to create major art.

But behind the gimmicks there is a version of the life that would reconcile euphoria with ecstasy. Wholeheartedness and psychic exaltation are to be cultivated in "a world which hurries by so rapidly that it is gone before we can enjoy it. But through 'awakening to the instant' one sees that this is the reverse of the truth." I am quoting from Alan Watts's *The Spirit of Zen* (1958) ; but it could be from Pater. The passage goes on to describe "that constant feeling of abandon, of giving oneself up to a driving force that exuberantly fructifies in every living thing"—which is more dynamic a view than Pater's, but fuses his main preoccupations: attending to and transcending the world about us. Pleasure is a word we must redeem; and in so far as the Beats attempt this they resume one of the oldest quests of creative endeavor, setting receptivity and spontaneity on a religious plane. Hence the Beat preference for Whitman and William Carlos Williams, for ragged poems, for the shaman-jazzman's extempore hot licks, for fond allusions to Frazer's *Golden Bough* and Dionysian rites, for a renewed oral tradition in poetry and for an informally gregarious society even in futility.

What the Beats never satisfactorily explain is why such reverent openness cannot be practiced eclectically in society at large, rather than in an enclave. In order to stick to his job the artist need not associate only with his own kind. But the Beats aim low: he who sleeps on the floor has no fear of falling out of bed. Equally, a fall now and then stimulates the artist more than floorboard caution ever does. In the last analysis the Beats can prove their originality only by pointing to their lack of ambition, and their hyperhumanity only by decrying the duped decency of the man in the street. The human and social condition catches up with all of us sooner or later. Why pretend to play truant from it? One is reminded of the strictures that Ortega passed on Goethe in *The Dehumanization of Art* (1948) : "Goethe becomes vegetable. The vegetable is the organic being which does not struggle with its surroundings. Hence it cannot live except in a favorable environment, sustained and coddled by its environment. Weimar was the silken cocoon. . . ." And, harsher and even more pertinent to the Beats, there is this: "Goethe became accustomed to floating on life—he forgot that he was shipwrecked." The cap fits; and the Beats have little solid work to show. Their contribution, I suggest, is pastoral; it is what they do when they have a congregation immediately and physically before them, even when the church is a university lecture-theater where, not long ago, Dylan Thomas and T. S. Eliot were reciting their own poems.

I cannot help thinking how the consolatory myths and disciplines evolved by intellectuals evoke the big modern desk that Karl Rossman's rich uncle gives him in Kafka's *Amerika:*

. . . there was also a regulator at one side and by turning a handle you could produce the most complicated combinations and permutations of the compartments to please yourself and suit your requirements. Thin panels sank slowly and formed the bottom of a new series or the top of existing drawers promoted from below; even after one turn of the handle the disposition of the whole was quite changed and the transformations took place slowly or at delirious speed according to the rate at which you wound the thing round. It was a very modern invention, yet it reminded Karl vividly of the traditional Christmas panorama which was shown to gaping children in the market place at home, where he too, well wrapped in his winter clothes, had often stood enthralled, closely comparing the movement of the handle, which was turned by an old man, with the changes in the scene, the jerky advance of the Three Holy Kings, the shining out of the Star and the humble life of the Holy Manger.

In the same novel that outrageous concept, "The Great Nature Theater of Oklahoma," repeats the motif, for Karl, "in this almost boundless theater" organized and financed by an invisible but powerful benefactor, is to accomplish miracles "as by a celestial spell." Kafka's trilogy of solitude has had enormous influence on the thought of our own time in which, perhaps, all intellectuals long for the "celestial spell" or myth which helps them to get things straight, to see life integrated and superb. Spell or no spell, they look for something permanent and inspiring—much as Malraux in *The Voices of Silence* and *The Walnut Trees of Altenburg* tries to establish the continuing identity of man. They appear to dread the prospect of fragmentariness and the possibility that not only our own individual lives but even those of civilizations and nations are mere unintegrated chaos. They look for a beauty of sorts; a beauty of recurring forms; and this they pit against the onset of possibilities. For what recurs comes to be a certain thing; what may or may not happen is best not considered. And it is in this respect that the Myth critics, turning a blind or at least a long-sighted eye to the manifold intricacies of everyday life, bring to mind the French existentialists.

Both groups have a keen longing for perdurable formulas: archetypes, condemnation to freedom, the existence-essence process. Both have a disturbed awareness of life's possibilities: the one group dulls that awareness by dealing in large generalities, the other by taking it all out in arcane theorizing. But the acute anguish of the existentialists hits the Myth critics not at all, for Myth criticism is really an academic etiolation of the existentialist drama, and its practitioners stop short of overt personal disclosure. Nevertheless, the Myth of the one, the abstract formulas of the other, do to a large extent what Wallace Stevens said poetry should do: ". . . take the place of empty heaven and its hymns." It was Stevens who spoke of ". . . the wonder and mystery of art, as indeed of religion" being in the last resort "the revelation of something wholly other by which the inexhaustible loneliness of thinking is broken and enriched. . . ." This is close to Pater's evocation of the brain-sick mystic weary of spiritual self-reliance, Babbitt's inner check, Santayana's view of the moral function of the imagination and the poetic nature of religion. Along with the American national myths goes a capacity for intense personal rebellion—albeit on a merely theoretical level: myth-mindedness emerges as the subtlest "revolt" of all.

This kind of revolt has shown up in a curious way in some critical notes introducing the poems of the French surrealist, Ivan Goll. Goll's cycle of poems, *Jean sans terre* (1960), is supplemented by a whole farrago of comment and decoration: a preface by W. H. Auden, "critical notes" from Louise Bogan, Clark Mills, Jules Romains and Allen Tate, and drawings by Chagall, Dali and Eugene Berman. The poems translated come from Ivan Goll's three volumes on the John Landless theme. John, says Auden, is an Everyman figure, but one to be interpreted in terms of such figures of our own time as the Unknown Soldier and the Collective Man who lives vicariously through the television set and the newspaper. But, from the very quality and trend of his thoughts, Jean sans terre is an intellectual: rootless, uncommitted, eclectic, liberal and voluptuously introspective. Goll's four critical intermediaries present Jean as an average man of our time, *sans* (as Auden says) traditions, *sans* belief, *sans* everything save "the Machine." Jean sans terre is rather the exemplar of recoiled intellectuals who find in refugees an analogue of their own predicament. Average or collective man would not endorse Auden's lament about the Machine ("it has made all lands its land, reduced all ways of living to its single way") or his assertions that "surrealism seems a very natural response to a world in which we must passively submit to a succession of incongruous and discontinuous experiences." No: Jean's Arcadian longings and his surrealisms hardly fit average man, refugee or otherwise; and what Auden and the other American contributors say about Jean reveals nothing so much as the Procrustean, secessive impulse of American brahmins, afraid of an increasingly rigidifying society that threatens to take them over or spurn them altogether. Goll's theme and texture spring from a tradition only too glad to admit how esoteric it is. Jean is the type of the impenitent, mooning misfit and, even in his American incarnation, is essentially a minority figure.

How odd, then, to find Allen Tate saying that Jean is not "a private fiction." For elsewhere Tate has suggested that "While the politician, in his cynical innocence, uses society, the man of letters disdainfully, or perhaps even absent-mindedly, withdraws from it." The figure which Tate calls "The Man of Letters in the Modern World" has a clear function: "To keep alive the knowledge of ourselves with which the literary arts continue to enlighten the more ignorant portion of mankind . . . to separate them from other indispensable forms of knowledge, and to define their limits, is the intellectual and thus the social function of the writer. Here the man of letters is the critic." To this personage "modern societies are machines." If the Man of Letters withdraws from this Modern World, he should not try to cover up by identifying his action with what *all* men would like to do. Buttressing his assertion that Jean "is not a private fiction," Tate peculiarly comments: ". . . he is based solidly upon an experience that began to be known a hundred years ago. Gérard de Nerval, Baudelaire, and Rimbaud would have understood him." True; but this is hardly to turn Jean into a public fiction. Tate and Auden are committing *mauvaise foi* in its supreme form. Perhaps in a culture that now finds literature its main cultural discipline, its organ of conscience and perfectionism, it is inevitable that self-deception on the grand scale should ensue. It is one thing to mythologize and genealogize your predicament; but quite another to regard the result as a microcosm of the world at large.

Self-deception of this kind is the aesthetic tradition at its most insidious. Hyperbole is the mainstay. What the Jungian-Aristotelian myth-seekers propose is something to counter the fear of possibility: the *carte blanche* of each individual life and not least the freedom of some men to turn the majority into unthinking conformists. Their revolt derives also from a sense of former possibilities that now are actualities. On the personal plane the myth-obsession derives from two related fears: first, that this is our only life; we do not wish to spoil it, but we cannot always know what to do for the best; second, that it is perhaps better to live our lives badly rather than waste them in endless deliberation over insoluble dilemmas. Not to choose is still a choice, an act. It is very difficult to be nothing; life's possibilities always drag us out of inaction; and our decisions are not always our own.

Hence the mind-game with literature and the compensatory disciplines of literary criticism. Hence, obviously, all forms of aestheticism and perfectionism; the mythophile's craving for the unvarying pattern, for a recurring constant with which he can make a safe although only cerebral acquaintance. An astonishing amount of modern American critical writing is devoted to the search for causes, for authentication. What is so passionately wanted is a mode of being beyond irresolution and some kind of action beyond indecision. It is not surprising that existentialism has caught on in America but has, in being adapted by critics and teachers, been given a new form which seizes on the theoretical impotence at its root. American Myth criticism, in giving us a new version of existentialism, can only too easily end up in a grandiose cerebrality. We should not be surprised when it does so. For such is the nature of this mature, mimetic, philosophical game.

Babbitt, a consummate Aristotelian and well aware of the great deal that Aristotle shares with Buddhism, himself recommended an existentialist view expressed in the *Nicomachean Ethics:* "Truth in matters of moral action is judged from facts and from actual life. . . . So what we should do is to examine the preceding statements [of Solon and others] by referring them to facts and to actual life, and when they harmonize with facts we may accept them; when they are at variance with them conceive of them as mere theories (1179a) ." It would be hard to fault this; "mere theory," significantly, was no tautology to Babbitt and is unlikely to seem one in the present century. It is "mere theory" that cushions us in our disciplines and eases us, however briefly, of the burden of action. But, as Babbitt pointed out, Aristotle himself occasionally dealt in mere theory without knowing it. "He fails," says Babbitt towards the end of *Rousseau and Romanticism,* "to bring out sufficiently the bond between the meditative or religious life that he describes at the end of his 'Ethics' and the humanistic life or life of meditation to which most of his work is devoted." The missing link is certainly no more than a gap in theory, but it is an important one. For it leads Babbitt to ask whether or not Aristotle's magnanimous man puts "human nature itself in its proper place." "Does he," persists Babbitt, "feel sufficiently its nothingness and helplessness, its dependence on a higher power?" And the answer is no: Aristotle made insufficient place for humility. It is humility that must eventually bridge the gap between the desirable and the impossible: no other attitude will do.

These reflections suggest the measure of American affinity with modern existentialism. The crucial difference is brought about by the gap between theory and mere theory, between action and velleity. Just as there is an existentialism that is a mode of conduct, so there is one which is a literary *mimesis.* As such, this second variety has to be tested against what Babbitt calls his "two main types of imagination": "the ethical type that gives high seriousness to creative writing and the Arcadian or dalliant type that does not raise it above the recreative level." The first, to which both Myth criticism and Sartre's fictions belong, must inevitably operate under suspicion of being the second. All theorizing is fun, whether it is about the nature of God or the private life of public figures. But there is a point at which serious

offering degenerates into the recreative, still good for us but at
odds with the purposes of serious literature. And in proportion as
the theorizing concerns character rather than situation, so it tends
to mean less and entertain us more. For situation is consolingly
fixed whilst character is mercurial, and it is easier to discuss
character in the light of "the human condition" than of "human
nature."

Man is cut off from anything abiding—except the human
condition. And surely it is this condition that the Myth critics try
to define in the wake of Babbitt, who knew all about these things.
Voltaire's stern maxim has to be set aside:

Les prêtres ne sont pas ce qu'un vain peuple pense;
Notre crédulité fait toute leur science.

But its principle persists. As Babbitt says, "civilization must rest
on the recognition of something abiding. It follows that the truths
on the survival of which civilization depends cannot be conveyed
to man directly but only through imaginative symbols." So men
justifiably hunt out the major patterns and present them imaginatively; perhaps just as justifiably as critics collect up the presenta-
tions and work out the highest common factors. The one can
easily end in private vision; the other in a peripheral and sterile
game that offers more in terms of situations than of individuals
fictional or otherwise. The work of the Myth critics is, in fact, that
of analysis toward not detail but generality.[1] In that process,
could it be that the savor of individual living is lost? Is the process

[1] Reviewing Ken Kesey's pop-square second novel, *Sometimes A Good Notion*, in *Bookweek* (2 August 1964) Leslie Fiedler found it "an account of
male heroism triumphant rather than defeated—not lobotomized out of existence by woman (as in the first novel)." Myth criticism does indeed seem
to be a specifically American way of confronting specific American worries.
Similar myth-hunting goes on also in Daniel Boorstin's *The Image: or What
Happened to the American Dream* (1963), which perceives a Disneyland
shadow between Americans and "the facts of life," and even in Stanley Edgar
Hyman's *The Tangled Bank: Darwin, Marx, Fraser and Freud as Imaginative
Writers* (1963), in which Mr. Hyman claims that science is modified by its
own rhetoric and must be regarded as one of the forms of metaphor. It is a
fascinating exercise. Perhaps, one day, we shall have to thank myth-minded
critics for simplifying science so much that all scientists take to the Snow-
road just to regain the sense of complexity.

not a supreme evasion of the agonies of self-definition, about which the Trillings and Sartres have written so animatedly? One wonders how much of myth-discovery amounts to mere transcendental idling: balm for simplifying souls. One recalls how blithely Plato coined his theory of forms in terms of *epistēmē, noēsis, dianoia, eikasia* and the allegory of the cave, but had considerable trouble in defining justice. The mind which is weary of personal troubles or has lost confidence in its own theories yearns for something external and authoritative. There is also the mind which suddenly realizes that man's shaping ability and life's quality must necessarily conflict. Thus a work of art is bound to misrepresent life; but perhaps life can be tolerated only when shaped by human agency. The same is true of the effort to define one's identity: no one wants to be perpetually what Marx calls an "accidental man"; everyone wants to shape himself somewhat, but cannot do it in the void. This explains the acute worry to be found in the writings of Trilling; for, feeling forced back upon his own resources, he finds himself in the predicament of the character in André Gorz's philosophical "novel" *The Traitor* (1958):

. . . I cannot enact a commitment and invent a reality for myself in isolation. I can only determine the direction and the side on which I exist and, once this is done, launch in that direction an action still necessarily without real weight, dependent on my fragile and solitary will. After that, I must wait and hope that others will return this action to me weighted with the reality they will have conferred upon it. This is my present hope. I cannot go further by myself. My reality is not within my power alone. . . .

Such is, for instance, the feeling of an author about his book: it is the arbitrary, seemingly undestined quality of its career that is appallingly fascinating. Most people, of course, develop their identities casually, without any existentialist self-analysis. Intellectuals analyze themselves, however, and try to live deliberately. The difficulty is that society at large traditionally repels the man of letters, involving him in the sloppiest of paradoxes: an identity established in isolation is a feeble thing; yet society alienates him. Hence the confused and often fruitless search for a middle way—a

way that Trilling has sought through an eclecticism based, apparently, on Arnold, Forster and Freud, the subjects of his formal
literary monographs. Many Americans, indeed, are haunted
by the figure of Jay Gatsby, the man who tried to re-create his
world, from the ground up, through relentless application of will,
dream and money. But, as Gatsby finds, and as the existentialists
are continually pointing out, one's freedom to create oneself is
constantly subject to the world's otherness, to obstacles of all
kinds. As Sartre says in *Existentialism and Humanism:*

. . . I cannot count upon men whom I do not know, I cannot
base my confidence upon human goodness or upon man's interest in the good of society, seeing that man is free and that there
is no human nature which I can take as foundational.

A later Sartre decided to cut his coat according to a certain
ideological cloth: the identity in isolation has proved inadequate.

Understandably, then, American intellectuals in particular
have experienced an atrophy of the will, a blurring of standards.
Peter Viereck's *Shame and Glory of the Intellectuals* (1953)
reveals the longing for an absolute of some kind; Walter P. Webb,
in *The Great Frontier* (1952), suggests that free individuality is
to be found only in association with the frontier spirit—in other
words, where inner-directed people have to impose their wills on
what David Riesman and his colleagues call the hardness of the
material world. But an absolute has to be found; a move from
atrophy and blurring towards some fixity that is not altogether
private. No wonder that existentialism has made such a sharp
appeal to the American man of letters; it accords with the
national sensitivity to myth and the acute sense of selfhood.

But the American version of it is rather remote, rather
academic; it amounts to a consolatory formal garden. European
existentialism is not so much a philosophy as a call to order, a
terse reminder of man's freedom in limitation. But, in so far as it
emerges in the work of the Myth critics, it approximates much
more nearly to a self-sufficient system than in the works of Sartre
who, for example, offers a gospel that has very much to do with
other men, and is therefore implicitly ethical. The archetypes of

the Myth critics have little to do with ethics. Their mode of self-realization is removed from the sphere of action, whereas Sartre proposes self-definition with attendant risks. The pursuit of myth defines and sublimates the pursuer, with sheer escapism as the only risk attendant. Sartre finds himself driven towards an externalized system; it gives him a sense of identity and authenticates him in so far as it constitutes a Cause. Myth criticism also offers an external pattern, but authenticates without reference to society. Sartre, in espousing his Cause, gains a measure of control—or at least part of a necessary illusion of control; myth too offers a mode of control, but generates none of the *Angst* of which Sartre says so much. Myth merely gives the thinking man a sense of guilt—the sense of guilt consequent upon all evasion. Sartre can deal in situations partially alterable by individual will; all the situations of myth are *faits accomplis* and final in form.

I am suggesting, by means of a comparison perhaps more hostile to Myth criticism than is fair, that whereas Sartre sees man as perpetually creating his own myth, the myth of himself, Myth criticism is a technique of freedom without any accompanying sense of the abyss. I mean the kind of abyss of absurdity presented so vividly by Huxley in *Those Barren Leaves:*

All you have got to do is to pause for a moment in your work and ask yourself: Why am I doing this? What is it all for? Did I come into the world, supplied with a soul which may very likely be immortal, for the sole purpose of sitting every day at this desk? Ask yourself these questions thoughtfully, seriously. Reflect even for a moment on their significance—and I can guarantee that, firmly seated though you may be in your hard or padded chair, you will feel all at once that the void has opened beneath you, that you are sliding headlong, fast and faster, into nothingness.

This is the sense that "everything's perfectly provisional and temporary," the sense which every existentialist thinker has stressed. All *raisons d'être* are mere excuses. We invent our self-justifications: some choose a serene *hortus inclusus* of literature or history. In the long run it matters little that one man has chosen an inevitably imperfect system of political action whilst another has chosen an inevitably impractical academic quest. Beyond the daily charity of one to another, prescription is impossible. And theorizing about man's condemnation to freedom is no more efficacious than theorizing about the basic archetypes in literature. The one, product of war, atrocity, political chaos, cannot but make the other look mild. Both are responses to environmental insecurity; both are the consequence of man's attempt to justify himself; both add to the great consolatory mound of the humanities; both expose the essentially spectatorial nature of literature. Of course both lead to self-deception: the theories of the existentialists are not the rationale of their fictional illustrations; the formulas extracted by the Myth critics are not clues to living. All men are responsible to others, but each has to seek his own peace. Existentialism provides a forum in which thinkers of many sects may meet; Myth criticism bears equally on all disciplines. For our own "decipherment of signs" (Sartre's phrase) each of us is wholly responsible. Sartre speaks of the need for "an absolute truth": "Our aim is precisely to establish the human kingdom as a pattern of values in distinction from the material world." This is the exact scope of the Myth critic; both schools of thought seek to define Man utterly. Man defined is the humanists' only possible absolute: this they may rely on in perpetuity. This is why both Myth critic and existentialist show more interest in the fixed human condition than in what each individual amounts to. Setting, rather than will, pre-empts their attention, but not their respect. "There is," says Sartre, "a human universality of *condition.*" He is really dealing in myths and archetypes: "What never vary are the necessities of being in the world, of having to labor and to die there. These limitations are neither subjective nor objective, or rather there is both a subjective and an objective aspect of them. . . . Every human purpose presents itself as an attempt either to surpass these limitations, or to widen them, or else to deny or to accommodate oneself to them."

One might almost conclude that both Sartre and the Myth critics are anxious to establish the human condition in order to study, actually or theoretically, the frontier epic of self-definition. As Babbitt said, life is a oneness that is always changing: but the human condition is fixed; human nature is almost fixed; and only individual personality remains undecided. Men invent laws that eventually become part of the human condition; such inven-

tion is every bit as creative as that which produces a work of ar
But deliberate creation necessarily assumes a fixed backgrour
—whether of critical principles or of social ethics. As Gorz pu
it in *The Traitor:*

To start from the personal choice, what would be the use o
wanting to change your condition if you didn't know what hac
made you choose it in the first place, establish yourself withir
it. . . .

I said he must start with this choice! A Hegelian-Marxist notion
that the human condition is man's own work; not because he has
created it *ex nihilo*, but because it is his only insofar as he has
already assumed it, chosen to live it, recognized himself in the
meaning he gives it.

We notice the ambiguity of "assume": we take such-and-such a
thing upon ourselves; we take something for granted; what we
have taken on we also rely upon.

But both existentialism and Myth criticism are transcendental forms of humanism. Sartre says that we cannot worship
man as an end in himself because "man is still to be determined";
and he goes on to talk of "transcendent aims," dismissing Coc-
teau's "Man is magnificent!" Similarly, Myth criticism defines
those patterns man transcends in his recurring efforts to achieve
aims of his own. Myths are of two kinds: those which reflect the
main features of the inescapable human condition and those
which reflect recurring human aspirations. And it is the simplest
humanism of all that sets up, as do Sartre and the Myth critics,
man's finest enterprises in such fields as government and letters.
For any humanism to be worthwhile, man has to transcend
himself. And in this sense the two schools of thought may be said
to concern themselves with the same phenomena.

There is, however, a sense in which Myth criticism is "uncommitted," just as, in his early days, Sartre was accused by Marxist
critics of trying to "re-instate a philosophy which, for all its
claims, refuses in the last resort to commit itself, not only from the
political or social standpoint, but also in the deeper philosophic
sense." Similar charges have been leveled at Christianity, Buddhism and the position of liberals. But these creeds deal with man

not in any particular epoch; they aim to restore to man an awareness of what Karl Mannheim, in *Diagnosis of Our Time* (1944), calls "paradigmatic experience" and "primordial images or archetypes." Mannheim extends his theory so far as to suggest that there is an "ontological hierarchy" in which some persistent, basic experiences assume the status of virtuous axioms. Ignorance of or disrespect for these axioms takes the center and the heart out of our own living:

Without them our universe of discourse loses its articulation, conduct falls to pieces, and only disconnected bits of successful behavior patterns and fragments of adjustment to an ever-changing environment remain.

Nothing damages the human psyche more than fragmentariness. When all experiences are equally important we are truly lost in the flux. An acquaintance with basic myths will at least train us into a sense of discrimination. We must be constantly on guard against succumbing to a kaleidoscopic concept of life. A common standard, such as is implicit in all myths whether of the human condition or of human endeavor, is indispensable to civilization. Without community of standards, anarchy prevails and each man becomes a solipsist. T. S. Eliot has argued along the same lines, asking for some kind of institutional attachment, or even only the kind of shared pattern that Joyce offers in *Ulysses*. In 1923 Eliot said:

In using the myth, in manipulating a continuous parallel between contemporaneity and antiquity, Mr. Joyce is pursuing a method which others must pursue after him. . . . It is simply a way of controlling, or ordering, of giving a shape and significance to the immense panorama of futility and anarchy which is contemporary history.

A private myth, as Eliot has observed of Blake and Hardy, is worse than none; what is offered as pattern must be a pattern held in common with one's fellowmen. A man may safely, today, resort to a pattern or myth of alienation, of excessive self-reliance, of insignificance in a crowded world, of powerlessness among conflicting ideologies, of escape into Arcadia, of harsh confrontations with the violent, of prosperous rootlessness. What the Myth critics propose is a quest for roots, for something with which to counter the spin of the daily world. It is possible, after immersing one's mind in the great works (as well as the lesser) of literature, to emerge with a congeries of myths in relation to which one can the more clearly sum up and comprehend oneself. Such an effort at personal coherence is no more, no less, than the existentialists propose in their more ingenious language. Babbitt, to whom all American humanists are indebted (whether for neo-Buddhism or the code of self-reliance, whether for applied Aristotle or a wise antiromanticism) described the goal clearly for all time:

The abiding human element exists, even though it cannot be exhausted by dogmas and creeds, is not subject to rules and refuses to be locked up in formulae. A knowledge of it results from experience—experience vivified by the imagination. To do justice to writing which has this note of centrality we ourselves need to be in some measure experienced and imaginative.

It is that "note of centrality" which counts. It is to such centrality that David Riesman's limitedly co-operative man may look; he has to look to something, for his is a life of torsion. Whether American intellectual or French existentialist, he has to flourish between imagination and experience, between myth and *mimesis,* between the *mimesis* of the life-game and the myths of inward pastoral. To counter his fear of possibility, he has to cling to something. Perhaps, like Vincent Berger in *The Walnut Trees of Altenburg,* he can say, "I know now what those ancient myths mean which tell of people snatched from the dead": the stores of the imagination teach us more than history does. Or perhaps, like Gorz's Traitor, he can assert that he "can never feel entirely real," and "at best . . . will never . . . be a great man of action; at best he will be an adventurer of action, impatient to get back to his desk to write what he has lived and thereby to recover the part of himself which action has left unrealized." But "Art is disidentifying; it contests the identity which society conjures up" for us. Imagination, in short, will not teach us how to live, but will enable us to live fairly serenely in the knowledge that experience or action cannot help us to realize our "selves" fully. Such is the common theme of Myth and existentialist schools.

The only differences are of intensity of emphasis, not of principle. All dissenting individuals mythologize privately. Where American Myth criticism, developed in the uninvaded homeland, offers an almost apostolic sense of vocation (quite separated from the American novelist's cult of raw experience), French existentialism, developed in Occupied France, offers the speculative sense of action. Where the one emphasizes the essential apartness of the intellectual and his problems of private identity, the other offers a thoughtful elaboration of an equally minimal state: existence. And where Americans supply the solace of a humanistic discipline, the French version offers the magical abstraction of essence. In the long run, both variations on the theme are only literary; which is the more realistic? Grandiose claims for Experience or the self-evident triumphs of Imagination? Eventually the former finds itself subsumed under the latter. We desperately need our sham communion, because we all have to adjust ourselves to the human law, arbitrary and accidental as it may be. Sham communion, the mind-game, the inward pastoral—call our Western self-consciousness what we will, it reminds us how even Mahāyāna Buddhism lapsed from practical affirmation into myth and metaphysics. Perhaps the most that either Myth criticism or existentialism can offer is a wise passivity. André Gorz's Traitor, himself the archetype of those who state an intelligent fear of possibility, has the last word in the penultimate paragraph of Gorz's "novel":

The reality of our "innocent" intentions has led us to be what we have not wanted to be. We have never done only what we wanted to do, but always what other people and history have decided we have done. Between the intellectual who, to escape this risk, isolates himself and wills his own inaction and those who with good intentions and pious hopes decline the reality which in fact they create, but of which they declare themselves prisoners, a way must be found.

The way seems to consist in trying to decipher the graffiti of previous prisoners, for we can never efface them with our own. This, and it is no small enterprise, we can do while waiting, as Gorz says, "for something better." The graffiti afford objects of study to both Myth critics and existentialists, who have been brought even closer together by what the French "new novel" has executed of Sartre's demand in *Situations* that the novel become as impersonal as a "toboggan." Both groups end up with the same objective patterns, the Myth critics, who come from a confident society, finding meanings everywhere, and the *chosistes,* who compose novels that read like madrigals to inertia, finding none at all, but discovering balm in the world's very impersonality.

An Ist Among the Isms

This is not facetious. It merely seems a convenient way of abbreviating the position of someone casting around for a belief. The person who remains an Ist is one who for all his intelligence, sensitivity, awareness, self-discipline, gifts, ambition, reasoning and intuitive power, ends up saying (1) the ultimate cause (God) and the essential nature of things are unknown or unknowable; (2) human knowledge is limited to experience and is uncertain even then. A dictionary will tell him all he believes in. On the other hand, the person who discovers how to prefix his Istness will hook onto the train he picks and go tooting over the horizon. I think such a person, having got this far, is rare. The Ist is more likely to remain an eclectic, favoring some views, or chances of intuition, more than others. Of course the day may come when he will write in his journal, as Gabriel Marcel did in his "Metaphysical Diaries," "Today I experienced grace for the first time." But I do not think of such eclecticism as I attempt here as either a conditioning for grace or as a substitute for it. Grace is merely one of the possibilities; one that we find described by such writers as Simone Weil, Eliot and Greene as being in God's favor or in direct communication. (Kierkegaard never sought it, resting content—as content as he could be—with indirect communication in subjectivity. He believed and he remained alone.) Sartre, like Heidegger, denies and remains alone. Marcel and Jaspers believe and insist on communication with others as part of belief. We can take our choice, if we are up to choosing. Or we can settle for something such as John Stuart Mill's reverence for individuality. Or we can simply think of grace as the Graces who preside over (and are) all beauty and charm in nature and humanity. And so it goes, the picking and the choosing, the half-befuddled, half-wilful groping after unverifiable answers to the ill-put question that typifies the discontent of being human. I will try to explain as succinctly as possible what has come my way from the writers included in the preceding pages, picking out those phrases or concepts that "hit" and helped me to see something more clearly or gave me a more articulate description of something that had been nagging at my own mind. Some of this will have to be personal, and I hope the reader will bear with me.

It is Lawrence who pushes mystique (or enthusiasm, inspiration, the Dionysian, the non-rational—call it what we will) as far as it will go, only to discover that everyday life is as inimical to mystique as mystique is to everyday life. He also discovers that, for such as himself, mystique satisfies a spiritual craving without changing the nature of life; life's essence is contrariety, and men learn how to live only in the act of coping with day-to-day dilemmas. A Lawrence can usually curb the wildness inherent in utopian vision, but the average man tends to use mystique (when it is handed down to him) only as a pretext for excess and travesty. In other words, mystique is autonomous and private and does not eventuate in codes of morality; indeed, it cannot be converted into morality although in the hands of such as Lawrence, informing and intensifying his polemic, it can serve to knock us out of too uncritical a pride in existing systems of morality. The force of Lawrence's anthems about blood-consciousness is to make people reconfront the mystery and the energy of life, but in that role it furthers a mood or a mental temper without conferring schemes to live by.

Man is so placed in this world that he cannot continually be transcending himself: what Simone Weil calls "gravity" keeps on getting in the way, and there are so many mundane and mechanical concerns that simply have to be taken as they are. The wish we find in *Howards End* ("Let Squalor be turned into Tragedy") finds an echo in many minds. It is understandable that men should feel insignificant and mild, that they should wish to make themselves recklessly and even disastrously bigger than they are instead of remaining ingenious, prolific animals scuttling around on the surface of an indifferent planet with no idea where they came from and where they will end up. But the fact remains: mystique quickens our apprehension, delights or captivates us privately, conducting us into the vital Now of Pater's quickened awareness, the ravishing totality of Yeats's *Vision*, the atavistic ecstasy of Forster and the responsible aesthetic thrill of a Berenson. But it belongs with, indeed it is, the poetry of life, and must remain a private solace. Lawrence saw this clearly (most of the time) and his crazier outbursts merely reveal the frustration of preaching an absolute in a world of warring influences. He is as negative as positive, realizing that mystique is not wholly, or even to any extent at all, pertinent to human society. So, like any prophet, he is dangerous and voluptuous as well as regenerative and tutelary. We can learn from him and his like to acknowledge and respect—even enjoy—the recurring passional springs within and outside us, whether we think of them as blood or spirit; but whatever we get along these lines, if it does not persuade us into becoming heroes, martyrs and saints and devils, will only feed and nourish the humdrum performances of everyday. Which is no small thing: to relish, without judging, everything that is, because the ultimate reason for its existence is beyond us.

Where mystique promotes the reverence for life, reason is at its best when it defines its own limits after doing all it can in its proper sphere. Santayana and Babbitt make this clear, especially the fact that the physical universe has no attitude towards us and functions according to laws very different from those we invent. Reason clarifies the disparity between what man has and what he would like, and into the gap it pops all kinds of what R. P. Blackmur once called "irregular metaphysics." The disciplined mind is bound, sooner or later, to doubt that God, if God exists, takes much interest in our fate on earth; to criticize Christianity for presuming to know so much—even on behalf of those people who are not asking for an institutionalized faith; to argue against Christian otherworldliness and antisecularism; and to object that the history of Christianity is a poor demonstration of its alleged power for good. We do not have to assume too critical a position in order to see that Christianity has made much theistic propaganda out of stoicisms and forbearances that are essentially feats of human courage based, not on any promise of eternal reward, but on the human capacity to suffer with dignity. But, of course, reason goes too far when it denies the existence of mystique; for reason cannot touch mystique any more than it can ensure action. Reason works very well to a certain point and then has to be shelved in the form of a system or put into action. And once in action in a world there men are not altogether rational or in control, it becomes modified. All very well to theorize, to propound systems and schemes; such things are splendid on the level of privacy and meditation. But finally we have to concede that whereas mystique is a private instrument almost incapable of adaptation to worldly purposes, reason is a public instrument which, taking into account the nonrational parts of human nature, has to do for us as much as it can, putting passion and energy to its least harmful purposes. Reason in world politics is the only thing we can trust, but it has to be reason from shared premises, two of which are that life is a gift and that individual liberty is a reflection of that gift. Reason also tells us that we live in a semideterministic world which is also not always to be controlled and that men, when relegated to the condition of their animal needs alone, are just as compelled as beasts.

These concluding remarks have already moved from reason to action. We may console ourselves with mystique when action has gone wrong, yet even that is a small reassurance: a trance for a mishap. Men cannot always manage to be what Faulkner calls "Knights of the Verities," and this is what Camus, Sartre, Malraux and Beauvoir teach us. Yet, notice, Camus and Malraux resort to mystiques of their own; Sartre appeals to the future in an oddly romantic manner, and Beauvoir alone contents herself with the hard fact that man has very few reassurances on this earth. The best they can manage is a mitigating stoicism which gives man more responsibility than it gives him power. All that we cause to happen is *our* fault even if we did not intend it to happen, unless we are bold enough to invoke luck or chance, as Beauvoir does. To what the "existential" French tell us about the omnipresence of *Angst* or pain or remorse, or the sapping effect of always having to choose, we should add the Christian existentialists' emphasis on communication. It is not communication with God that will save us, but communication—on the levels of love, friendship, shared interests, principles stood by communally— with one another. Non-stop, we witness the life-process and, so long as we admit that any constructive communication is life-enhancing, we can dispense with foolish dichotomies between art and life, between criticism and creativity, between aloofness and political engagement. All that we do comes under the heading of "action." Nearly everything we do has some kind of repercussion somewhere, and we can hardly ever predict all the repercussions of all we do.

What is clear is true of both literature and living: a man without imagination is safer to himself than one with it. But to have it at all is to live riskily, because imagination starts us maximizing our humanity until we don't know where to stop. He is a clod indeed who cannot see the magic of man, the magic of what man is and the magic of the fact that he exists at all. He is an obscurantist who cannot see the presence in man of reason and the obligation to exercise it. And he is a maniac who tries to act without taking into account both the magic and the possibilities of reason. If we respect man at all it is for his capacity to live in tension without disintegrating; and Lawrence, Santayana and Camus, none of whom, of course, is perfect, display according to their own emphases the strain and the demands of being imaginatively heretical. Mix the best of the three and you have the makings of a tolerable humanism in which Lawrence expresses (although much less simply than we have been accustomed to think) the point of view of blood, Santayana "the point of view of the grave" (his own phrase) and Camus the sane stoicism of being in between: the point of view of one who has not lost hope but does not hope for too much. Ultimately, of course, thought leads to action and action extends thought, and the one thing we all have to act on constantly is the necessity of being a person, of having an identity. It is not enough to retreat into hipster mystique or, in the manner of the *chosiste* novelists, to evade the pain and responsibility of the *pour-soi* for obsessive tabulation of the *en-soi*. What has to be managed is something similar to Leavis's "vital capacity for experience, a kind of reverent openness before life" without his emphasis on "marked moral intensity." If we are going to be moral ourselves, then by all means be intense about it; but when we begin to judge others intensely for their morals—assuming they are not plotting or committing genocide or felony—we have no right to be intense or even to judge absolutely: we never know all the facts, and reason tells us so if we heed it. There is a way of behaving which relies very largely on the intuitions we vaguely call considerateness, sympathy and fellow feelings; and this way is in some aspects what we call Christian. But it is much more than that; it is positivist and it is what Camus asks for when he says Christian values are *human* values of the kind we must have to go on living at all.

The main thing, as we learn by reading and living, is not to become an accidental person, but to live life deliberately without missing its tragic magic. Whatever identity we achieve has to exist in tension; it can never be a static thing, and we have to achieve it for ourselves. We must live as we expect others to live. We cannot offer ourselves (as we say) to others until we have some self-esteem. We cannot have self-esteem until we have achieved a reverence for all created life and adjusted our longings to its paradoxes. We need not go as far as Santayana's "Pleasure must first cease to attract and pain to repel," but we have to school ourselves to tailor hope to the possible and always, no matter how much torment may ensue, remain open to experience: feeling things sharply and complicatedly. It is no use setting up a moral code for ourselves or for others: all moral decisions are *en situation* and quite often it is luck or impulse or sheer stalling that decides. The best we can achieve is to be aware of everything that we are feeling or doing and to remember that we are part of a process we do not always understand even when we help it along. This is where the imagination is heretical inasmuch as it takes us beyond immediate concerns and all formulas. It is the only restorative each man has that is entirely his own; it is the most benign form of anarchy and, as I said at the beginning, it is the inevitable answer to the inevitable absurdity of man's not having created himself. All man can do is to *re*-create himself, each within his own limits, taking his mystique where he finds it without expecting morals from it, being as rational as he can without lapsing into arid formulas, and acting with as full a sense of responsibility as he can manage in a world where he is always in motion. To remain a coherent person entails always an effort of imagination, for imagination is the only means we have of going beyond minimal awareness. To be ourselves is to deal with ourselves on the move between inexplicable birth and inexplicable death; and imagination, whether we call it mystique or reason or action, is the only weapon we have against death. It helps us to cope in whatever way we choose with the fact of physical death and the possibility of that other death, the death of the mind, which is not inevitable until physical death. Unless, of course, we invite it by declining to exercise the faculties with which we have, inexplicably, been equipped. Life has no ready-made meaning but we can, if we wish, force meaning upon it or into it. And even the act of declaring life an absurd meander defeats absurdity by trapping it in words and thus humanizing it. Imagination, trite and presumptuous as it may seem to express the fact, is the only source of the meaning our life can have. At the same time we have to remember that what we create through imagination is something we *invent* which exists independently of the world about us. Certainly it bears some resemblances to that world, but it is parallel without being identical. And whatever we imagine in order to console ourselves for our baffled condition in this world, we must remember that the imagined cannot *become* the world any more than it can come out of anything but an imaginative mind. That is the burden we bear for being men only, and it is the only safeguard we have against dreaming we have re-created Creation when, in fact, we have only added something of our own.